A Trilogy bringing tog
are also individu:

MW01120351

The Modern Debacle

Containing close readings of work by Beckett, Hemingway, and T.S. Eliot; Tennessee Williams, Chekhov, Arthur Miller, and Brecht; Plath, Hughes, and Robert Graves, and W.B. Yeats.

*"beautifully and fluently written and
ingenious in its combination of catastrophes"*

—Anthony Gash, Drama Head, The University of East Anglia

Myth, Depravity, Impasse

An in-depth study of Robert Graves, the modern theory of myth, and Ted Hughes, with further reference to Shakespeare and to Keats.

*"I am very sympathetic to the cause of myth and
especially in relation to literature"*

—Michael Bell, author of *Literature,
Modernism and Myth* in a letter to John O'Meara

This Life, This Death

An extensive study of Wordsworth's great life-crisis, with additional reference to S.T. Coleridge, and to P.B. Shelley.

*"Of this Wordsworth book, one recognizes its truth, its breadth
of coverage and awareness, and above all its depth…"*

—Richard Ramsbotham, editor of *Vernon Watkins,
New Selected Poems,* Carcanet Press.

JOHN O'MEARA taught for over 20 years at the University of Toronto and the University of Ottawa.

On
Shakespeare, the Goddess, and Modernity

"O'Meara's work shines utterly clear light on the path of understanding we may re-win with regard to myth, forcing the reader to face the incredible starkness of the prospect we face—and the lack of options—ever closing in—and also giving the reader the necessary clues to follow, particularly Barfield, Shakespeare and Rudolf Steiner."

—Richard Ramsbotham, author of *Who Wrote Bacon?*
William Shakespeare, Francis Bacon and James I

Also by John O'Meara

Shakespeare, the Goddess, and Modernity

Visit the author's website at
johnomeara.squarespace.com

Details from
Adam and Eve
by
Albrecht Durer
Museo del Prado, Madrid

ON Nature & THE Goddess

in Romantic and post-Romantic Literature

John O'Meara

iUniverse, Inc.
Bloomington

iUniverse books may be ordered through booksellers or by contacting:

iUniverse
1663 Liberty Drive
Bloomington, IN 47403
www.iuniverse.com
1-800-Authors (1-800-288-4677)

ISBN: 978-1-4759-4291-0 (sc)
ISBN: 978-1-4759-4292-7 (hc)
ISBN: 978-1-4759-4293-4 (e)

Printed in the United States of America

iUniverse rev. date: 8/17/2012

CONTENTS

The longer her hour is postponed...the narrower
the scope of action that she grants...

Robert Graves
from *The White Goddess*

Will no one tell me what she sings?

William Wordsworth
from "The Solitary Reaper"

PART ONE

THE MODERN DEBACLE

John O'Meara

iUniverse, Inc.
Bloomington

THE MODERN DEBACLE

AND OUR HOPE IN THE GODDESS:
A LITERARY TESTAMENT

John O'Meara

iUniverse, Inc.
Bloomington

Quotations from Sartre from *Nausea*, tr. Lloyd Alexander (New York: New Directions, 1964). All quotations from Beckett from *The Collected Works* (New York: Grove Press, 1970); from Hemingway from *The Short Stories* (New York: Scribner, 1995); from Eliot from the *Collected Poems* (London: Faber, 1974); from Williams from *The Glass Menagerie* (New York: New Directions, 1999); from Chekhov from *The Plays of Chekhov* (New York: Illustrated Editions, 1935); from Miller from *Death of a Salesman* (New York: Viking, 1971); from Brecht from *Mother Courage and Her Children* (New York: Grove Press, 1963); from Hughes from *Birthday Letters* (London: Faber, 1998) and from the *Collected Poems* (New York: Farrar, Strauss and Giroux, 2003); from Plath from *The Colossus* (London: Faber, 1972) and *Ariel* (NewYork: Harper and Row, 1966); from Graves from the *Complete Poems* (London: Penguin, 2003); from Yeats from *The Collected Poems* (London: Macmillan, 1977).

Am I yielding to the meanness of our times, to naked trees and the winter of the world?

But this very nostalgia for light is my justification: it speaks to me of another world, of my true homeland.

—Albert Camus
"Prometheus in the Underworld"

FOR
ALL LOVERS OF
LITERATURE, NATURE, AND THE GODDESS

Contents

Preface

I have subtitled this book "A Literary Testament" because the literature I cover one could say is now behind us, so that what it has to offer, by way of a view of the modern world, today may seem more in the nature of a testament out of that time, and with an application strictly to that time. The period covered ranges from the early part of the 20th century right through to the end of the 20th—roughly from the death of Chekhov to that of Ted Hughes. But, with *this* testament we may feel haunted by what *has* come down to us, and wonder if the vision of the modern world that opened up to these authors does not still apply in our own time. I found myself consequently involved, when presenting this literature, in a use of "we", "our" and "us", as if this literature were present to us the way it was to the readers of that time and as if "we" felt that it applied to us still.—Perhaps it will be felt that it still does, that we are still living in the throes of what I have called the debacle.

I otherwise speak of a "literary" testament because the focus in these pages is on what this literature is saying almost strictly out of itself, as a comprehensive digest and record of that time. I assume that the reader will be more than ready to be reading through many poems, a few short stories, and some plays as if it mattered that we did look very carefully at what the language of these works is presenting. Ideally, the reader will have just come from a fresh reading of the work that is treated and have that work opened up to the right page, to see for her/himself how the readings I propose arise from it. The terms of my exposition are, consequently, those that arise from the work itself, so that how the "mind" comes into it, or what form or forms "thinking" takes, at any stage of my exposition, will be in relation to how these terms suggest themselves from the author's own concern with them as expressed through the detail of the writing. I have not sought theoretical justification for these terms outside the work of these authors, so that my method suggests close reading, but with an eye to bringing out the inner visionary direction these works take.

My idea of "modernity" is thus bound up with how these authors are making an approach to it from inside the work they are fashioning. This assumes an idea of the relation between history and literature the inverse of that propounded today. It is to go too far to say that literature is creative of history; it is to fall short of the method suggested here to say that literature offers only its own history. Rather, literature provides the great authors with their medium for saying how history—in broader epochal terms—is actually unfolding (notwithstanding the fashionable ways in which we suppose history is unfolding). These authors do so, what's more, out of inward senses that are their own evidence, without the further impulse to dictate social-historical form. It thus remains for *us* to gather what we wish to make of the inner vision these authors bestow upon us—whether we wish to pursue these matters any further with ourselves, OR move on from them unchanged though perhaps the more vulnerable for it.

John O'Meara

Introduction

Nietzsche's declaration that "God is dead" could equally have been spoken by T.S. Eliot somewhere in the course of his writing of *The Waste Land*. Somewhere along the line Eliot would have come to recognize that the world of Revelation, which had provided so many prophets and artists with their inspirations over the course of long Tradition, could no longer be accessed—that, it had, in a word, shut its doors. His subsequent *recovery* of that world—achieved through the very intricate process he describes in *Ash-Wednesday* and in the *Quartets*—we must see, accordingly, as one of the extraordinary feats in the spiritual history of the twentieth-century, especially as that century was generally moving in a diametrically opposite direction—towards inevitable social secularization. Even so, Eliot found himself, in spite of his superhuman achievement, progressively coming to terms with the fact that the world *had* altered decisively and seemed to be drifting into a no-man's land of terminal metaphysical inconsequence.

Hemingway, although a radically different writer and of radically different background, had come, over roughly the same period, into the same perception of utter metaphysical inconsequence, which he likewise experienced as a final alteration in the state of the world. Hemingway's inspiration derives not from a form of residual connection to Revelation as in the case of Eliot but from a peculiarly American susceptibility to the environment of Nature that is connected initially with the Native American Indian experience of Nature as "the good place". Starting from such radically separate inspirational origins, both authors nevertheless meet in the same post-war environment that would come to proclaim the ultimate reality of modern nothingness.

It is of course tempting to think of the phenomenon of modern nothingness as dictated strictly by the effects of the 1st World War and its dark aftermath, but the evidence points to the fact that we come into a whole new *world* with its own defiant laws of space and time—laws that are entirely self-referential. Hence, the irrelevance of *all* past realities that Sartre is proclaiming in the ground-breaking novel, *Nausea*:

1

> *The true nature of the past revealed itself: it was what exists, and all that was not*
> *present did not exist. The past did not exist. Not at all, not in things, not even in*
> *my thoughts.*

Nor could one attribute any consequence either to one's thoughts in the *present*
world or to that world itself:

> *I exist—the world exists—and I know that the world exists. That's all ... Now I*
> *knew: things are entirely what they appear to be—and behind them ... there is*
> *nothing ...*

The period of *l'entre deux guerres* is dominated by this irreversible, so-called "existential" event, and it was to be drastically *added* to by the forces of social-economic history that, coming out of the past, continued to work themselves out relentlessly, bringing in the further catastrophe of the 2nd World War.

As far back as 1922, W.B. Yeats, in responding to the events of the Irish Civil War, could already anticipate the inexorable course that the century would take again towards World War. At least Yeats could see that a wilful choice of hateful violence in the disposition of modern politics would remain the pattern, and already he could predict, from that pattern, the end of a whole epoch of civilization and the historical ascendancy of a new dark age that was coming in—as he puts it,

> *spreading wide*
> *For the embrace of nothing.*

But, in any case, the effects of a choice of Realpolitik over Culture in the West, as this had come down from the Renaissance, were bound to be overriding—as Brecht's *Mother Courage* searingly illustrates. These effects would carry over beyond the 2nd World War directly into the era of the Cold War and the Atomic Threat that constitutes the context of Beckett's plays of the 1950's. To *his* presentation of the now advanced effects of modern nothingness Beckett would add his own peculiarly disturbing perception of a civilization that had become *denuded* of its vital forces. Nature, and the very Universe, seemed to be menaced with annihilation, and the order of Power—or the institution of Realpolitik—itself threatened, ironically, with terminal disintegration.

All of these developments, together, constitute what I have called "the modern debacle". They would be taken up further and brought to a head by Sylvia Plath in the poetry she wrote towards the end of the 50's and the early 60's. Plath would then proceed, through her suicide, to her inimitable act of indictment both of the age and of the civilization that had brought things *to* this dark pass. Whatever we may think of the case, Plath saw herself as performing, by her death, the direct or indirect will of the Goddess, whom we are asked to conceive as having no other way of intervening in the madness of that age and of that civilization. Equally extraordinary of this most fateful of centuries, indeed, is the way at a certain point the Great Mother or Goddess comes into it. It is as if, when faced with the prospect of utter hopelessness, authors would *have* to invoke the helping presence of the one Power on Whom humankind can rely to see them through the worst. The most outspoken proponent of the Goddess in that century, Robert Graves, definitely held to this view.

The nature of Her intercession, on the other hand, reflects the desperate nature of the case. She is Herself compelled to suffer through the debacle. She is directly associated with the world of Nature so vulgarly denied by the big Western industrial economic machine and the military which it supports and which supports it. However, it is one of its saving graces that the modern literature that is presented here should continue to retain a connection and to reach back heroically to the great *experience* of Nature as this comes down to us from before the straitened confines of the 20th century. *Then* Nature was still alive in the thinking of man[1]. It is the experience the *modern* man would deny at the risk of cutting himself off from the one life-giving source that he has. So that, Graves could see no hope of recovery except through some form of catastrophic breakdown in the great machine. Thus, he concludes,

> there seems no escape from our difficulties until the industrial system breaks down for some reason or other, as it nearly did in Europe during the Second World War, and Nature re-asserts herself with grass and trees among the ruins....
>
> I forsee no change for the better until everything gets far worse.

In the meantime, post-modern man continues profoundly disoriented—for what can his thinking avail without the further connection *back* to Nature, or to Revelation, from which that thinking derives? How to overcome those limits that have been put on our thinking—challenged as this thinking has been since the onslaught of the modern age—by the blighting effects of our seemingly final dissociation from Nature and from Revelation? What remains that is superhumanly possible, despite all appearances that nothing more and nothing new is left to man to break through with? Such are the questions that the event of the modern debacle leaves us struggling with—with what idea of their continued relevance today only the effect of the literature will show.

1

Eliot's Route Through the Debacle and the Comparison with Beckett and with Hemingway

Beckett's *Godot* haunts us with its suggestions of a depth of inconsequence that is already with us. "[I]n the midst of nothingness" is how Vladimir puts it, already with only forms of "diversion" for himself and Estragon to work with. The "repertory" of crank actions, at which they work so hard, is extended as far as it can, until even these actions seem to come to an end. Space is a void, experienced as such from moment to moment, while the problem with time is that *it* has not "stopped", so that Estragon at one point can protest "I'm tired breathing". All the diversion exists in the end to "keep from thinking" all this, and to keep from hearing "all the dead voices" who have gone before, for whom "to have lived is not enough" and "to have died is not enough", so that "they have to talk" about their lives. All is by way of implying that history has been of no consequence, though even these thoughtful considerations are turned into forms of diversion to keep from really thinking the reality. And yet, as Estragon puts it, "You think all the same", and the "worst", as Vladimir puts it is "To *have* thought".

Here, for Beckett, is the paradox of the modern condition. Nothing goes any more, *except that* thinking perpetuates itself. Nor is it as if we have reached the end: the consciousness of what has been remains, and Beckett himself is bound to that consciousness; he himself is still involved—in spite of the appalling inconsequence—in a structuring effort of significant analytical consequence (in part the result of his own classical intellectual training). In the many attitudes and frames of mind shared out between Vladimir and Estragon, we recognize the experience of the modern-day Everyman, and in Pozzo what European Realpolitik (Power) has come to in its sadistic relation to the devastated remnants of Western Culture, represented in Lucky. *He* was once Lucky—in every way favored—but is now, in a tragically ironic development of history, too obviously no longer so.

There was a time, long ago, when the world of Power still deferred to the world of Culture, as when Pozzo says of Lucky:

> But for him all of my thoughts, all my feelings, would have been of common things … Beauty, grace, truth of the first water, I knew they were all beyond me.

We are told that

> That was nearly sixty years ago …

But elsewhere in the play, "sixty years ago" (which takes us back, from the play itself, to the "nineties" of the previous century) feels like "a million", and a world in which Power once deferred to Culture might just as well have existed only as the idea of it. Contrasting with the optimum grandeur of that "original" relationship, today Pozzo is bringing Lucky "to the fair, where I hope to get a good price for him".

Much is made of Pozzo possibly being Godot. The "God" on whom this world is waiting is thus (momentarily) reduced to what Power determines of us. But Beckett was taking the matter further, offering us an elaborate and evolved analysis of where Power stands inwardly with itself. In Pozzo a preposterous form of self-serving egoism is dissociating wildly. In relation to that spectacle, Vladimir and Estragon feel a form of moral superiority but are unable to alter anything; in fact, they *need* that spectacle to dwell on and to attach themselves to, to divert from the scene of utter inconsequence that is ravaging *them*.

We understand precisely where things have come to, but Beckett's analysis does not transform into anything else. Everything has gotten stuck there and is *comprehensively* falling apart. Thinking offers the possibility of shaping an understanding of experience, and so being diverted from it, but the picture which that understanding obtrudes is of a truth that is terminally incapacitating. This is the Hamlet-like burden of thinking in *our* time; in fact, a whole additional effort of thinking is going into preventing reason from foundering, when already, for as long as one can remember, reason has been straying:

> But has it not long been straying in the night without end of the abyssal depths? That is what I sometimes wonder.

Beckett does not see an absurd creative joy emerging from this scene, in spite of all the diversionary fun. What remains, to confound, is the need to think order, the rational ideal persisting with a vengeance. It is not that one wants to continue to think; thinking continues to be forced upon one, and yet one is coming to the end of *what* one can think, except for thinking on a dissociating universe. In *Endgame* the effort to contend with where things have come is both more heroic and infinitely more strained. Hamm's attitude is a direct derivative from the heroic past with which we associate high tragedy:

> Can there be misery—[he yawns]—loftier than mine? No doubt. Formerly. But now? ... No, all is a—[yawns]—bsolute, [proudly] the bigger a man is the fuller he is. [Pause. Gloomily.] And the emptier.

Thus Hamm's blindness, in comparison with Pozzo's, is a deeper thing, and of much longer duration:

> *my eyes …*
> *it seems they've gone all white.*

The end, in this case, came much farther back, and Hamm's persistence, because it grew hopeless long ago, is a greater thing, though for that reason is infinitely more decadent. Spectacularly, the situation of a dissociating Nature can only be referred by Hamm to himself, as there can only be, for him, such a Nature as always waited on him; because of this, even now, in its dissociation and failure of influence, it can only give ongoing proof of its existence:

> Hamm. *Nature has forgotten us.*
> Clov. *There's no more nature.*
> Hamm. *No more nature. You exaggerate.*
> Clov. *In the vicinity.*
> Hamm. *But we breathe, we change! We lose our hair, our teeth! Our bloom! Our ideals!*
> Clov. *Then she hasn't forgotten us.*
> Hamm. *But you say there is none.*
> Clov. [Sadly] *No one that ever lived thought so crooked as we.*
> Hamm. *We do what we can.*
> Clov. *We shouldn't.*

Hamm must turn within, to his dreams, to recover his eyes and the Nature that once supported him so fully—if only the *in*verted influence of Nature today would let him sleep:

> *If I could sleep I might make love. I'd go into the woods. My eyes could see … the sky, the earth, I'd run, run, they wouldn't catch me. [Pause] Nature!*

At least *some* inner life remains, as yet untouched, or not so fully touched, in the general debacle; on the outer plane, however,

> *Nothing stirs. All is …*
> *…*
> *Corpsed*

while over the sea, the light is

Light black. From pole to pole.

In spite of this universal hopelessness, Hamm insists on asking the question:

> *Do you know what's happened? [Pause] Clov.*
> …
> *Do you know what's happened?*
> Clov. *When? Where?*
> Hamm. *[Violently] When! What's happened! Use your head, can't you! What has happened?*
> Clov. *What for Christ's sake does it matter?*
> *[He looks out of window.]*
> Hamm. *I don't know.*

It has only, in fact, ever been an

> *Old endgame, lost of old, …*
> *play and lose and have done with losing.*

and all Hamm is left with in the end are

> *Moments for nothing, now as always, time was never and time is over*

And it seems to him that he

> *was never there …*
> …
> *Absent, always. It all happened without me.*

◆   ◆   ◆

A whole generation earlier, Hemingway had had his own profound sense of being hopelessly on the verge of the modern inconsequence. In "A Clean Well-Lighted Place", every inverted effort is made to keep from doing the thinking that can only draw one into an inchoate mass of undifferentiated thought:

> *What did he fear? It was not fear or dread. It was a nothing that he knew too well. It was all a nothing and man was nothing too.*

That is what thought, on the one hand, and thinking, on the other, had come to. There was a time when one still had a *world* of thought to think, dictated by tradition, as in the case of the tradition of prayer pre-eminently and characteristically. However, all that might be "thought" in those terms now can only leave one the more vulnerable to the "nada" that is taking over, because those terms no longer offer any grounds for thought. One has to *keep thinking* that this is so, or else risk being taken over by the "nada" without realizing it; hence, the transformation of the traditional prayer in Hemingway's story—

> *Our nada, who art in nada.*

That *only* the "nada" is there is the one thought, however, one must retain, for to otherwise let the mind go is to allow a process of thinking to take over that can only confound frighteningly, because no stable thoughts will support it.

◆   ◆   ◆

However, one has to turn to other work by Hemingway to be made aware of *his* more characteristic background, out of which *another* idea of thinking emerges. It is an idea of thinking that makes of Hemingway, initially, a Romantic. Elsewhere one is given *another* picture—of Nature's extraordinary role in Hemingway's idea of the mental life. This is in "Big Two-Hearted River"; there Nature appears as the "good place" where "Nothing could touch him". In this story the suggestion is strong that it is *out* of this "place" that one finds the restoring power that allows one to apply oneself properly to life's tragedies, here that one learns the art of reality, of waiting and of looking and of working carefully. It is from an impulse of that sort that Nick, and Hemingway himself, then turns to his writing, which becomes in this view the application of Nature's power *to* life's tragedies—what Nick calls "the tragic adventure".

Nature's power is still being impressively characterised in "Fathers and Sons", where it evokes for Nick the memory of his youth once shared with his father:

> *Hunting this country for quail as his father had taught him, Nicholas Adams started thinking about his father…. Nick could not write about him yet, although he would later, but the quail country made him remember him as he was when Nick was a boy …*

Nick's father otherwise suppressed Nature in himself, and killed himself in consequence—a classic case of modern repression, and hinting at this tragedy Nick
cannot find solace or pleasure in such remembering. He is determined to suppress
such thinking, but, so overwhelming is the associationist power, he cannot keep
himself from continuing to think:

> *His father came back to him in the fall of the year, or in the early spring ... or*
> *when he saw shocks of corn, or when he saw a lake ...*

Here is thinking of another sort than the kind that only leads to nothingness. It is
a thinking that remains full of content, full of thought to think about—though
that only renders Nick's mental life more difficult.

Then there is the thinking that represents Nick's effort, *before* writing, to
retain mental coherence in the midst of tragedy, as in "A Way You'll Never Be".
Hence, Nick's deliberate effort to take stock of every detail of the scene of massa-
cre he is re-viewing at the beginning of this story. His fear is that if he does not
apply himself in this way, that scene will return to undermine his coherence, as
has already happened, and *is* happening, from the influence of the scene in which
he himself was hit by shrapnel:

> *That was why he noticed everything in such detail to keep it all straight so he*
> *would know just where he was ...*

There is something madly heroic about this effort to absorb war's scene of
destruction, which Hemingway is considering because it had become *part* of the
modern scene and had thus to be contended with. But the effort to put the mind
around that scene or to take hold of it must appear to be utterly futile, "a way
you'll never *be*". Hemingway would return to war's scene of destruction in "The
Snows of Kilimanjaro", with the same notion of being challenged, though far
beyond every possible hope in this case:

> *Later he had seen the things that he could never think of and later still he had seen*
> *much worse.*

But by then Hemingway had become more decisively aware of the limits to
which the human mind had come in taking on the realities of the modern world
through which he had lived.

No story would clarify more where Hemingway stood in all this than "The Snows of Kilimanjaro", arguably his masterwork of art, his great work of summation, in which, as he put it, "I put all the true stuff in". Hemingway's two fundamental experiences—of the Romantic and the modern—come to a head here. Harry, the writer, comes into the story's scene out of an "old life" the remnants of which he has "traded away". (In "Big Two-Hearted River" Nick speaks of regaining, out in the scene of Nature, "all the old feeling".) "Vitality" is the word Harry uses for it, in which he is all but "sold" out, having "sold" it "in one form or another all his life". And for some time now he has been unable to write, hardly has the prospect of even thinking about what he could write, since death now stands before him. He thinks back also on all that he did not write, which it seems to him he could have written, and he asks himself why he didn't, why he couldn't. And he tells himself that the "talent" he had had from the first was in any case only in potential:

> *It was never what he had done but always what he could do.*

His "affections", his "love", his "demands", arising out of his "old life", he has worn out, and he sees himself ultimately as the destroyer of his own talent "by not using it". The choice not to use it came with a growing sense that it was easier to live *without* an application to writing, more personally profitable and also more comfortable for others. "Trading" on his talent then, he had come into another life of "comfort", the last artificial attempt to flee from which has only brought death. (Harry infects himself and is now dying of gangrene, after hoping that a return to an "uncomfortable" way of living in Africa might spark some form of resurgence in his writing career.)

Hemingway's Romantic "life" has here reached its limits. Harry has both "worn" it out and not "used" it, so that it has seemed to him as if it were only a creative "potential" in the first place. That course of life propels him to ask finally "why":

> *"Why what, dear?"*
> *"Why nothing?"*

Why the modern nothingness, the inconsequence, that has overwhelmed him and defeated him? Except that here also is the effort to fight on, the effort to gather up somehow what should have been written, and to sum *up* the whole tragic import of the transition into the modern, because:

> *There was so much to write. He had seen the world change; not just the events; although he had seen many of them and had watched the people, but he had seen the subtler change and he could remember how the people were at different times. He had been in it and he had watched it and it was his duty to write of it; but now he never would.*

That "death" awaits him now that is the inner strike and overwhelming by the modern inconsequence, but overwhelmed as he is in the debacle, which Hemingway connects with the appearance of the locusts in the *Apocalypse*[2], it seems to him yet that he is being taken back, could only ever go back to Nature's primordial scene, in which alone he has his being:

> *and looking down he saw a pink sifting cloud, moving over the ground, and in the air, like the first snow in a blizzard, that comes from nowhere, and he knew the locusts were coming up from the South. Then they began to climb and they were going to the East, it seemed, and then it darkened and they were in a storm, the rain so thick it seemed like flying through a waterfall, and then they were out and Compie turned his head and grinned and pointed and there, ahead, all he could see, as wide as all the world, great, high, and unbelievably white in the sun, was the square top of Kilimanjaro. And then he knew that there was where he was going.*

II

In early Eliot (in poems like "Sweeney Among the Nightingales", Burbank and Bleistein", "Sweeney Erect" and "Whispers of Immortality") we find insisted upon values of revelation, heroic action, conscience, and the thinking spirit, from which in the modern world there has been a very dramatic decline. In *The Waste Land* still more is gathered up out of the past that is being brought to bear on the modern world, including the superior ideal points of view that are invoked out of the world of Dante, Spenser, Shakespeare, and many others. However, Eliot realized, as he was going along, that he could not continue in that same effort of thinking spirit that had occupied great minds over centuries—out of what he called the ideal order of Tradition.[3] Out of that order all great authors of the past had drawn for inspiration: mythology attests to that order, as do all testamental religions and indeed all artistic traditions. In short, it is the world of Revelation, and each author is assumed to have drawn from this ideal world of

Revelation in a different way for his/her own purposes at the time. Eliot wanted to see himself as part of that ideal order out of which the great authors of the past had written, but, as a modern, he too was dissociating from that world. In *The Waste Land*, seeking to realize a more direct connection to this world of Revelation, Eliot discovers that he is incapable of a further connection, that this ideal world has passed beyond him:

> ... *for you know only*
> *A heap of broken images, where the sun beats,*
> *And the dead tree gives no shelter. The cricket no relief,*
> *And the dry stone no sound of water.*

In *Ash-Wednesday*, Eliot will speak of his "reign", and "[t]he infirm glory of the positive hour", because he felt at one time connected *with* this ideal world of the past, with the "face" and the "voice" of ideal creation. But he has understood that it is now no longer possible to "think" creatively in the old way, that it is no longer possible to "drink" from that world:

> *Because I do not hope to know again*
> *The infirm glory of the positive hour*
> *Because I do not think*
> *Because I know I shall not know*
> *The one veritable transitory power*
> *Because I cannot drink*
> *There, where trees flower, and springs flow, for there is*
> *nothing again.*

The extensive reality of consciousness that links such creative thinking back to the underlying presence of the "I", and an ideal creative order to which this "I" is connected, is here re-lived from the point of view of its having once been. It is seen from the point of view of continued hope, continued desire for what is passing beyond, and continued repulse. The turn towards modern nothingness has caught up with Eliot. He then steps *back* from identifying with the classical thinking of the past and its remnants, this desire-to-think-order, this will-to-think-order, in which Hemingway and Beckett continue—steps back from this thinking that is going nowhere. Over-attachment to this kind of thinking has only brought breakdown, and in a *new* spirit of renunciation, relentlessly pursued by Eliot, in the second section of the poem breakdown assumes another guise:

what seemed like disaster is now a blessing; the desert landscape of *The Waste-Land* is in process of transforming.

From this point onwards, Eliot was moving out in his own direction, to offer us one of the most profoundly original meditations through the modern inconsequence. For disaster to turn into blessing, a new saving force had had to enter, represented by the Lady of Eliot's poem, and on her intercession with God Eliot now depends to progress from here. The contrast with Hemingway *circa* 1930 is astonishing, since Eliot is *re*-discovering the power of religion, which Hemingway in "A Clean, Well-Lighted Place" is assuming was dead. As a poet at least, Eliot's focus is not on religion's content but on its method. He is learning that religion teaches something other than a direct success with creative thinking. The way to successful creative thinking today is, rather, roundabout and goes *through* the acceptance and deeper penetration also of all that we are or are not *apart* from the creative thinking we aspire to. And this the Lady of the poem can do; she can go the route back to thinking *through* the modern non-thinking, ultimately combining both worlds into a unity. Non-thinking in Eliot represents paradoxically its own reality. Eliot's mind reaches *into* the sphere of non-thinking and of inconsequence along with his Lady, and he finds in that route the answer to modern anxiety.

"Memory" in the context of this poem is remembrance of the ideal order, and "forgetfulness" the route back to "memory". Hence the prayer of this section, in which, in litany form, the poet appeals to the Lady to intercede out of her power to combine both worlds:

> *Lady of silences*
> *Calm and distressed*
> *Torn and most whole*
> *Rose of memory*
> *Rose of forgetfulness*
> *Exhausted and life-gving*
> *Worried reposeful*
> *The single Rose*
> *Is now the Garden*
> *Where all loves end*
> *Terminate torment*
> *Of love unsatisfied*
> *The greater torment*
> *O love satisfied*
> *End of the endless*
> *Journey to no end*

> *Conclusion of all that*
> *Is inconclusible*
> *Speech without word and*
> *Word of no speech*
> *Grace to the Mother*
> *For the Garden*
> *Where all love ends.*

Eliot's sublime Lady is already accomplishing all this, but in the meantime himself is mired in the struggle. The poem's third section describes this awful struggle: Eliot is slowly, strenuously rising above himself, terrified by what continues to drag him down:

> *… the devil of the stairs who wears*
> *The deceitful face of hope and of despair.*

What this imagery decribes is the futile way in which creative thinking is being engaged in the modern present. In contrast with Eliot's struggle, in the poem's fourth section we are given what the Lady is already accomplishing, the Lady at work among us. The poem's fifth section places Eliot's struggle back in the context of a world that militates against the meditative path, which for Eliot can be the only route through our time. Finally, in the sixth section Eliot has his first intimations of the return of a creative thinking that is now newly harmonized with a self that has become capable also of reaching into the sphere of so-called non-thinking. The route back to thinking from non-thinking has been found.

With Eliot, then, we learn that one doesn't just *have* a connection to the ideal world as one did in the past, when it flowed into writers and flowed for them; it is a question now of our *working* back into it, recovering a relation to the ideal world in a new way. Our task becomes: how to find again the connection to the ideal world, to the world of Revelation, not directly through the thinking that we want to do but getting back to that thinking indirectly, through a meditative engagement that takes place *first* within the sphere of non-thinking. Contrasting with this is the *over*-identification with thinking that continues in Hemingway and in Beckett, which we may see as a case of thinking that is attempting to carry on without Revelation. Thinking separated from Revelation takes its course nowhere; it *must*, in Eliot's view, be a matter of recovering the relation to Revelation. The way the ideal world once presented itself has passed away, but the ideal world as such has not passed away; it has slipped beyond us into its own sphere apart, and it becomes, for Eliot, a matter of finding a new way of living back to that ideal world before we can go on.

◆   ◆   ◆

To this end Eliot's "Lady" or modern-day "silent sister" displaces the "broad-backed figure" of ancient religious-literary Tradition. *He* is "the garden god" whose flute is now "breathless" because *his* form of creation has passed away. Withdrawing, in the poem's second section,

> *... to contemplation, in a white gown*

the poem's Lady re-appears, in the poem's fourth section,

> *... wearing*
> *White light folded, sheathed about her, folded.*

This "light" she brings back with her from the sphere of so-called non-thinking or inconsequence, which Eliot presents as the sphere of "darkness". To quote from the later *Burnt Norton*, by the power of this "light"

> *past and future are gathered*

making possible once again a full creation out of the present. What Eliot finally experiences in the way of such creation, in the sixth section of *Ash-Wednesday*, is made possible by the Lady's intercession. When Eliot himself proposes to conjure the inner power into being, the attempt fails, as in the opening of the fifth section. But what Eliot cannot accomplish in *Ash-Wednesday*, he does manage for himself in the opening of the second section of *Burnt Norton*[4]. Here himself has reached "the still point of the turning world", by whose "white light" Eliot will go on to measure every other form of human experience we know.

◆   ◆   ◆

Contrasting with the possibility of a new present emerging from "the still point of the turning world" is another present that is more recognizably modern. It is the experience we have for the most part, from the tragic consciousness of the difference between "what might have been and what has been". Much of the *Four*

Quartets is concerned with measuring the extent of that tragedy. In the first section of *Burnt Norton*, Eliot's focus is on "what might have been". This takes him back to the world of early childhood when it seemed to us that we shared life with elders who, in an ideal form of sympathy, moved with us, the world reflecting back to us at that time an informing consciousness that spoke directly to us. The impression was of an informing love that could suddenly fill the emptiness of ordinary consciousness with the full "light" of its creating presence:

> *And the pool was filled with water out of sunlight.*
> ...
> *The surface glittered out of heart of light.*
> *And they were behind us reflected in the pool.*

The question this section then raises (in an echo of Wordsworth's recollections of early childhood) is "where is it now?"; "what has that creative potential come to?" At the end of *Burnt Norton* Eliot returns fitfully to this world; it breaks in on him again only to elicit his despair over "the waste sad time/Stretching before and after" that has overtaken him. How, then, to re-connect with this ideal potential out of the past, which seemed to portend an equally ideal future? The answer has come to Eliot along the meditative path that he has broken open, by which this "light" is, from time to time, recovered. For the rest of the time that "light" offers at least a focal point around which Eliot can further pursue his meditations on the world.

There is thus, on the one hand, an ideal "point" where "past and future are gathered" and, on the other, a "time past and time future" which represent between them the consequence of living in the tragedy of the gap between what might have been and what has been. The act of consciousness itself is bound up with a drama of "heaven and damnation" that can barely be endured while it lasts. The suggestion is that we have dispossessed ourselves of a connection to the ideal world to that extent, that in every moment of recovering it, we must live out the full conflict between our momentary possession of it and our fundamental condition of dispossession, and this especially in modern times when we are threatened with being dispossessed for good. There is in the meantime a continual prayerful attending on the event of saving consciousness, while the other dutiful task is imposed, while waiting, of making sense of the world in the "light" of that event. That sense, typically of Eliot in his last phase, is almost continually a tragic one, as if our experience of the world is one that could only be imbued from moment to moment with the spirit of tragedy.

◆   ◆   ◆

Eliot's poetic technique corresponds exactly to his image of "the kingfisher's wing", which answers "light to light", while there *is* illumination; otherwise, Eliot falls back upon "waiting", as long as the primal "light" is "still". When illuminated from within, the poet can give himself to the creation of an art that reflects that "light" directly, even if at a remove:

> *Investing form with lucid stillness*
> *Turning shadow into transient beauty*
> *With slow rotation suggesting permanence.*

Alternately, there is the "darkness" into which one is plunged while waiting for illumination. However, *that* experience is just as significant for Eliot, so long as it is the authentic thing, so long as the apparent nothingness is directly engaged as an occasion for purifying one's soul:

> *Emptying the sensual with deprivation*
> *Cleansing affection from the temporal.*

One only engages the nothingness properly by seeing that it is not a world to accept or to live in, but rather "that which is *not* world", and itself only a "way" *back* to the "light".

The poet's art, when centred, will otherwise be engaged in reflecting the tragic distance worldly, historical realities assume *from* the "light" of grace on which salvation hinges. Hence, "the *sultry* light" of nature and the dark realities of generation of "East Coker", which are implicitly presented as a fall from grace ("Now the light falls"). A new strength of vision allows Eliot to see even the "darkness" of generation in its proper, reflected "light", as the indifferent ground upon which one comes into the world:

> *I am here*
> *Or there, or elsewhere. In my beginning.*

There is something otherwise frightful about the driving impulse of generation as it draws one into its own powerful rhythms of earthly necessity:

> *Lifting heavy feet in clumsy shoes,*
> *Earth feet, loam feet,*

One might even find oneself tiredly driven by an impulse to create that derives *from* this reduced existence, as in Eliot's dull attempts to transcend himself in this poem's next section, which testify to his own engrossment in "the scheme of generation".

Already for Eliot, at the time of the writing of this poem, such existence has led to the "deliberate hebetude" connected with the aging process. This has left him for the most part in a condition of creative "darkness" or emptiness that he sees as an ironic form of "humility". All are destined for the darkness that is ultimately death, except for the one thought that is reserved that out of such "darkness" there shall *yet* come the "light"; the soul will have found a "way", in the midst of this "darkness", to be "still" and to "wait" and to let this "darkness" come upon it as "the darkness of God". All stems from the understanding of the negative "way", to which Eliot has been devoted from the time of his initial success in *Ash-Wednesday*, for

> *In order to possess what you do not possess*
>   *You must go by the way of dispossession.*
> *In order to arrive at what you are not*
>   *You must go through the way in which you are not.*

◆   ◆   ◆

Within this wider, *generational* context there remains

>   *what there is to conquer*
> *By strength and submission.*
> *...*
>   *... **and now**, under conditions*
> *That seem unpropitious.*

The modern debacle, in addition to the problem of generation, makes the process of recovering the ideal world today especially arduous, almost impossible. And it almost seems that by the time we reach the end of "East Coker" Eliot has become resigned to a form of *defeated* creative life; the outer world presents itself to the uncreative poet more and more as a vast terrain of impenetrable realities:

Old stones that cannot be deciphered.

It is true that what proceeds from "the still point of the turning world" is not forsaken. As Eliot exhorts us, at the end of "East Coker":

We must be still and still moving

looking ahead to

> *... another intensity*
> *... a deeper communion*

But the route to that farther point of creative success will be for the moment

Through the dark cold and the empty desolation
The wave cry, the wind cry, the vast waters
Of the petrel and the porpoise.

"The Dry Salvages" associates this scene of outer desolation with the great multitude of tragic human destinies that, especially in modern times, are being played out all over the world:

> *The sea howl*
> *And the sea yelp, are different voices*
> *Often together heard: the whine in the rigging,*
> *The menace and carress of wave that breaks on water,*
> *The distant rote in the granite teeth,*

"[T]he sea is all about us", Eliot declares, and it speaks, cryptically, of the world's alienness to our purposes. There are

Its hints of earlier and other creation ...

but, for the most part, there are

Our losses, the torne seine
The shattered lobsterpot, the broken oar,
And the gear of foreign dead men.

"The river" that "is within us", which pours into this "sea" of tragic human destinies, is

> *destroyer, reminder*
> *Of what men choose to forget.*

Men wilfully turn away from the one rhythmic time-experience that alone drives the world forward from its world-creative source as

> *the unhurried*
> *Ground swell*

that

> *Clangs*
> *… the bell of the last annunciation.*

And within this whole vast scene of human unsuccess that leads to death—the scope of which is limitless and appalling—one finds, in fact,

> *Only the hardly, barely prayable,*
> *Prayer of the one Annunciation.*

◆   ◆   ◆

Experience of the primal "light" remains for Eliot, nevertheless, the one indisputable positive fact of human history:

> *Here the impossible union*
> *Of spheres of existence is actual,*
> *Here the past and future*
> *Are conquered and reconciled*

And it is part of this understanding that much will continue to be made of the effort, from generation to generation, to enshrine the meaning of this experience in works of art. For, as Eliot will put it, in the end of the *Quartets*:

> *A people without history*
> *Is not redeemed from time, for history is a pattern*
> *Of timeless moments.*

However, Eliot's attention, from a certain point in the *Quartets*, would seem to be directed just as much towards all that opposes and even overwhelms that task, as he considers, e.g., the "permanence" of "the agony" that "abides", or the innumerable range of fates that at one point or another bring everyone to "the world's end" where one confronts

> *a husk of meaning*
> *From which the purpose breaks only when it is fulfilled*
> *If at all.*

This other focus involves Eliot in an attitude of deep philosophical consolation that finally settles in a view *other than* that of the negative way that leads back *to* the light. Thus he exhorts us to

> *consider the future*
> *And the past with an equal mind*

and

> *Not fare well,*
> *But fare forward.*

The ideal *remains* as to how to find

> *freedom*
> *From past and future*

but, as Eliot also puts it,

> *For most of us, this is the aim*
> *Never here to be realized;*
> *Who are only undefeated*
> *Because we have gone on trying.*

Eliot's final focus thus becomes

the constitution of [baffled] silence

In it, all who have struggled to find the way, in one form or another, are united—in death. This will be so until more can come of history. And what Eliot finally settles into is a kind of formal partnership with us *about* this, through the "rightness" of the words he himself has set down in his verse

> *(where every word is at home,*
> *Taking its place to support the others,*

These words are finally placed there as a reminder of that seeking after the action that

> *Is a step to the block, to the fire, down the sea's throat*
> *Or to an illegible stone*

which is continually

> *where we start*

from.

2

Opposing Nature to Modern Economics/The Struggle of the Goddess in Modern Drama: Williams, Chekhov, Miller, Brecht

Among the profound achievements of modern American literature, *The Glass Menagerie* also brings us to the edge of what was possible in the modern age. The case of the Wingfield family is not an isolated one but is rather universally symptomatic: human hope is at its last gasp, and a final desperation has installed itself. A world economic situation that the play traces to the capitalistic abuses of a reigning gangster mentality, which has left the masses in the strictest economic distress, has brought on the last of what the human spirit can achieve in its resilient attempt to survive. "I'm at the end of my patience", Amanda pleads, to be echoed directly by her struggling son who is doing all *he* can to avert economic ruin, far beyond the capacity of his young years:

> Aren't *I* supposed to have any patience to reach the end of, Mother?

The father absconded long ago, unable to abide the pressure of supporting his family without the relief of any other identity or satisfaction beyond the rigor of that role. His young son, at twenty-one, himself forced to assume this role, will be compelled in the end to go the same route. It is a world that has made a desperate thing of the human heart, as Amanda confides to her son:

> There's so many things in my heart that I cannot describe to you!

to which the son echoes the same sentiments:

> You say there is so much in your heart that you can't describe to me. That's true of me too. There's so much in my heart that I can't describe to you!

The repression of the heart has reached, as it were, this point of no return. The needs of the heart have grown irrelevant to the direction the world is taking, so that these needs are now compelled to hide themselves, abandoned to depths of private obsession that can no longer be shared.

It is the point to which Western realpolitik had driven the world. In Europe there was sufficient resistance, in one quarter at least, to justify the name of revolution, as in Spain where there was Guernica; but in America, there was

> only shouting and confusion ... disturbances of labor, sometimes pretty violent, in otherwise peaceful cities like Chicago, Cleveland, St. Louis.

Tom's implied cynicism about the failure of the masses to rise up against this situation has *some* justification. They acquiesce in the illusory forms of escape that are left them to siphon off rebellious energy—among which are:

> *hot swing music and liquor, dance halls, bars, and movies, and sex that hung in the gloom like a chandelier and flooded the world with brief, deceptive rainbows ...*

But Tom's view is ultimately sympathetic, his cynicism fundamental, reflecting a situation that is hopeless. He himself will seek a form of parasitic adventure that *depends* on the war effort, itself the expression of a concept of economic survival dictated by Western realpolitik.

In the complementary exchange between Amanda and Tom about "hearts", Williams in the meantime invokes another dimension to this scene, and out of this a great *counter*-action develops. How to satisfy once again the life of the heart, crucial to which, as we learn, is the perpetuation of Nature's life? Thus we get the scene where Amanda recalls her jonquil gathering, before the meeting between Laura and Jim. Here is the image of the Great Mother, in her latest phase, gathering all the life-giving forces of Nature to Herself, in order to bestow them *once again* upon modern man:

> *Evenings, dances!—Afternoon, long, long rides! Picnics—lovely—So lovely, that country in May.—All lacy with dogwood, literally flooded with jonquils.—That was the spring I had the craze for jonquils. Jonquils became an absolute obsession. Mother said, "Honey, there's no more room for jonquils." And still I kept bringing in more jonquils. Whenever, wherever I saw them, I'd say, "Stop! Stop! I see jonquils!" I made the young men help me gather the jonquils! It was a joke, Amanda and her jonquils! Finally there were no more vases to hold them, every available space was filled with jonquils, No vases to hold them? All right, I'll hold them myself! And then I—met your father!*

The situation in which Amanda once met her prospective husband *repeats* itself in the meeting she has brought into being between Laura and Jim. The sequence of inspiration/nature's creative life/love, as embodied in Amanda's meeting with her husband:

> *Malaria fever and jonquils and then—this—boy ...*

again appears in the situation that is created around her daughter's meeting with the "boy" *she* loves, across the parallel sequence of dandelion wine/jonquils/love. And the full transition from past to present is almost accomplished! Jim, as modern man, through whom, depending on *his* choice, a full transition will be accomplished or not, brings himself to the point of "kissing" Laura, in a momentous re-working of the conventional romantic climax. A triumphant "romance" is suggested—only to collapse immediately, because of the choice Jim has already made. At the cost of his emotional life, he has committed to a woman who will ensure his success in the new modern age of:

Knowledge … Money … Power!

"the cycle" that he tells us "democracy is built on."

It is astonishing, and tremendously unsettling, to see that the blame for Jim's situation should be laid to Tom. It is Amanda who blames him for deceiving them about Jim. It does not appear that Tom knew of Jim's situation, and yet the effect is to insist, in spite of this, that it *is* his fault. Certainly one notes the insouciance of Tom's role in this momentous meeting between Laura and Jim. He assumes *before*hand that nothing will come of it: he has already made *his* choice to leave the situation that binds him to Amanda and to Laura. Williams's view of it is that the modern writer (Tom) has predetermined the outcome, having neglected to fight the good fight, on behalf of the Goddess, to win the modern man over. The modern writer's *cynicism* is to blame, and Williams sees him paying dearly for it. Departing from the Mother and her daughter, Tom finds himself suddenly radically displaced, from the one source that alone could have sustained him. He follows in his father's footsteps, only to discover that his life has become a form of perpetually distracted movement substituting hopelessly for the one source of life-giving Nature that has passed beyond him:

> *I descended the steps of this fire-escape for a last time and followed, from then on, in my father's footsteps,* **attempting to find in motion what was lost in space**—*I travelled around a great deal. The cities swept about me like dead leaves, leaves that were brightly colored but torn away from the branches.*

The modern writer has inherited this world by pretending, in his proud assertion of his own life, to break away prematurely from the Mother. Subsequently, it is the modern writer's fate to be continually haunted, by that part of his own soul that he has left behind with the Mother. It is what the daughter, Laura, represents: the living essence of the human soul life, without whose delicate, transparent medium the world's experiences cannot acquire any grace, though the connection to this materially unexploitable essence has shattered for the modern man:

> *I would have stopped but I was pursued by something. It always came upon me unawares, taking me altogether by surprise. Perhaps it was a familiar bit of music. Perhaps it was only a piece of transparent glass—Perhaps I am walking along a street at night, in some strange city, before I have found companions. I pass the lighted window of a shop where perfume is sold. The window is filled with pieces of colored glass, tiny transparent bottles in delicate colors, like bits of a shattered rainbow. Then all at once my sister touches my shoulder. I turn around and look into her eyes ...*

It is the very notion of being called *back* to the essence of Nature's creation that drives the modern, anxiously and desperately, to continue in his escape from it, in his despair of reversing the pattern. But his bewildered self is nevertheless reached, for he remains, in spite of himself, connected to what he is in his essence:

> *O Laura, Laura, I tried to leave you behind me, but I am more faithful than I intended to be!*

The despair of recovering this condition, however, is what prevails, and it drives the modern to that ultimate, terrible position of wishing his final separation from himself—anticipating that, with ultimate severance, anxiety will cease:

> *I reach for a cigarette, I cross the street, I run into the movies or a bar, I buy a drink, I speak to the nearest stranger—anything that can blow your candles out! (Laura bends over the candles.) ... Blow your candles, Laura—and so goodbye ... (She blows the candles out.)*

It is, however, a futile undertaking—leaving the modern soul all the more tragically bewildered—because, even as the candles are blown out, Laura, we realize, remains.

II

Amanda's direct precursor in the modern drama is Lyubov who, likewise, holds the key to the equation between past and present, in an *earlier* phase of the modern debacle. Lyubov's "return" to the Cherry Orchard—as it were, suddenly again, *into* the world of the great Nature-Past—is of very great moment, if itself already too late. From the depths of her own despair—from her own initial, miscarrying commitment to modern man (represented by the man who follows her to Paris), which brings her to the verge of suicide—Lyubov has had the thought of returning to all that she has known and been. For what will be the last time, all are again gathered around her, who are already dispersing; characters who would otherwise be drifting separately, lost in their own worlds, suddenly see themselves restored in her. Chekhov allows for this great re-centring process, accomplished in the play's first act, to take place wittily around Lyubov's modern practice of having coffee, but it is Lyubov herself who is the centre. Not only does her return amongst this company coincide with an effect of the rising sun, She Herself in Her splendid influence *is* that sun, which Chekhov has taken discrete pains to establish is the sun of the Easter season.

Lyubov, as the Great Mother, has "returned" from death—from the universal death that threatened, from Her first, tragically sad encounter with modernity. Lyubov's overwhelming quality as the Great Mother is Her uncritical, all-giving nature, which drives Her passionately to love this modern man without condition, at a great risk to Her own being:

> *I love him, that's plain. I love him, I love him ... My love is like a stone tied round my neck; it's dragging me down to the bottom; but I love my stone; I can't live without it.*

This modern man, ingrateful as he is, has otherwise no support:

> *He's ill. he's lonely, he's unhappy. Who is to look after him? Who is to keep him from doing stupid things?*

In the circumstances, it is a very great gift of Herself, if historically inevitable. How, in the meantime, to accomplish the momentous transition from Nature's Past to the modern experience, oblivious as this experience is to Nature's indispensible support?

That transition is bound up with an extent of social chaos for which the ruling classes of the past are to blame. The power of Nature Chekhov acknowledges mystically belonged to these classes at one time, but it never properly channeled, into forms of social organization that would have brought about the transition to a fairly disposed, naturally empowered, egalitarian future. Trofimov makes the symbolic point in speaking to Pishtchik:

> *If the energy which you have spent in the course of your life in looking for money to pay the interest on your loans had been diverted to some other purpose, you would have had enough of it, I dare say, to turn the world upside down.*

As a consequence, as Trofimov symbolically expresses it, it has become necessary to "work" all the harder at accomplishing the transition, which Trofimov (echoing Chekhov's hope) supposes is still possible.

It is a matter of coming to terms with the burden of guilt that has accumulated from a past that involved the wilful oppression of serfs. For Trofimov this now demands a species of re-education that includes a painful facing up to the consequences of oppression, but also a new intellectual "work", of self-growth, in which everyone must engage beyond the resolution of the political tragedy:

> *It is so plain that, before we can live in the present, we must first redeem the past, and have done with it; and it is only by suffering that we can redeem it, only by strenuous, unremitting toil.*

Another set of factors is left out of Trofimov's account, however, which Lyubov brings forward in herself, for it is a matter of really suffering *through* the historical process. This it devolves upon *her* to accomplish; it is not principally Trofimov's (Peter's) burden:

> *You settle every important question so boldly; but tell me, Peter, isn't that because you're young, because you never solved any question of your own as yet by suffering.*

Nor is this process of suffering connected simply with Lyubov's cultural affiliations. Beyond such affiliations is her identity with that deeper creative order of Nature that has gone hand in hand with those affiliations:

> *You are bolder, honester, deeper than we are, but reflect, show me just a finger's breadth of consideration, take pity on me. Don't you see. I was born here, my father and mother lived here, and my grandfather; I love this house; without this cherry orchard my life has no meaning for me, and if it must be sold, then for heaven's sake sell me too!*

What, then, of those deeper creative forces of Nature that stand to be squandered in the transition? Trofimov's vision does not clarify how, or whether at all, these forces will also carry over or find their proper conversion in the new social order. Lyubov herself has no clear vision of how to go over with them, and it does look like a case of great tragic loss. It is all the *more* extraordinary, then, that Trofimov should be allowed such hopefulness as he expresses, which seems to take on even *this* prospect of deprivation, as if Chekhov were supposing it possible to recover these forces even through such a loss:

> *I am sick, anxious, poor as a beggar. Fate has tossed me hither and thither; I have been everywhere, everywhere. But wherever I have been, every minute, day and night, my soul has been full of mysterious anticipations, I feel the approach of happiness.*

All this must seem very paradoxical in the face of the immediate evidence of tragic bafflement, as this concentrates itself in Lyubov. When the cherry orchard is sold, she collapses on stage alone, huddled to herself, weeping bitterly. The Great Mother Herself has been tragically and ignominiously sold off—to the symbolic "new" owner of the cherry orchard, the modern entrepreneur, Lopakhin. *His* first thought is to cut the orchard down, to make management of the estate more profitable in modern terms. No regard is given to the deeper reality of Nature's life or to the tragedy associated with it—which symbolically extends to the death of Lyubov's boy, in that same river that Lopakhin can only recognize for its marketing value:

> *and if only you will cut up the cherry orchard and the land along the river into building lots ... It'll all be snapped up. In two words, I congratulate you; you are saved. It's a first class-site, with a good deep river.*

There is a kind of historical triumph in Lopakhin's possession of the orchard. The enslaved classes of the past, to whom his family belonged, have by his action been vindicated. But Lophakhin also betrays his ignorance of his terms, inasmuch as these bear on the reality of Nature's life:

> *the cherry orchard is mine! ... a property that hasn't its equal anywhere in the whole world! ... Come everyone and see Yermolai Lopakhin lay his axe to the cherry orchard, come and see the trees fall down! We'll fill the place with villas; ...*

In the end Chekhov acknowledges *the two* patterns, but it is clear that, for him, the political resolution plays a secondary role. There is the more essential task of working through to an awakened consciousness that would be truly redemptive of the world's woes. It is, however, equally clear that for Chekhov an awakened consciousness of this sort, for the moment, lies beyond the comprehending power of everyone.

III

Lopakhin's decisive role in the disposition of events anticipates the coming in of the modern profiteer, who looms so large in Williams's account of the modern event. Indeed by Williams's time no room is left for a proper resolution of the deeper issues that concern the relationship of past and present. By then, all is determined by economic tyranny; all idealism has fallen away from those in control of the forces of history. In offering their respective accounts of the modern event, Chekhov and Williams focus attention on those who find themselves victims of this process *on the outside*. To some extent, Arthur Miller, in *Death of a Salesman*, does so as well (in the case of Biff), but with him the focus is more on one (Willy) destroyed by the process from within, as Tom or Tom's father might have been, had they continued at their post. Miller's engagement is more head-on and one might suppose therefore deeper: the difference corresponds to Miller's immediate engagement with this process as a Marxist at the time of the writing of this play. The monster-bull is taken by the horns, and the tragic "effect", which Miller famously sought to achieve with his play, would serve the purpose of political rousing, as if some significant social action might come from it.

Involved in Miller's fiercely direct indictment of the economic order is his own presentation of our tragic separation from Nature. It is the life of Nature of a former time that has fed the view that a natural creative energy will suffice to bring success in the business world. In the meantime that world grounds itself on *other* forms of capitalistic expedients that radically escape the natural man. The famous American Dream, that all can be had from sheer natural creative will or desire, comes into it directly—for it really seemed at one time that all *could* be had in this way. It is the grandeur of this Dream that Miller recovers where America's universal symbolic Father is brought in :

> *Father was a very great and very wild-hearted man. We would start in Boston, and he'd toss the whole family into the wagon, and then he'd drive the team right across the country; through Ohio, and Indiana, Michigan, Illinois, and all the*

Western states. And we'd stop in the towns and sell the flutes that he'd made along
the way. Great inventor, Father. With one gadget he made more in a week than a
man like you could make in a lifetime.

The American Dream originates in the image of such a free-roaming frontier
culture, when success, it was thought, could be had directly on the basis of the
naturally creative personality. Something of this tendency would appear to have
been assimilated into the modern American idea of business, and Miller, along
with Willy, laments that business practice did not continue to pride itself on it
and to leave room for it. But, in any case, a divarication of worlds had taken
place. There had been no conscious transitional "work", to achieve the balance of
forces that was needed. In the meantime, the forces of the personality survive at
least to this point, that Willy can convincingly assert the possession of a residual
"greatness" of "spirit" that sets him and Biff apart from the circumstances that
tragically claim them. In Biff, the potential for grandeur is unmistakeable:

Willy. *When that team came out—he was the tallest, remember?*
Linda. *Oh. yes. And in gold.*
Willy. *Like a young god. Hercules—something like that. And the sun, the sun all*
around him.

But such energies can no longer be properly channelled, and in Willy's case
especially the process by which they are displaced takes a radical form. They reap-
pear as the wild fantasies of hope and relived expectations that drive Willy outside
the bounds of reality, ultimately to suicide. These energies find their consumma-
tion in his death, and the tragic effect would serve, in Miller's intention, to purge
American culture of its contradictions. The effect goes far beyond Charley's sim-
ple-minded eulogy on behalf of the struggling salesman. Working, as it were,
from *within* the cultural experience of this period—taking us, via Willy, *through*
the tragedy of this time—Miller was seeking to free America from the residual
claims of both the creative past and the economic present. Both of these worlds
seemed to him radically inappropriate, while the contradiction represented
between them, in his Marxist view, would have to resolve itself in the emergence
of a new possibility that grows out of it.

This new world Miller defines through Biff, who pretends from the tragedy to
have learned who he is in terms other than those Willy had determined for him.
He has finally purged himself of his embroilment in Willy's contradictions. The
play is *also* an elegy on the decline from Nature's past, and Miller, like many
other authors of this epoch, had the vision to see that much had been lost in the

transition. But what remains for him—which Biff is confirmed in—is a *new* form of natural life, one that has clarified from the deeper energies that could not carry over. Biff's intention is to take up a simple life on a ranch. Whether *this* survival finally satisfies our idea of the creative life, or what we feel we *should* be making of Nature's Past, that was the Marxist solution Miller was presenting as a dialectic alternative to an inhuman economics that in the meantime had run away with itself.

IV

Both Chekhov and Williams could be said to stand well *outside* the economic takeover of our modern experience, desperate as *they* were to maintain in its original grandeur that other experience of Nature's Past, our final severance from which denies all value to modernity. Miller, in comparison, takes us (from a point of view that likewise connects with this Past) more directly into the throes of the modern economic experience. Nevertheless, Miller himself only takes us so far into this experience, concentrating on the impact on the common man of an economic order whose power source still lies at some distance from his presentation.

The same cannot be said of Brecht in *Mother Courage and Her Children*. Though the war is never brought directly on stage, here we are set in the very midst of that source whose inexorable unfolding threatens the annihilation of our humanity. At the same time Brecht has retained, in spite of himself, the strictest connection back to the Great Mother, Who continues to preside over the modern scene through the worst degradation.[5] The Great Mother in Williams, as in Chekhov, remains tragically baffled yet scrupulously aloof from the modern realities that threaten. It is a matter for these authors of supposing that the modern debacle can still be resisted, right through the tragic eventuality of the historically final moment. Relative to them, Miller presents a situation in which the Mother (reflected in Willy's wife, Linda) has given *over* any grand saving role, except for ordinarily (if honorably) seeing Willy through to his end. In Brecht the Great Mother is still battling on. Historically compromised as never before, and indeed *plunged* in the morass of modern economic destruction, Mother Courage represents what is *left* of the Mother in the historical process. Radically subjected, Her effort consists now in seeking whatever ground She may find to withstand Her own extinction. In this desperate process, She shares in man's own efforts to avert the final loss of *his* humanity. She is in this case what *we* have become as a result of allowing our own subjection; She is the image of our own condition, as we are thrown back upon the grotesque need to come out of a ruthless modern economics alive. Much has already been sacrificed in this effort, and the indications are that more will be, as long as such economics continue; nor is there any suggestion in the play that these will alter.

Brecht's displacement of the action to the early seventeenth century suggests that these economic realities have been upon us since the Renaissance when the plunge into realpolitik was first made. But Brecht also targets the sad collusion of the masses in this grotesque breakdown:

> *To hear the big fellows talk, they wage war from fear of God and for all things bright and beautiful, but just look into it, and you'll see they're not so silly: they want a good profit out of it, or else the little fellows like you and me wouldn't back 'em up.*

Courage, in this context, assumes a whole new, diabolically ironic meaning:

> *The poor need courage. Why? ... They have to hang each other one by one and slaughter each other in the lump, so if they want to look each other in the face once in a while, well, it takes courage. That they put up with an Emperor and a Pope, that takes an unnatural amount of courage, for they cost you your life.*

This position is voiced by Mother Courage with a significant measure of knowing irony. The conditions under which she labors and to which she is exposed are stubbornly resisted, even when, in her effort to save her son and while trying to stave off ruin (appealing to strange mercies) she must count on the corruptibility of her oppressors:

> *Thanks be to God they're corruptible. They're not wolves, they're human and after money. God is merciful and men are bribable.... Corruption is our only hope. As long as there's corruption, there'll be merciful judges and even the innocent may get off.*

Haggling over the life of her son—from the need to reserve something for herself—Mother Courage loses the gamble, plunging into murkier depths in seeking to survive. With the direct attacks on her canteen, she stops to consider capitulation, before forms of degradation that grow more and more extreme. Injustice overwhelms, and we are forced to view destructive realities from the inside of subjection. What is finally presented is the tragic irony of a "survival" that constitutes the negation of our humanity. It is the deep burden of the Great Mother in our time, who has been tragically reduced to that ignominious condition.

Brecht is unsparing in pursuing the logic of this subjection, making a powerfully ironic case for the idea that

> *you can't be sure the war will ever end*

There are also no limits to what humankind will grow accustomed to. Being fruitful and multiplying, Brecht insists, continues also through war, because

> *Nothing can keep you from it [multiplying] very long in any event. And so the war has your offspring and can carry on.*

We are challenged to see the grotesque absurdity of any accommodation to war, at the same time as we are compelled to acknowledge that humankind will continue to propagate itself regardless. The grotesquerie lies all in that impossible, irreduceable meeting of facts. To this ultimate lowpoint in the play's logic (which we reach about halfway through), Brecht adds yet a further argument: there is also no *logical* necessity for war to end:

> *Why should it end?*

the chaplain says, who is the one to speak all of these thoughts about war.

That he is the one to do so undermines, of course, the whole Western idealistic-humanistic tradition for which he stands, anticipating Brecht's satiric exposure later of the "great virtues" of wisdom, bravery, honesty, unselfishness and the pretension to godliness (in the extraordinary "Song of the Great Souls of this Earth"). All of these, Brecht suggests, have come to nothing. The social-economic realities have led the world to another point:

> *Yes, we're told to be unselfish and share what we have, but what if we have nothing? And those who do share it don't have an easy time either, for what's left when you're through sharing?*

Ironically, this view is voiced by the Cook when he and Mother Courage are reduced to begging for food, but dramatically it is the Cook's idea that the history of idealism has *led* them to this point that prompts a "Voice (from above)" to offer them the minimal "soup".

War *had*, at one point, seemed to offer more as a prospect of survival:

> *Destroys the weak, does it? Well, what does peace do for 'em, huh? War feeds its people better.*

Thus, when peace announces itself, Mother Courage ironically clings to war. Meanwhile, the Chaplain's jealousy—he is in a love-struggle over Courage with the Cook, drives him to say about her, ironically in light of his recent thoughts on war:

> *You have no respect for peace, Courage. You're a hyena of the battlefield!*

Nevertheless, Mother Courage still responds to the idea of peace, even when it threatens her with economic ruin:

> *I'm glad about the peace even though I'm ruined. At least I've got two of my children through the war.*

But then the war is on again, and it only leads to a worse penury, reducing them all to beggary.

Brecht at this point brings forward one option that is left in the midst of this impossible dialectic: the symbolic option of getting away from it all, with the unique chance of settling down. The Cook is in the position to offer Mother Courage a "stable" life of work at an inn far away from the war. But the offer is made with the understanding that, if they are to survive, Kattrin, Mother Courage's daughter, must be left out. Mother Courage cannot accept the Cook's terms, not because she cannot tear herself away from the war, but because she cannot leave Kattrin. Kattrin is singled out in this play for her "good heart" and her "pity"; *she* continues to represent a center of pure resistance to the war:

> *The war frightens her. She can't bear it. She has terrible dreams. I hear her groan at night, especially after battles. What she sees in her dreams I don't know. She suffers from sheer pity.*

The mother's commitment to her daughter is symbolic, reflecting Mother Courage's underlying status as Great Mother. She Herself has been brought to a great lowpoint in Her subjection but has nevertheless retained sufficient connection to what She has been to continue in a relation to Her daughter, in whom the final hope resides.

In the end, this is the hope in sacrificial action. Recovering peace has been Kattrin's hope, but this particular hope has passed. Too much has been lost along the way. The possibility remains, however, even in the midst of war, of transforming to good, by the kind of action to which Kattrin commits. Knowing that an ambush has been planned on an unsuspecting village, and that silence will certainly ensure that the people of the village are wiped out (while noting at the same time that all around her who know would maintain silence in order to save their lives), Kattrin flies in the face of this choice of "survival". She climbs to the top of a roof and, in desperation of what is at stake—knowing that she risks her life but that many other lives, including the lives of children, will be lost—frantically beats her drum, managing to alert the village in time to save some. This is at the cost, however, of her own life. In this way, Kattrin by her action redeems and preserves at least the concept of humanity.

But Brecht would appear to be suggesting more—that it is possible by such sacrificial action to *redeem* the process of history, though Brecht was hardly writing as a Christian. For him it is simply what the dialectical process, in part by means of such confrontation, would achieve. Brecht at the same time had continued to link himself to the tradition of the Great Mother, and by that connection his drama suggests still deeper forces at work in history that are the result of the continued *intercession* of the Great Mother in our subjection. She Herself is baffled for now but can still work through the sacrificial action of her offspring, the heroic "daughter" who proceeds to take the burden of the historical struggle upon herself.

◆   ◆   ◆

This is precisely the role that Sylvia Plath in her unique way would later assume, as I shall now proceed to show, admittedly at quite another level of the historical process. Plath herself spoke of her work as "deflections" from an influence on her that came directly from "the issues of our time"[6], nor was her association of "herself and her sufferings with historical events"[7], which once made her poetry so controversial, a gratuitous one.[8] A poem like "Daddy", says one critic, "by extending itself through historical images ... defines the *age* as schizophrenic, torn between brutality and a love which in the end can only manifest itself, today, in images of violence."[9] And it was George Steiner who said of this poem: "In "Daddy" she wrote one of the very few poems I know of in any language to come near the last horror."[10]

3

Plath and Hughes: A Comparative View of Their Poetry Through the Goddess-Theme

The crushing realities of Western realpolitik continue to be represented well into our own time, but not often have the lives of poets and their work been so bound up with these realities as in the case of Sylvia Plath and Ted Hughes. Hughes's poems establish clearly how Plath became both a victim of these realities and their sternest judge, taking them upon herself in an absolute effort to come to terms that turned into one of their century's most daunting challenges to our capacity for evasion of the historical/creative task. Hughes's poem, "The Tender Place", fully dramatizes the influence of modern-day realpolitik on Plath's psyche. She is depicted as literally possessed by its realities, fitfully bombed and electrocuted as it were from within, *made* to explode or just waiting to be violently subdued again by "the god" in possession of her at the least hint of recovered sensation. What could be left of a voice born into such circumstances? What sort of voice could a poet who was subjected to such violence have, if not a voice

> *over-exposed, like an X-ray,*

with words

> *reversed from the light,*
> *Holding in their entrails?*

In "The God", Plath's dark progress towards a new poetry of inverted realities is meticulously outlined, Hughes's account emphasizing that himself saw it forced into being, to his very great dismay. Plath would have to find her *own* way out of the condition imposed upon her by the unnatural "God" in possession of her, who was paradoxically a

> *non-existent God. A dead God*
> *With a terrible voice.*

A totally desperate emptiness, imposed upon her by his violence, which had brought nothing into being and perpetuated nothingness, would constitute the *prima materia* of her poetry. Much is (implicitly) made of the inverse contrast Plath's situation makes with another view of the encounter with modern emptiness more traditionally conceived, of the kind that Eliot is working through in *The Waste Land* and in *Ash-Wednesday*. Plath had no use for the deep meditative method Eliot reserved for dealing further with the emptiness, which was too far gone in her case, hers being an age far more evolved in hopelessness than was

Eliot's. Plath's "panic of emptiness" alone would have to become the supportive "God" or the main motive force behind her breakthrough. Out of this "God", who was her own inversion of the God who possessed her, Plath managed strenuously to bring to birth a new dynamic *counter*-poetry of revolt. In this poetry insomnia plays a key role (an insomnia that Plath would later link up to one of the components of the experience those in concentration camps had known) and a new kind of creative process emerges from it:

> *Soon*
> *Your silent howl through the night*
> *Had made itself a moon, a fiery idol*
> *Of your God.*
> *Your crying carried its moon*
> *Like a woman a dead child.*

An *inverted* creation now comes to life, in which, miraculously if morbidly, the realities of violent inconsequence begin to unfold further:

> *Till the child stirred.*

And thus a god is born, whose inspirations begin to dictate a drastically new poetry. It is composed of the very elements of devastation that had once had Plath in their grip but are now in hers. "Everybody" is referred to this process of truth, Plath herself being involved by the "sacrifice" of her own life, through which alone that truth could be laid bare. The process implicates everyone in a ghoulish form of inverted life (of guilt) in which everything is judged from the point of view of her death; in the meanwhile Hughes, in horror, was left

> *Watching everything go up*
> *In the flames of your sacrifice*
> *That finally caught you too till you*
> *Vanished, exploding*
> *Into the flames*
> *Of the story of your God*

II

"The Colossus" is the poem in which Plath formally gives up on a traditional ideal of poetic creation. It all seems to her a sterile imposition that could only engage the modern poet in a monumental patchwork business, full of inexpressive noises, defying mending or any reconstuctive effort:

> *I shall never get you put together entirely,*
> *Pieced, glued, and properly jointed.*
> *Mule-bray, pig-grunt and bawdy cackles*
> *Proceed from your great lips.*

Contrasting with this false path is the kind of poetry she can now see herself committing to, which takes its precise start from the ruinous fate of her father. In *his* ignominious end[11] Plath sees the symbol of a Nature that is now essentially and fundamentally ruined, dispossessed of any former inspiriting grandeur:

> *O father, all by yourself*
> *You are pithy and historical ...*
> *I open my lunch on a hill of black cypress.*
> *Your fluted bones and acanthine hair are littered*
>
> *In their old anarchy to the horizon-line.*
> *It would take more than a lightning-stroke*
> *To create such a ruin.*

In this now clearly seen "ruin" or "anarchy" of history, there could only be marriage to the "shadow" of inverted realities, Nature appearing merely as the ghastly thing that is seen through the eyes of sleeplessness:

> *Nights, I squat ...*
> *... out of the wind*
>
> *Counting the red stars and those of plum-color.*
> *The sun rises under the pillar of your tongue.*
> *My hours are married to shadow.*

Hers had become, in fact, the sublime anguish of the Goddess forced to remove Herself from the paltry scene of her hero, man, who had failed things. The Goddess she can now *hear* calling out to her, out of the prospect of her own death. In "Elm" all has become clear, in the capacious knowledge the Goddess reserves about these things from the removed sphere of the death that would indict them for what they are:

I know the bottom, she says. I know it with my great tap root:
It is what you fear.
I do not fear it: I have been there.

Is it the sea you hear in me,
Its dissatisfactions?
Or the voice of nothing, that was your madness?

Love is a shadow
How you lie and cry after it
Listen: these are its hooves: it has gone off, like a horse.

All night I shall gallop thus, impetuously,
Til your head is a stone, your pillow a little turf.
Echoing, echoing.

The Goddess is helping Plath to imagine how or why it is she must be "galloping" to her death, where she shall "echo" the knowledge of the Goddess. The power of "love" can only be recovered *there*. It is the disaster of modern history, and the world's anarchy or the "sea"'s "dissatisfactions", that are driving her there. She is driven there most immediately out of the emptiness in nature that correlates to that world's horror and is directly perceived in sleeplessness:

Or shall I bring you the sound of poisons?
This is rain now, this big hush.
And this is the fruit of it: tin-white, like arsenic.

I have suffered the atrocity of sunsets.

(after a former night of sleeplessness, looking towards another).

This poem also highlights Plath's explosions from within, which now express themselves *freely* and are the basis of a rage that is the motive force behind her drive towards death:

Scorched to the root
My red filaments burn and stand, a hand of wires.

Now I break up in pieces that fly about like clubs.
A wind of such violence
Will tolerate no bystanding: I must shriek.

The moon, also, is merciless: she would drag me
Cruelly, being barren.
Her radiance scathes me. Or perhaps I have caught her.

The point of view of the poem then alters: slowly, the Goddess, who is the poem's speaker, merges with the voice of Plath's personal anguish in life—the real happenings in *her* going into feeding the Goddess's growing power over her:

> *How your bad dreams possess and endow me.*

The sublime motive force behind the drive towards death in "Elm" is rage. Overpowering the "faces of love"—for whom Plath has lived, who have become "pale irretrievables"—is the one "face" from which she can still learn. This is the "face" of "murderous" entanglement that is in possession of her psyche and involves her in the rage that alone can deal with it. The poem's final lines—"that kill, that kill, that kill"—ironically echo and appropriate to that cause, which in this case is a woman's cause, the burning rage of Lear. In "The Birthday Present" (written five months later) Plath can *already* project into her death the "calm" after "all passion spent". *Out* of this "calm" Plath speaks now as herself, in full identification with the purposes of the Goddess. She is here addressing *another* part of herself that continues to resist and doubt the rightness of her projected death by suicide:

> *I know why you will not give it to me,*
> *You are terrified*
>
> *The world will go up in a shriek, and your head with it,*
> *Bossed, brazen, an antique shield,*
>
> *A marvel to your great-grandchildren.*
> *Do not be afraid, it is not so.*
>
> *I will only take it and go aside quietly.*
> *You will not hear me opening it, no paper crackle,*
>
> *No falling ribbons, no scream at the end.*
> *I do not think you credit me with this discretion.*

The poem is, to my mind, along with "Ariel" and "Edge", among the best and the most haunting of her poems. One is overwhelmed by the echo of the voice of Christ in "Do not be afraid". This phrase brings to a climax a series of similar phrases, which clarify that it is up to the part of Plath that still resists to provide the right kind of act of death through the suicide:

> *Do not be ashamed—I do not mind if it is small.*

Do not be mean—I am ready for enormity.

The reasoning tone with which Plath continues to confront the part of herself that resists is sublime in its power of paradox:

> *Is it impossible for you to let something go and have it go whole?*
> *Must you stamp each piece in purple,*
>
> *Must you kill what you can?*

The rage that had impelled "Elm" and had led to the final absorption of Lear's rage, in the lines:

> *These are the isolate, slow faults*
> *That kill, that kill, that kill.*

is, in the calm of "Birthday Present", now fully contained:

> *Only let down the veil, the veil, the veil.*

◆   ◆   ◆

One has to turn to "Daddy" and to "Lady Lazarus" to be put in mind again of the depth of oppression, by Western realpolitik and male tradition, that Plath was throwing off in her drive toward suicide—poems that, considering their fame and popularity, do not require extensive comment. What should be re-emphasized, however, is the literalness of the psychological oppression with which Plath had had to contend. Especially impressive is her attempt, in "Daddy", to reach through to the *root* of the oppression, which, being diffuse, finally defies location:

> *In the German tongue, in the Polish town*
> *Scraped flat by the roller*
> *Of wars, wars, wars.*
> *But the name of the town is common.*
> *My Polack friend,*
> *Says there are a dozen or two.*
> *So I never could tell where you*
> *Put your foot, your root,*
> *I never could talk to you.*
> *The tongue stuck in my jaw.*

There is an allusion, in that last line, back to the trials through which she was put in trying to locate her voice, when she supposed her voice ought to have been that of tradition. Also relevant is the way Plath, in some of her most haunting lines, involves us in the idea of a world she thinks they all might yet have shared in, had the standard of Nature been truly and authentically embraced:

> *Where it pours bean green over blue*
> *In the waters off beautiful Nauset.*

Here, in fact, is the voice of the Goddess yearningly coming through, as if to remind, in the midst of the horror, of a still greater possibility, which might yet have been discovered, beyond the tragic facts and the anarchic direction of the present age.

"Lady Lazarus", for its part, is the poem to be turning to, before plunging with Plath into her death, to recover the sense of the tremendous power *over* her life, death, and rebirth she had always envisioned. That power over herself is here openly displayed, to the degree of a Coleridgean ecstatic revelation (with its echoes of the ending of "Kubla Khan"):

> *Herr God Herr Lucifer*
> *Beware*
> *Beware.*
>
> *Out of the ash,*
> *I rise with my red hair*
> *And I eat men like air.*

The final plunge towards death is taken in "Ariel". It is a sublime imagination of passage, with its concentrated evocation, first, of the element through which one passes from life into death:

> *Stasis of darkness*

—the receding world of death already crystallizing and opening out to us in

> *the substanceless blue*
> *pour of tor and distances.*

Ariel, as "horse", is the vehicular drive by which Plath is *propelled* into death, but, as "God's lioness", this drive is, at the same time, the whole of the new world that now unfolds before her vision. The world into which Plath is penetrating ("furrow") and the vehicle by which she is penetrating that world ("arc") are cognate, everything unfolding by virtue of an inner law and motion all its own, with which she could not interfere even if she wished to:

> *The furrow*
> *Splits and passes, sister to*
> *The brown arc*
> *Of the neck I cannot catch.*

As "White/Godiva"/Goddess, Plath sees herself possessed by a power that allows her to "unpeel", and unbind, even from her condition as a corpse and a victim of historical "stringencies":

> *White*
> *Godiva, I unpeel—*
> *Dead hands, dead stringencies.*

And by her putting off death, a whole new creation unfolds before us that lies beyond the judgment of the present one, as a "child's cry" *from* that present world is daringly left behind:

> *And now I*
> *Foam to wheat, a glitter of seas.*
> *The child's cry*
> *Melts in the wall.*
> *And I*
> *Am the arrow,*
>
> *The dew that flies,*
> *Suicidal, at one with the drive*
> *Into the red*
>
> *Eye, the cauldron of morning.*

In plunging to her death, Plath was drawing back into herself the power that, as a woman, she reserved of bestowing life, each breast becoming—in "Edge"—the focal point of the child she might be nursing, who is pictured as dead because she has now withdrawn that power. In death her breasts are returned to the body from which they drew their power to bestow life:

> *as petals*
> *Of a rose close when the garden*
>
> *Stiffens and odors bleed*
> *From the sweet, deep throats of the night flower.*

With this final withdrawing of life, menstruation also ceases, but not before one last, drastic version of it in the act and moment of death itself. Beyond this last experience of returning pain, the "night flower" of life's deep source, from which death also comes, breathes on intact, from out of that transcendent world of renewed creation into which Plath has plunged. Nor has the "moon", who governs the process of menstruation, anything to be "sad about" in the case of this death, for here is the usual process by which "*Her* blacks crackle and drag." By then, however, Plath has assumed complete control over this horrible process of imposed pain, with which she had been living for so long.

III

Plath had in the meantime laid down the deepest challenge, to Hughes most directly, to live back with her into the deepest sources of creation, where life has recovered itself from death. Only—death, her death, now stood in the way. A situation of utter dispossession and annihilation comes down upon Hughes: her death is, first and foremost, a judgment on him who, more than any other, experienced that death as the negation it had taken upon itself and had imposed upon others. To this would be added for him the later suicide of Assia Wevill and the death of their daughter, Shura—for all of which Hughes would, in fact, be socially much maligned.

In "A Flayed Crow in the Hall of Judgment", Hughes dramatizes himself as

> *A condensation, a gleam simplification*
> *Of all that pertained*

to those realities. Like a Miltonic devil, gasping in hell, Hughes asks of his condition:

> *Is this everlasting? Is it*
> *Stoppage and the start of nothing?*

That which remains of consciousness, as he continues to stand in life, leads him to wonder, *without* intimation of hope or purpose:

> *Or am I under attention?*
> *Do purposeful cares incubate me?*
> *Am I the self of some spore*
> *In this white of death blackness,*
> *This yoke of afterlife?*

There is the final assumption of a Lear-like submission to being overwhelmed (on the other side of his legendary rage), as Hughes is heard saying:

> *I shall not fight*
> *Against whatever is allotted to me.*

Hughes has entered a world in which "The Executioner"

> *Fills up*
> *Sun, moon, stars, he fills them up*
> *With his hemlock—*

Everything is now informed with the poison of these realities that he has been asked to drink, like an anti-Socrates dispossessed of his integrity, so that

> *You have no idea what has happened*
> *To what is no longer yours.*

In "The Executioner" and "Bedtime Anecdote", Hughes runs through a whole litany of forms of an alienated existence that is now ubiquitous. In the latter poem, he relates the impression that seemingly living things now have the effect, in his consciousness, of being merely

> *what was left of a picture*
> *In a book*
> *Under a monsoon downpour*
> *In a ruinous hut*
>
> *From which years ago his body was lifted by a leopard.*

◆   ◆   ◆

Steeped now in *his* experience of dispossession, Hughes would feel compelled to evolve his own mythology of the world's horror and inconsequence, and the result was the famous *Crow* poems, of which one, "Crow Tyrannosauros" dramatizes how it now appears as if

> *Creation quaked voices—*
> *It was a cortege of mourning and lament*

Innumerable instances of violent death and of being preyed upon to the point of death are listed, nor do this mourning and lament lead to harmonious resolution; they converge, rather, on a grotesque and inchoate cacophany of outcrying voices, as in the case of

> *the dog ... a bulging filterbag*
> *Of all the deaths it had gulped ...*
> *It could not digest their screeching finales.*
> *Its shapeless cry was a blort of all those voices.*

There is also the indifference of man, as a whole, in this widespread scene of lament and outcry:

> *Even man he was a walking*
> *Abbatoir*
> *Of innocents—*
> *His brain incinerating their outcry.*

Crow—the power in control of such a Creation—cynically entertains the idea that perhaps he should convert to the light but, at the sight of more victims, is inspired to maintain the destructive action that defines his Creation. He is indifferent, as always, to the "weeping" that meets the violence he oversees. An overwhelming violence within the whole of the Creation, transferred to the image of the sea breaking against the shore, one might suppose would have some effect in awakening Crow to the consciousness of a suffering world, and in "Crow on the Beach" Hughes imagines for a moment that it almost seems to. However, that "awakening" only leads to perplexed incomprehension that anything could be afflicting the Creation thus:

He knew he was the wrong listener unwanted
To understand or help—
His utmost gaping of brain in his tiny skull
Was just enough to wonder, about the sea,

What could be hurting so much?

◆   ◆   ◆

In "The Scream" Hughes returns to how the Creation once appeared to him, from the time of his youth—as One magnificent and busy Life, into which Death itself seemed inscribed. The facts of violent death then seemed naturally to belong to the *wheel of the galaxy*—Creation's great cycle of Life and Death. This was the fundamental idiom of Hughes's early work (an idiom far-reaching in its own right) right up to the time of Plath's suicide. At one time, he was only made the *more* "brave and creaturely" on witnessing the spectacles of violent death in the Creation. Then it happened to *him*, and he might have thought that, as in the case of a "mate" who was once greatly afflicted physically, he too could come through with a song of triumphant courage:

But a silence wedged **my** *gullet.*
. . .
The scream
Vomited itself.

Beyond affliction, *negation* in his case overwhelmed, bringing in a grotesque, shapeless chaos of unmanaged hopelessness. Contradicting the grandeur of the claims Plath had made with her death was the symbolic evidence of her corpse, which Hughes poignantly visited in the morgue. It could only seem to him that her action had gone too far, that her "hardly-used beauty" and the power of Life itself had been wasted when she took it all "away from everybody". In this view, Hughes could only see fallibility in her claims, since, now dead, she was no longer able to serve those claims herself. The terrible paradox of her effort to affirm these claims is what is highlighted in *I know well/You are not infallible*":

And I had to lift your hand for you

While your chin sank to your chest
With the sheer weariness

Of taking away from everybody
Your envied beauty, your much-desired beauty

Your hardly used beauty

Of lifting away yourself
from yourself
And weeping from the ache of the effort.

In "Prospero and Sycorax" (a title which bitterly projects Hughes and Plath in these roles), Hughes is confident in asserting that Plath must *know* that it is over for them both, that he cannot find it in him to fulfil the role assigned to him by her out of the sphere of her death, and that they remain, rather, *locked into* the human tragedy—in one projection of it as Cordelia to Lear:

She knows, like Cordelia,
He is not himself now,
And what speaks through him must be discounted—
Though it will be the end of them both.

Not that Hughes cannot contemplate his assigned role clearly, but, in his hope-lessness and his weakness, he only wishes to be re-united with her, looks ahead to his own death, when he will join her again, as

Something
Easier to live with

with some suggestion that, in any case, he could only fulfil his assigned role *in* his death, just as the challenge to assume that role comes to him out of her death.

Hughes knows and fully understands, in mythical poetical terms, that in her death Plath has been recovered into The Tree of Life, that *there* all is well:

The oak is in bliss.

and

I see the oak's bride in the oak's grasp.

There, because the Tree of Life reaches down to it all, all violence in the Creation is re-absorbed:

> *Its roots*
> *Lift arms that are a supplication*
> *Crippled with stigmata.*
> *Like the sea-carved cliffs earth lifts*
> *Loaded with dumb, uttering effigies*
> *The oak seems to die and to be dead*
> *In its love-act.*

But, as for himself, continuing in life, Hughes knows only his own pathetically remote distance from that prospect:

> *As **I** lie under it*
>
> *In a brown leaf nostalgia*
> *only,*
> *An acorn stupor.*

Hughes looks out into great Creating Nature and sees evidence everywhere of a productive re-building from the world's corruptible matter, as in "*The swallow—re-building—/Collects the lot*":

> *But what **I** did only shifted the dust about.*
> *And what crossed my mind*
> *Crossed into outer space.*

He is unable to *re-create* from her death—is rather, Donne-like, in *her* absence an absence to himself, and he feels caught in a reverse form of relationship of falcon to falconer, unable to penetrate back to the place whence his falconer now beckons to him, from the other side of death.

IV

Hughes, as a poet, would finally confess himself unable to fulfil the role Plath had challenged of him by her death. One might say that he comes into a kind of acceptance of this fact and of the judgment that has left him drastically without devices, as in "Prometheus on the Crag #2":

> *The blue wedge through his breastbone, into the rock*
> *Unadjusted by vision or prayer—so*

Surrendering to this kind of helplessness, he can yet sense a recovery of strength of a sort. He can find a *form* of identification with Prometheus, inasmuch as Hughes bears in *himself* the secret by which a significant resolution might be found—if only *he* could "be let stir", as in "#9". Only, the "man" he had fashioned—the man of weakness who is subjected to judgment—and the "god" of destiny who has insisted on this judgment

> *Dare not let [him] stir.*

It is impossible to think he could come into the power involved in the role that Plath has challenged of him. In the meantime, he can free himself enough, can recover enough strength, to shout, as in "#3":

> *a world's end shout.*

This scatters his maligners, who would suffocate all creativity that is left, and by his shout they are themselves thrown into dismay as to those elusive "holy, happy notions" of fulfilled promise from which, along with himself, all have now been banished.

◆   ◆   ◆

Nevertheless, Hughes has also been sensing, if ever so tenuously, that

> *When everything that can fall has fallen,*
> *Something rises.*

and in "The Guide" he testifies to an experience beyond the emptying (by *the red wind*) and the long scouring (by *the black wind*), when

> *the non-wind, the least breath,*
> *Fills you from easy sources.*

In "The Risen" there is a new experience of "standing" and of "lifting" again, and he can even identify the *shape* of this further power, which has re-emerged from the disaster, sensing it soaring above the world as

> *a cross, eaten by light*
> *On the Creator's face.*

He adds that

> *Where he [this power] alights*
> *A skin sloughs from a leafless apocalypse.*

There is a throwing off of the disaster, and a *re-creation* from the apparent nothingness, as

> *Each atom*

that yet remains

> *engraves with a diamond.*

and

> *The dirt becomes God*

again. Hughes, however, must ask a further question:

> *But when will he land*
> *On a man's wrist?*

When and how will he find himself no longer the dispossessed falcon to Plath's falconer beyond death? He himself must be the falconer to the falcon of this new power that he senses now working within him, from within the experience he has undergone because of her.

◆   ◆   ◆

In "Chinese History of Colden Water" Hughes supposes a condition of Creation that is possessed of the power to support him through what he has known, because unconsciously *it* has lived through

> *The bloody matter of the Cross*

It has also lived through the nightmare of puritanical judgment from his society that met the fate Hughes inherited. This judgment he relates to a corrupt civilization that has fallen away from the ways in which the Creation works. The re-affirmation of this abiding condition of the Creation, right through the tragedy he has known, recovers him, in Faust-like fashion, as it

> *washed and washed at his eye.*
> *Washed from his ear*

> *All but the laughter of foxes.*

He might have written "all but the abiding Life of the Creation". It is *another* form of Life, however, that Hughes is celebrating in a poem like "Swifts", where he notes that

> *the globe's still working, the Creation's*
> *Still waking refreshed.*

Here self-renewing Life, as a thrilling and momentarily consoling distraction, is still being observed outside himself. It is, in fact, the *old* Hughes one finds momentarily flexing himself again here.

One has to turn, rather, to another form of poem to get the measure of the Hughes in whom a *new* perception of Creation's Life has emerged. "Salmon Eggs" and "October Salmon" offer that perception, which comes to a head in the newly found revelation that

> *"Only birth matters".*

In the former poem, this perception concentrates around a view that

> *Something else is going on in the river*
> *More vital than death ...*
> *... more grave than life*

The poem speaks of a *telling* and of *tidings* that are heard from within the river's

> *melt of mouthing silence*

and

> *the charge of light*
> *Dumb with immensity.*

as well as of

> *The nameless*
> *Teeming inside atoms—and inside the haze,*
> *And inside the sun and inside the earth.*

The whole of the Creation in fact concentrates itself on

> *Swaddling the egg.*

in *one* expression of

> *the liturgy*
> *Of Earth's advent—harrowing, crowned ...*

Here we might say the new power Hughes was celebrating in "Risen" *has* finally landed on his wrist, showing itself fully now from within the Creation of which Hughes has himself become an expression.

The *other* side to his newly found understanding, one might say, is that death does *not* matter, and in "October Salmon" we have one final measure of all that that can mean, in relation to the life Hughes has suffered. It may be the finest poem he wrote, Hughes's old, pervasive focus on the Creation taking on here an entirely new *form*, since he has been through an evolution. The October salmon has returned to its source to breed new life, to carry on with what matters. We see in him what has *become* of the Great Creating Life that was once bestowed upon the egg:

> *Such sweet months, so richly embroidered into earth's beauty dress,*
> *Her life-robe ...*
> *...*
> *Hangs in the flow, a frayed scarf.*

Favored once so richly by the Goddess, he is now the model sufferer, utterly resigned both to historical subjection and to man's more incidental (mean) violence, ready to be exposed and to be made utterly vulnerable for the only thing that matters:

What a death-in-life—to be his own spectre!
…
He haunts his own staring vigil
And suffers the subjection, and the dumbness,
And the humiliation of the role!

Hughes's search has come that far, and it is in no obvious triumphant way that he has responded to Plath's challenge. Her death has, finally, yielded new life, but in the most tenuous form of renewed purpose. Hughes has worked his way into a new influence in the Creation only because his longsuffering of that death continues. Her death is giving birth to a new perception of Creation's ceaseless power of *re*-creation, and we have come into a new evolutionary dimension, of which "The Risen" is the testament and poems like "Salmon Eggs" and "October Salmon" are the first creations. A new scion of the Creation has been added to what there is, and, with poems such as these, human consciousness itself has become a new thing, endowed with an access of fresh evolutionary power. Likewise as a literary critic[1] Hughes was driving progressively forward in his understanding of the Goddess's forbidding claims on our lives, which he, for one, knew remain, to challenge us from the very midst of the condition of nothingness of our time.

---

1.   In *Shakespeare and the Goddess of Complete Being* and in his Introduction to *A Choice of Coleridge's Verse*.

4

Graves and the Goddess

It was, of course, Graves who, over this period, gave renewed currency to the Goddess whose existence, as he shows, has always been implicit in the development of human evolution.[12] To turn from Plath and Hughes to Graves is to be made aware of the confidence with which Graves proclaimed *his* purpose of living for and with the Goddess, in spite of the immense difficulties he also faced in knowing Her. Nor is *he* oblivious to the historical struggle occasioned by the Goddess's deep subjection to the forces of Western realpolitik and economic dictation. He knew as well as anyone what was at stake, or all that would have to be un-done, before one could see a general return of the Goddess in Her proper form, as the primal Spirit Who reigns in and through Nature's Creation[13]. But he had very early been through a reckoning with historical matters, and he is at a certain point rightly boastful of his hard-earned emancipation from them[14]. What his life's work consequently offers is an intensely privileged understanding of what ought to have been possible to us for some time and what he is proclaiming is now possible, if only we were ready to devote ourselves to what the Goddess requires of us.

Not that the effort to know the Goddess again as She really is in Her Creation, beyond Her historical subjection, does not demand the most strenuous application of the poetic spirit or, indeed, the continuous support of a poetic faith gleaned from a mythical past that we must labor to learn from once again. What *is* possible, by way of this effort, is the sort of *conscious* recognition between the poet and his Muse that *will* begin to open up the Goddess's influences to us again. In "The Unnamed Spell", the "spell" in which the poet-hero and his Muse are caught originates in an "act" of recognition between them whose effect has been to sow in the "heart" of his Muse the "more than tree" that the poet goes on to celebrate in its luxuriating "Seven ells above earth". This shared "heart", concentrating itself in a "kiss", is then represented as the sun, the

> *All heal, golden surprise*

that suddenly blazes up from within the environment of this "tree" as the

> *Wakeful glory*

now set off against the austere natural setting without, where

> *the grove winters*

The possibility of such inner "wakeful glory", even in the midst of nature's desolation, will explain what Graves intends where he speaks, in "The White Goddess", of being

> ... *gifted, even in November,*
> *Rawest of seasons, with so huge a sense*
> *Of her nakedly worn magnificence,*
> *We forget cruelty and past betrayal*

The threat of cruelty from, and betrayal by, the Goddess, which comes from the stringency of her demands on the Imagination, has been cast aside in "The Unnamed Spell". The problematic nature of the Imaginative engagement over which She presides has been (momentarily) transcended, the reflection of Graves's personal success with his Muse at this time.[15]

If he merely "likens" the spell to a "tree" "luxuriating/Seven ells above earth" or to "A branch Hell-harrowing", this is because Graves remains otherwise baffled by the literal import of the world he is penetrating, must have recourse, in the last analysis, to how this world has been represented in mythical accounts of it in the past. He stands, in the meantime, poised for a deeper movement into that world into which former heroes have proceeded. The threshhold of that world is represented as an "arch" (of the creative intelligence) in which he lies suspended, anticipating his own entrance through. In "The Gorge" the metaphor is altered to the "bridge" that hangs "concealed from view/Even in sunlight" with "the gorge bottomless" beneath him. The great risk of the Imagination, that one may fall into mental disorder from a presumptuous venturing, is again invoked, but is nevertheless countered by the Imaginative strength the poet puts forth, propelled by his honest need.

Supported in such strength, the poet succeeds in evoking, through the suggestion that the bridge

> *Swings and echoes*

an Imaginative potency that draws towards it echoes of the inner world that he would penetrate. Graves continues to insist on this "crossing", even though he has admitted that the Goddess lies "beyond all hopes of access", acknowledging therein an essential ignorance of her mythical status. In the meantime he has added another understanding of his distance from Her. "Between us", he says, *howl phantoms of the long dead*

who died in despair in their own presumption to know Her, but whose fate he temerariously denies by insisting on his own crossing over to Her now.

In moments when the poet's Muse *wavers* in her commitment, the Goddess's presence insists on asserting itself despite the poet's readiness to think himself freed of his own commitment (because of the burden he feels from it himself). In "A Restless Ghost", the poet weakens before his realization that his "heart" is still engaged. He is already imagining, from his presumed *dis*engagement, that, in any case, "hills" and "coast" will continue to echo splendidly the effects of the Goddess's presence after his Muse is gone. It will then be for the poet an easier life with the Goddess, among the nostalgic relics of Her visitation:

> *Alas for obstinate doubt: the dread*
> *Of error in supposing my heart freed,*
> *All care for her stone dead!*
> *Ineffably will shine the hills and radiant coast*
> *Of early morning when she is gone indeed,*
> *Her divine elements disbanded, disembodied*
> *And through the misty orchards in love spread—*
> *When she is gone indeed—*

But the poet remains aware that that moment has not come, and it is out of his very imagining of those relics that the poet succeeds in evoking for us the power of Her presence at the moment:

> *But still among them moves her restless ghost.*

In this image Muse and Goddess *remain* one, the uncertainty (or restlessness) with which the Muse is assuming her role as medium for the Goddess being a measure of the intensity of the Goddess's presence. The difficulty of engagement, for both Muse and poet, continues.

The Goddess's presence is conveyed in this poem amidst Nature's phenomenal scene, which the Goddess informs, but She makes Her presence felt more directly in the Muse herself. In "The Intrusion" the poet happens unsuspectingly upon his Muse in her private anguish, and is overwhelmed by the Goddess's presence: She suddenly manifests in the Muse in a "Divine mourning for what cannot be." The Muse herself has been taken up by the Goddess directly, as reflected in her "white motionless face and folded hands/Framed in such thunderclouds of sorrow." Confronted with this development the poet recognizes his powerlessness in averting it, and it redounds to his faithfulness to the process the Goddess commands that he can acknowledge, at the cost of his own good fortune, what the Goddess has spoken. For

> *This is the dark edge of her double-axe*

That axe is now sharpened against the incapacities both poet and Muse have betrayed in relation to Her creation.

In "Apple Island", the severity of the Goddess's will is measured by the cruel side of Nature's scene, the "Wrecking" seas and "dangerously clear" shining of the moon that overwhelm the capacity of the Imagination to see its way to the basis of Her creation. This the poet mythically places in the sphere of "Apple Island" beyond that scene, where the poet says "I may not hope to dwell apart with you", his Muse. To find his way there, the poet would have to submit to that horrible "death" at the Goddess's hands, of which Graves speaks so extensively elsewhere:

> *Unless my breast be docile to the dart—*

This is in some sense a literal death, evoking the language of "The White Goddess" where the poet saw himself amongst those who are

> *Heedless of where [Her] next bright bolt may fall.*

The poet's temerarious spirit has altered in "Apple Island" to an honest confession of baffled limitation. The poet does not in this instance feel that he is worthy of the venture, but he does not for that reason feel any less committed to the vision. There is in any case no other life to be had, which is why in the end there can be no fear of the forces that, for now, range themselves against him. They themselves are but a part of the great whole over which the Goddess has command, a thought that paradoxically leads the poet back to a new Imagination of the "death" for which he might yet make himself worthy:

> *And though I may not hope to dwell apart*
> *With you on Apple Island*
> *Unless my breast be docile to the dart—*

Why should I fear your element, the sea,
Or the full moon, your mirror,
Or the halved apple from your holy tree?

In the cut or "halved" apple is represented that mythical death that *would* link the poet from this life to the other where the whole is to be had, along the lines of the death of the mythical Curoi, whose soul was said to be *in* the apple[16].

There is in any case much consciousness in Graves that we now inhabit a world that has cut us off from our mythical destiny. No longer is there in our modern civilization any "envy" of the hero who once managed the "journey" to the Goddess's "island paradise", as expressed in "The Hero":

No blood is poured now at the hero's tomb,
No prayers intoned,
The island paradise is unfrequented,
And neither Finn, nor Ogier, nor Arthur,
Returns to prophesy our common doom.

Much store is set, consequently, by the legendary evidence of success from the past, into which the poet's Imagination feels free to enter, as it strongly evokes to itself the experience it would encompass. It was the hero's distinction that *he* submitted to "death" at the Goddess's hands in a spirit of faith that transcended the baffled sorrow of his society:

For he alone, amid excessive keening,
Might voyage to that island paradise,
In the red West,
Where bees[17] come thronging to the apple flow
And thrice three damsels in a tall house
Tend the mead-vat of inspiration.

"In Her Praise" is the poem in which Graves formally acknowledges that no single woman, as the poet's Muse, for long supports the Goddess's presence in her. However, She Herself "abides", and the consequence for the poet is that he is called:

                    to live on
To parley with the pure, oracular dead,
To hear the wild pack whimpering overhead,
To watch the moon tugging at her cold tides.

Nature's challenging enigma continues to engage the poet's creative intelligence, in spite of the bafflement with which he finds himself contending on every hand. Then, in a late phase of Graves's struggle, it appears as if a breakthrough has finally come. Once again, as in "The Unnamed Spell", the moment coincides with his new success with his personal Muse of *that* period.[18]

◆   ◆   ◆

What difficulty Graves had known in finding a stable basis in the commitment shared between himself and his Muse had always been connected with the uncertain cycle of life and death (harvest and drought; abundance and barrenness) in which the Goddess operates.[19] Also, life and death stand radically opposed, so that it remained literally impossible for the poet to find his way to the Goddess with his Muse from this life to the other. That more must be possible at a certain point overwhelmed the poet, and out of that intuition came Graves' discovery of the Black Goddess, access to whom in the past had been sought by the poet only after he had passed "uncomplaining through all the passionate ordeals to which the White Goddess may subject him"[20]. What the Black Goddess promised was a "miraculous certitude in love"[21] that went beyond the "unpredictable vagaries" of his dependence on the White Goddess.[22] This extraordinary possibility was then uncannily fulfilled in Graves's life with a new prospect of love between himself and his Muse, for the first time experienced as a "joint venture"[23]. In this case, a "perfection of *reciprocal* understanding between the lovers" had materialized. It was now a case of the Muse acting with full consciousness of her role.[24]

And so, in "Deliverance", as the poet and his new Muse lie "disembodied under the trees", a greater world opens up for the first time, in which they feel themselves transported beyond the confines of the created universe, "beyond the stellar mill", into "blue pastures":

> *Lying disembodied under the trees*
> *(Their slender trunks converged above us*
> *Like rays of a five-fold star) we heard*
> *A sudden whinnying from the dark hill.*
>
> *Our implacable demon, foaled by love,*
> *Never knew rein or saddle; though he drank*
> *From a stream winding by, his blue pastures*
> *Ranged far out beyond the stellar mill.*

He had seared us two so close together
That death itself might not disjoin us;
It was impossible you could love me less,
It was impossible I could love you more.

The "blue pastures" evoke a creative "eternity"[25] still very much associated with their present life in the terrestrial world. The creative power (of their love) in which they have expanded, is replenished from a source in the world in which they live ("a stream winding by"). Expansion has come from the dark womb—or "dark hill"—of their creative engendering and, itself a young effect, is tenderly associated with a young foal whose roaming into another world takes them up with itself. The Imaginative breakthrough is symbolically marked by the "five-fold star" which the trees above the lovers figure forth in their heights—literal trees in this case that, yet, announce the passage through "love" into that other world. Such "five-foldness" is the mark of the halved apple at its centre that has always been mythically associated with a breakthrough into immortality.[26] Only the closest working together of the poet and his Muse, of a sort that Graves had not experienced before, could achieve such a breakthrough, which has finally cracked open the enigma of "death":

He had seared us two so close together
That death itself might not disjoin us;

That the problem of death would appear to have been resolved is, among other ways in which this is emphasized to us, also deduced from the fact that the lovers could not love each other more or with a more perfect reciprocity:

It was impossible you could love me less,
It was impossible I could love you more.

In "Deliverance" the lovers are very much in control of their experience, but in "This Holy Month", that control is momentarily lost, and both lovers are sorely plagued in consequence. The poet confesses to being physically thrown about:

Flung … at midnight into filthy ditches

while his Muse finds herself incapacitated to the point of paralysis:

> *... sleeplessness, dismay and darkness,*
> *Paralyzed ...*

The way in which they are plagued is in direct relation to their capacity for exaltation. The demon or creative power that in moments of control fills their lives so fully is said to be the same who, in their denial of him, would subject them to affliction. And from *this* evidence the poet rallies them to a fresh commitment, as if release from affliction were only a matter of their again finding the right spin on their experience, especially as they cannot avoid their involvement with the power they've released. This exhortation becomes for the poet and his Muse an occasion for living *back* into what they have known of a world that from its otherworldly source now fills wholly with the Goddess's influence:

> *We both know well he was the same demon*
> *...*
> *Who ...*
> *Astonishes us with blossom, silvers the hills*
> *With more than moonlight, summons bees in swarms*
> *From the Lion's mouth to fill our hives with honey*
> *Turns flesh into fire, and eyes into deep lakes;*
> *And so may do once more, this holy month.*

The Goddess expresses Herself in the natural world around them in a way that now outdoes the presence of Her influence in the past—for now She

> *silvers the hills*
> *With <u>more</u> than moonlight*

"[A]stonishes" is also intended to convey this greater influence. At the same time, She creates through the lovers themselves, and in a more complete way than before, because out of a direct link now from Her mythic source, which has always been related to the "bees" that "[throng] to the apple flow" of Her "island paradise" (to quote again from "The Hero"). These "bees" have been summoned from the dark normally unyielding abyss of the Imagination—the "Lion's mouth"—to work their potency directly in the lovers' passion. It is a passion possessed of qualities—"flesh" turning to "fire" and "eyes" into "deep lakes"—that fix it in a complete circuitry, incorporating also the natural world around. In "Tomorrow's Envy of Today", this achievement—of completeness of their passions won—is celebrated openly; it is celebrated in defiance of the judgments of those to come who will look back upon it as a wild, historically unsubstantiated claim. The claimed achievement will have ceased with the lovers themselves, but the lovers know that they experience it now, and the poet insists on their completeness in this moment, which makes of them

> *... flowers that never fade,*
> *Leaves that never shrivel, truth persistent*
> *Not as a prophecy of bliss to fall*
> *A thousand generations hence on lovers*
> *More fortunately circumstanced than we,*
> *But as a golden interlock of power*
> *Looped about every bush and branching tree.*

The completeness of the circuitry that involves the lovers, in their passion, with "every" outgrowth of burgeoning life in the natural world is insisted on again here. Behind this complete interpenetration of worlds lies the completeness of the influence of the Goddess's order in which the further mystery of an eternal, incorruptible life is contained. That influence being now complete, it pre-empts the future, inasmuch as no greater creative evolution can be imagined. All has been achieved finally on the basis of that "miraculous certitude" that has come from:

> *... the close engagement*
> *Of Moon and Lion that we have witnessed*
> *Here in this lair,*

Goddess, or Moon, has in this latest phase of the poet's life allowed Herself to be completely engaged by the poet's Imagination or Lion ("close" possessing the additional sense of "contained" as well as "intimate"). The implied contrast, crystallizing out of the poet's oeuvre, is with that chronic condition of *dis*possession in which the poet (as Her "lion lover") had travailed in the past, because of the Goddess's inconstant influence, which had always been mediated principally by the Moon.[27]

Finally, we come to "Conjunction", in which Graves wonders what shall happen to himself and his Muse "afterwards", which is to say, in their common afterlife. If the poet affirms at once: "none need enquire", this is because poet and Muse are *already* living out their life in the world to come. The condition in which they shall one day find themselves in death can already be deduced directly from their present situation. Thus, what is offered as a projection of their afterlife

condition resounds with their achievement in the immediate present which trans-
ports them directly into that sphere that had formerly seemed accessible to
Graves only in mythical accounts from the past:

> *They are poised there in conjunction, beyond time,*
> *At an oak-tree top level with Paradise:*
> *Its leafy tester unshaken where they stand*
> *Palm to palm, mouth to mouth, beyond desire*
> *Perpetuating lark song, perfume, colour,*
> *And the tremulous gasp of watchful winds,*
>
> *Past all unbelief, we know them held*
> *By peace and light and irrefragable love—*
> *Twin paragons, our final selves,*

Here again is the perfection of the Goddess's circuitry, which now courses
through the lovers simultaneously out of nature *and* the otherworld, so that life
on earth is interchangeably taken for life in death. The Goddess's will has come
to fulfillment in how the poet and Muse are now engaged.

But what in the meantime has become of the mythological structure in which
Graves had once supported himself so strongly, over that long period of trial
when the poet felt less fortunately endowed with the Goddess's favor, yet when
far more of the otherworldly landscape was delineated for us? In the later phase,
Graves's representation of the Goddess's influence comes to a head in the final,
unitary image of the oak-tree which, as it were, bodies forth that perfect unfolding of experience, out of this world into the other, into which poet and Muse
have worked themselves.[28] A similar unfolding of himself and his Muse in the
earlier phase was imagined by the poet in "The Unnamed Spell" where the poet
says of the creative "spell" that has overcome them:

> *liken it only*
> *To the more than tree luxuriating*
> *Seven ells above earth:*

However, there the further mythological setting was retained:

> *A branch Hell-harrowing*

—one might suppose, because the mythological setting is still depended on, in
the more limited Imaginative effort of that time. Certainly there is progression in

Graves's quest: from an earlier dependency on myth to a more self-reliant approach in the later phase that would appear to bode more in the way of a literal achievement. The later representation has been seen as precisely that: an advancement in the development of Graves's experience, with a "difference" in relation to the earlier representation "only of degree", but of "degree" nevertheless. The "poetic trance" of the earlier phase (identified with the "mythical" trance) is thus distinguished from "the trance of mystical illumination which has developed out of it."[29]

But what if this final relegating of the poetic, mythological setting turned out to be a limitation? To turn back to "The White Goddess" is to be reminded of the motive out of which Graves initially pursued his quest. It was originally a matter not of coming into possession of Her influence in the self only or primarily, but of knowing *Her*; to break *through* Nature's desolation was to emerge into a direct vision of the Goddess Herself:

> *It was a virtue not to stay,*
> *To go our headstrong and heroic way*
> *Seeking her out at the volcano's head,*
> *Among pack ice, or where the track had faded*
> *Beyond the cavern of the seven sleepers:*
> *Whose broad high brow was white as any leper's*
> *Whose eyes were blue, with rowan-berry lips*
> *With hair curled honey-coloured to white hips.*

Where the poet arrives at the extreme reaches of Nature's scene—beyond the place where the Imagination has transformed out of its own inner potentiality ("the seven sleepers") and where "the track" of the Imaginative quest *leaves* this world—the Goddess Herself arises. One need not dwell on what it signified for Graves, after the in-depth research into the Goddess material he'd offered in his book[1], to be finally bringing forward this concentrated picture of Who She was, as it were as a distillation of his living over many years with the wide-ranging depictions of Her existence through numerous mythical cultures.

In "To Juan", this effort to finally bring the Goddess into view is as extensive and as great as anywhere in Graves's work. The effort is especially connected here with the attempt to do justice to the whole *range* of Her creation, with something surviving in this presentation of the depth of Graves's recent research, and as if it could only be a case, with the vision of Her, of the *whole* creation coming into

---

1.   *The White Goddess.*

view at once. Compare with this the form in which She is given to us in the later phase, where nothing of Herself comes into view and without any further evocation of the particularities of Her otherworldly order, except for that centralizing configuration of the oak-tree in which experience in this world and experience of the other are said to unite. The natural scene has in the meantime also retired from view except for what is retained from it of the mysteries of burgeoning life that are eternally assured by the action of the Goddess. The scene of nature's desolation has itself been left behind.

In "To Juan" Graves narrates how it is a case of bringing to expression the influence of the Goddess first as She manifests through the several worlds of nature that include trees, beasts and birds—as well as the starry worlds. All of these worlds are then harmoniously referred to the encircling Zodiac and the Goddess's "Triple Will" that concerns life, death and their further union, and in which She expresses Herself out of Her three worlds of Earth, the Underworld and Sky or Heaven:

> *Is it of trees you tell, their months and virtues,*
> *Or strange beasts that beset you,*
> *Of birds that croak at you the Triple Will?*
> *Or of the Zodiac*

To take stock of the Goddess's creation is to be made aware, at the same time, of an immediate *doubleness* to Her form, as She reaches out both to the world of Heaven above and to the Underworld beneath, the influences of these opposed worlds combining in the vision of the Goddess possessed of a "silver beauty" but with the form of "fish below the thighs", as She has always mythically been seen. Which is to say that She combines in Her form both the upper and the lower aspects of the *Earthly* creation that most immediately express the two sides of Her otherworldly influence.

In "The White Goddess" She appears strictly in Her upper form, though with the additional reflection in the tone of Her skin of the "whiteness" of disease and death. I would suggest that She only appears thus there because the breakthrough enacted is in a *first* stage; there the personal Imagination has only initially broken through the confines of Nature. But in the mythopoeic Imagination on which Graves is building in "To Juan", death itself is engaged, and it is as if a vision of the Goddess in a *second* stage were being mediated: She appears in the doubleness of Her creation just before the Imaginative spirit takes the plunge into death. She transforms yet again, suddenly bearing the "leafy quince" of the Love-Goddess

Aphrodite in one hand while with the other She beckons Her appointed disciple in sinister fashion, though smilingly, to death. She appears, thus, in all the attractiveness She exercises in Her reigning power over life, and, in that same vision, as the jealous Crone of the Underworld Who summons Her disciple unto death but Who communicates, by Her smile, that the route *will* be back from death to life.

And so Her disciple *takes* that plunge into death, engages the great "snake" of the "ocean" of death, out of which the Goddess's own "fish" form is shaped[30], for he knows that he will be returned from death[31]:

> *Or of the undying snake from chaos hatched,*
> *Whose coils contain the ocean,*
> *Into whose chops with naked sword he springs,*
> *Then in black water, tangled by the reeds,*
> *Battles three days and nights,*
> *To be spewed up beside her scalloped shore?*

At which point the poet suddenly returns to the immediate scene in nature that he shares with his son:

> *Much snow is falling, winds roar hollowly,*

—the dire question being raised: how, then, to bridge the gap, between one's immediate place in nature and the astounding prospect of a mythical destiny truly shared with the Goddess? For us, from our position in the world, it *must* be a case of "fear", that one must *go* to one's death. There is also bound to be a crying out for the "love" that will support one through that forbidding fate and ultimately save us from it. It *is* a case of living, from moment to moment, in the sorrow of consuming oneself, as one moves inexorably towards death. However, even the log in the fireplace that consumes itself as it burns knows that only in being consumed can the fire finally burn:

> *Fear in your heart cries to the loving-cup:*
> *Sorrow to sorrow as the sparks fly upward.*
> *The log groans and confesses:*
> *There is one story and one story only.*

It is a matter, consequently, of "dwell"-ing on what the Goddess, in Her "graciousness" and by her "smiling", has "promised" as the reward for the journey through death with Her. The certainty is that the "flowers", which have gone under or been trampled on by the "great boar" of Her deathly will, will invariably return. For it is *with Her* that we return Who Herself demonstrates the power of rising again from that "sea" of death where She lives also, "wild" with the power of Her certain emergence back from that dire realm:

> Dwell on her graciousness, dwell on her smiling,
> Do not forget what flowers
> The great boar trampled down in ivy time.
> Her brow was creamy as the crested wave,
> Her sea-grey eyes were wild
> But nothing promised that is not performed.

In spite of Graves's claim, in the later phase, to an experience of completeness—of a sort that appears to place him outside the repeated cycle of death and rebirth, from the presentation offered in the earlier phase it is clear that that cycle is not so easily transcended. The weight of evidence points rather to the idea that one continues to submit to it, as well one must if it is a matter of *growth* in knowledge, from one's present uninformed experience. The knowledge of death awaits us, but if it is to be of use to us here, where we have life, that knowledge we must bring back with us. If we assume, what's more, that in any given life we can only have a more or less developed consciousness of the cycle, then it may be that many deaths will be required of us before we can reach the kind of consciousness that the Imaginative hero of old brought with him into *his* death, that gave him such assurance of his fate. Then the hero reaches the point at which Graves can imagine him breaking free of the cycle, having become perfect in his knowledge along with the Goddess. What Graves would appear to be sensing is that some intimation, however faint, of that final condition may be had even now, though this is to project a condition that stands far ahead in the future. In the meantime, the Goddess might make use of Her emissary—as in the case of Sylvia Plath—to challenge us more directly back to Her creation, insisting through Her emissary on a more substantial effort than at present is being made—that it *must* be a matter of restoring ourselves to the Creation and that it must be by the un-doing of the social-economic oppression that Graves himself saw as the chief enemy to the return of the Goddess in our lives.

5

The Visionary Bitterness of Yeats

We may well ask what form an actual culture of the Goddess would take, and the question would often be put to Graves though he was at pains to say that it would only be answered after things got much worse.[32] One thing he could say with some assurance:

> The Goddess is no townswoman: she is the Lady of the Wild Things, haunting the wooded hill-tops ...[33]

However, a change for the better could not be put off for very long, for

> the longer her hour is postponed, and therefore the more exhausted by man's irreligious improvidence the natural resources of the soil and sea become, the less merciful will her five-fold mask be, and the narrower the scope of action that she grants to whichever demi-god she chooses to take as her temporary consort in godhead.

Graves's inclination is to respond with a poem ("The Return of the Goddess"):

> Let us placate her in advance by assuming the cannibalistic worst:

> Under your Milky Way,
> And slow-revolving Bear,
> Frogs from the alder-thicket pray
> In terror of the judgment day,
> Loud with repentance there.

> The frog they crowned as king
> Grew sodden, lurched and sank.
> Dark waters bubble from the spring,
> An owl floats by on silent wing,
> They invoke you from each bank.

> At dawn you shall appear,
> A gaunt, red-wattled crane,
> She whom they know too well for fear,
> Lunging your beak down like a spear
> To fetch them home again.

It was also Yeats's view that what the Goddess had to offer would have to be worked out through man's *suffering* of the process of history, though here the Goddess might occasionally condescend to join man *in* his struggle. Hence, the prototypic significance Yeats attached to Helen of Troy through whom the Goddess once made Her dramatic appearance in history. She had appeared again (see

"The Sorrow of Love") in the figure of Maud Gonne who had brought both earth and man back to their former condition, in a direct relationship to Her for the bringing in of Whose reign the world was once again "laboring":

> *And then you came with those red mournful lips,*
> *And with you came the whole of the world's tears,*
> *And all the trouble of her labouring ships,*
> *And all the trouble of her myriad years.*

Yeats's scene would cloud over, however, when Gonne would stray from their purposes to entertain violent politics as the way to bring about the transformation of their society they both sought. In his first view of it (in "Reconciliation"), Yeats would see this tragic divagation as the consequence of Gonne's being in possession of an excess of promise in conflict with an age unfit to respond with the cultured work required to see that transformation through:

> *Why should I blame her that she filled my days*
> *With misery, or that she would of late*
> *Have taught to ignorant men most violent ways,*
> *Or hurled the little streets upon the great,*
> *Had they but courage equal to their desire?*
> *What could have made her peaceful with a mind*
> *That nobleness made simple as a fire,*
> *With beauty like a tightened bow, a kind*
> *That is not natural in an age like this,*
> *Being high and solitary and most stern?*
> *...*
> *Was there another Troy for her to burn?*

Later Yeats would not be so generous, and his former Muse he would see (in "A Prayer for My Daughter") as bearing violent qualities that were the antithesis of those he knew were indispensible to authentic cultural evolution:

> *Have I not seen the loveliest woman born*
> *Out of the mouth of Plenty's horn,*
> *Because of her opinionated mind,*
> *Barter that horn and every good*
> *By quiet natures understood*
> *For an old bellows full of angry wind?*

There loomed in Yeats's mind the deep foreboding of historical forces that were coming to subvert the cultural values with which he had aligned himself, and he saw these forces foreshadowed already in the political direction Maud Gonne had taken. Hence the "angry wind" of her violent politics and its corresponding extension in the "wind" that—coming from the "sea"—now "screams" around the "tower" in which Yeats ensconces himself along with his daughter. Yeats projects into this "wind" all the violent forces of the future that are now coming towards them:

> *Once more the storm is howling, …*
> *…*
> *And for an hour I have walked and prayed*
> *Because of the great gloom that is in my mind.*
>
> *I have walked and prayed for this young child an hour*
> *And heard the sea-wind scream upon the tower*
> *And under the arches of the bridge, and scream*
> *In the elms above the flooded stream;*
> *Imagining in excited reverie*
> *That the future years had come,*
> *Dancing to a frenzied drum,*
> *Out of the murderous innocence of the sea.*

The "storm" on which Yeats concentrates here is, no less, the storm of modern political violence and the extreme hatred that would fuel it. That hatred and the violence Yeats thought historically inevitable, as his phrase suggests—"the murderous innocence of the sea". Out of the "sea" of history comes at once both innocence *and* murderousness, as alternating epochs, so that in "The Second Coming" Yeats could clearly imagine how in the next phase of civilization something terrible was destined to be born, some monstrous inversion of the Birth of Christ that had inaugurated the epoch in which all had lived up to that point:

> *And what rough beast, its hour come round at last,*
> *Slouches toward Bethlehem to be born?*

More and more Yeats would insist on the inevitability of the pattern, but that is not to say that he did not see his emergence into the epoch of violence as overwhelmingly tragic.

By "Nineteen Hundred and Nineteen", Yeats's great cultural hopes are dramatically giving way *to* the modern turn towards violence. In these hopes was contained the reflection of committed service to the Goddess. The "ingenious lovely things" to which Yeats, in the artistic culture he had promoted, had given expression had reflected the effort of man to bring the Goddess's earthly order into being, "beauty" to birth through "laboring", and "love" through "sorrow". "Man is in love" declares Yeats, although nothing could be done about the historical subjection that follows. To live into that subjection with Yeats is to be reminded of the deep challenge the modern debacle would pose, beyond the many heroic efforts to withstand it. He himself had personally much to lose, and his attitude was dismay and bitterness. It is not that he continues to affirm the cultural hope in spite of the violence, for as he notes now decisively:

> *No work can stand.*

It is truer to say that his cultural faith must now contend directly with the force of violence in nature that has overcome it. He has now come to a fuller conclusion:

> *Man is in love and loves what vanishes*

There is also a strained attempt to work his way into an acceptance of inevitable reality:

> *What more is there to say?*

But it is clear that Yeats is here still rationalizing the tragic defeat to himself, overwhelmed by the fact that it is now actually happening.

Defeat on this scale, he is finding, is not so easy to live with. There is a peculiar hysterical strain in his response to the violence that shows he is not yet the equal of the reality in which he is now immersed. It was still a case, at this point, of his asserting a *view* of it, as where he declares:

> *All men are dancers, and their tread*
> *Goes to the barbarous clangour of a gong.*

How the two dimensions (of dancing and barbarousness) coincide has not been grasped in historical terms, even though by then Yeats could grasp well how the creative spirit only expresses itself as a result of a mysterious act of struggling free that is inwardly *dependent* on the process of its subjection, as in "Demon and Beast":

Yet I am certain as can be
That every natural victory
Belongs to beast or demon,
That never yet had freeman
Right mastery of natural things.

Yeats had long since moved past the Romantic view that "the solitary soul" could find itself in a direct act of self-fulfilment in nature (as "Ego Dominuus Tuus" bears witness). Even so, it remained difficult for him to comprehend how the soul was not still made for delight, so that while he now sees that it may also be made for desolation, he has only *begun* to imagine how it must contend with that reality. He looks towards the "night" of desolation as to a still distant fate with which he has *yet* to contend: "Satisfied if a troubled mirror show [the solitary soul]":

Before that brief gleam of its life be gone,
An image of its state;
The wings half-spread for flight,
The breast thrust out in pride
Whether to play, or to ride
Those winds that clamour of approaching night.

Yeats's pride of soul, for all its assumed heroism, is put on as an attitude, and as an attitude it soon crumbles before a more direct and complete consideration of the reality that now besets him. To console himself he had thought to embrace the view that cultural "triumph" would still leave one with the necessity of coping with one's "solitude" in nature. This view had seemed to him a way of reconciling himself to the cultural defeat he was now living through. But it now occurs to him that the process of subjection might go further and include subjection to emptiness in death. Yeats's most cherished notion had always been that in death one would inherit the complete reality of one's creative efforts which only manifested in a kind of *half*-form of realization in nature (a view predicated on a residual dualism of mind and body). If nature's desolation *did* extend into death, then there could be nothing left to stand by or support oneself with. This thought throws Yeats into a rage of uncertainty unlike anything he has known before, and at this point he collapses, into a complete dismissal of his laborious cultural efforts hitherto:

The swan has leaped into a desolate heaven:
That image can bring wildness, bring a rage
To end all things, to end
What my laborious life imagined, even
The half-imagined, the half-written page;
O but we dreamed to mend
Whatever mischief seemed
To afflict mankind, but now
That winds of winter blow
Learn that we were crack-pated when we dreamed.

Thrown into a complete despair, he now calls on all to mock the "great", the "wise" and the "good", because their efforts have been unable to withstand the forces of historical desolation. However, he is careful to include also all mockers as objects of mockery, for it is they, he implies, who ought to have helped "the good, wise or great/To bar that foul storm out". At the same time, having passed on to the complete disavowal of culture, he makes himself ready to confront more directly the forces of historical breakdown. Suddenly he sees the perpetrators of violence as they appear in their native element. Though morally horrified, nevertheless he acknowledges that on them *is* bestowed the power to express themselves in all the lust of their historical ascendancy:

A sudden blast of dusty wind and after
Thunder of feet, tumult of images,
Their purpose in the labyrinth of the wind;
And should some crazy hand dare touch a daughter
All turn with amorous cries, or angry cries,
According to the wind, for all are blind.

◆   ◆   ◆

By the time he is writing "Meditations in Time of Civil War" (some four years later) Yeats had fully taken the plunge into a new world. He had moved well past his old attachment to the material effects of culture. The form of creation by which he stands is rather a purely spiritual act, "bitter"-ly and "violent"-ly conceived out of the subjection to chaos. What matters is no longer what is materially produced in the effort to soothe and to ennoble (the "silken clothes and stately walk" one cultivates) but rather (like Hughes later) *that chaos continues to be engaged.* Hence his readiness now to *steep* himself in the desolation of nature, in his own adversity in which he has become culturally forgotten, and in an extreme form of loneliness that is without cultural hope. He has now comprehended that it is only out of the "bitter and violent" encounter with those elements, amidst a finally desolate nature, that that symbolic "flower"-ing of the spirit can emerge on which a new artistic expression will be based. He is now ready and able to think his way into, and to embrace, the prospect of the desolation of *all* of his efforts:

> *May this laborious stair and this stark tower*
> *Become a roofless ruin ...*

and when faced with the *immediate* effects of violence

> *That dead young soldier in his blood*

responds with his anticipation of a new form of culture that will one day come to fill the present emptiness:

> *O honey-bees*
> *Come build in the empty house of the stare.*

What Yeats was entertaining here was the idea of a creation that will have successfully absorbed modern violence and will *one day* appear out of it as a new thing. Not, however, that this notion is for long sustained, for he allows the modern scene to impress itself on him still more intensely:

> *In cloud-pale rags, or in lace,*
> *The rage-driven, rage-tormented, and rage-hungry troop,*
> *Trooper after trooper, biting at arm or at face,*
> *Plunges towards nothing, arms and fingers spreading wide*
> *For the embrace of nothing;*

Highly developed as his vision is here, it is finally insupportable; the contrast with what *was* is too great, and he is compelled to fall back once again on what he feels he could have done:

> *I turn away and shut the door, and on the stair*
> *Wonder how many times I could have proved my worth*
> *In something that all others understand or share;*

But he knows now that that effort could never have borne fruit historically, and that consequently he could never have fulfilled himself in it, and in the meantime has *re-instated* his old cherished view that what there is to accomplish can be accomplished in half-measure only:

> *The abstract joy*
> *The half-read wisdom of daemonic images,*
> *Suffice the aging man as once the growing boy.*

◆   ◆   ◆

From here, right through to the end of his life, Yeats's creative effort will branch off in several directions. First, there will be a falling back into himself, a reaching back to the creative sources that he feels are still intensely present in him, and to when these last worked in directly into history, and so a "sailing away" as it were to "Byzantium", a "sailing away" that is a "looking back". On the other hand, he will not allow himself to turn away from the world in any final sense, as "Dialogue between Self and Soul" testifies; he rather looks forward to the time when he will plunge back into life to offer his creative effort *again*—assuming the idea of his reincarnation. Contrasting further with this "looking forward" is then *another* form of "looking back", to a more recent past, expressed in the monumental "Coole Park and Ballylee". Here Yeats re-lives from the point of view of his desolate present the symbolic import of Coole and the Lake he had made famous, and all that this represented once of great cultural hope. Now all is desolate, though it is a desolation that he has accepted as historically inevitable; in the meantime he still derives lessons about the creative purity of the incarnating soul and how *that* remains, in spite of life's transiency and the historical failure. Thus at "sudden thunder of the mounting swan", he declares:

> *Another emblem there. That stormy white*
> *But seems a concentration of the sky;*
> *And like the soul, it sails into the sight*
> *And in the morning's gone, no man knows why;*
> *And is so lovely that it sets to right*
> *What knowledge or its lack had set awry,*

Nevertheless it is the historical facts that prevail, and these challenge heroic faith by their suggestion that we *are* drifting back into another dark age:

But all is changed, that high horse riderless,
Though mounted in that saddle Homer rode
Where the swan drifts upon a darkening flood.

◆   ◆   ◆

Beyond these presentations Yeats will offer still vaster perspectives that propose our necessary disengagement from human tragedy when this is seen as a feature of the historical cycle. Like his Chinamen in "Lapis Lazuli", we too can assume hope in the re-creation of our world from the ruins of historical desolation—however bad things appear at present. In any case, there will continue to be the inevitable engagement of great souls in the occurrences of history, whatever the conditions that oppose them, as in the case of the Caesar and Michelangelo of "A Long-Legged Fly". "Under Ben Bulben" is also about the hope we have in looking forward—in our *re*-incarnation—to a new effort to create human civilization when we return. However, sudden doubt and despair enter into Yeats's view in "Man and Echo". Perhaps in the end there is nothing to look forward to in death and all we have is whatever consciousness of hope we possess while we are still alive to speak of it, and it might even appear, as "The Circus Animals' Desertion" suggests, as if what had engaged us were mere dreams.

Afterword

Four pictures have presented themselves over the course of the close readings that have been offered in this book. Beginning with the last of these from Yeats, one picture that emerges is of the tragic defeat of the Goddess for the moment, until history shall have worked through its cycle a little further and come back to its creative phase. Here a sort of Nietzchean idea of the eternal recurrence would seem to be implied, and a fatalistic notion of a perpetually cyclical historical happening embraced. Graves is ultimately more optimistic, projecting a definite time for the Goddess's decisive return in "a few centuries"[1]. It does look, also, as if Yeats was himself building on a late *survival* of the Goddess idea as lived out by many at this time out of a pre-modern experience that was fast dying out. However, this hardly seems the case with Graves, in whom an experience of the Goddess is so evolved one has the sense rather of a *future* reign manifesting itself proleptically in him.

A third picture presents itself in Sylvia Plath's tremendous tragic *agon* in mid-century, in which the Goddess's essential hold on Her creation is paradoxically re-affirmed, in the form of an appalling challenge to live one's way back to Her. Ted Hughes took up this challenge, having no room to do otherwise. Overwhelmed by it as he is—his struggle with it leads to one of the great tragic expressions in modern poetry—Hughes finally does make his way through again to the Goddess, but in a *difficult* form of existence that would seem to herald a new *resurrected* Creation, of which we are given but the first, tenuous intimations, and which will strike us as bafflingly remote from our experience at present.

At the other end from this excruciating, forward-moving venture lies the great nostalgic farewell to the Goddess's *old* Creation in which many of the authors in the earlier part of the century found themselves implicated, with the coming in of the modern debacle. This was our fourth picture. *Something* of the Goddess's Creation, as this survived from the past, would not be able to make it through, and this could only entail for Tennessee Williams a drastic separation from our

---

1. By which time we shall have also learned how to transcend "the cautiously abstract titles" we give to the Goddess now, among which Graves cites 'Nature', 'Truth', 'Beauty' and 'Poetry'. See *The White Goddess*, p. 503.

full humanity. Chekhov projects a recovery of our full humanity in the distant future; Miller pretends to be able to get on without it. For his part, Brecht is more than determined to hang onto this humanity, by way of a relentless critique of the historical forces that underlie the debacle. In this respect I have boldly associated Brecht with Plath.

But in any case all the authors that have been covered here are united in the uncompromising way in which they face and actively take on the debacle in one form or another. Beckett presents the effects of the debacle in its bare bones as it were, assuming a humanity that has become virtually dispossessed, or is on the verge of being disposessed, of any fighting spirit that may be left. In this way, he alerts us to an outcome that we must only wish to counteract in the best way we can. Hemingway wrote in an age when it was still possible for him to return to Nature, thus heroically *defying* historical time. Eliot lies as it were suspended *in* time, as if maintaining the crucial balance of awareness both of the menace and the hope out of which all further solutions might be fashioned, so that it is to him that we can always go back, to recover ourselves for the fresh task of taking on the lingering effects of the debacle.

Endnotes

[1]. To borrow a phrase from Owen Barfield from a broader historical context, from *Poetic Diction* (London: Faber, 1952).

[2]. See *The Johannine Books* in The Temple Bible series (Dent, 1902): "And he opened the bottomless pit; and there arose a smoke out of the pit, as the smoke of a great furnace; and the sun and the air were darkened by reason of the smoke of the pit. And there came out of the smoke locusts upon the earth: and unto them was given power, as the scorpions of the earth have power ..." (106-107)

[3]. See "Tradition and the Individual Talent" from *T.S. Eliot: Poems and Prose* (New York: Knopf, 1998).

[4]. Eliot will fail yet again in the opening of the second section of "East Coker".

[5]. It is doubtful that Brecht, as a self-proclaimed Marxist, would have <u>consciously</u> seen himself as mediating the Mother.

[6]. In *Johnny Panic and the Bible of Dreams* (London: Faber and Faber, 1979) p. 92.

[7]. See C.B. Cox and A.R. Jones, "After the Tranquilized Fifties", *Critical Quarterly* 6 (Summer, 1964), pp. 99-100.

[8]. Alan Sinfeld, e.g., has shown how "Plath's anxieties about war, militarism and state violence were by no means sudden. Despite what most critics say, she had long expressed political commitment." (In *Literature, Politics and Culture in Postwar Britain* (Oxford: Blackwell, 1989), p. 222. There is also Plath's own word about this; among the "issues of our time" that preoccupied her were "the terrifying mad, omnipotent marriage of big business and the military in America". (*Johnny Panic*, p. 92).

[9]. Cox and Jones, pp. 99-100.

[10]. See *Language and Silence* (London, Faber and Faber, 1967) p. 331.

[11]. Plath's father died of diabetes, which he in part deliberately brought on.

[12]. See *The White Goddess* (London: Faber and Faber, 1997).

[13]. See. e.g., his lecture on Mammon to the London School of Economics in *Mammon and the Black Goddess* (London: Cassell, 1965), or the many pages from *The White Goddess* in which Graves addresses the long history of our patriarchal oppression. Of this latter book D.N.G. Carter (in *Robert Graves: The Lasting Poetic Achievement* (London: Macmillan, 1989, p. 206) notes: "The book's conclusion is that our civilization has in its arrogance travelled so far from the principles of sanity and order implicit in the Goddess-oriented society that there is now no way back to them except through harrowing catastrophe."

[14]. See Carter, *Robert Graves*: "Having suffered more than most what the age can inflict, he publically washes his hands of it and turns to what he consider the poet's "real tale", the story of the true poet's love for the Muse, beyond the vicissitudes of time and history."

[15]. That this Muse was Margot Callas is confirmed in the account of the literal episode by Richard Perceval Graves that seems to have inspired Graves's poem: "Robert was on his way to the sea for an early-morning swim, when he found Margot "posted/Under the pine trees" by the side of his path. She looked as though she had stepped straight out of the magical world of poetic myth about which he had written in *The White Goddess*". See *Robert Graves and The White Goddess 1940-1985* (London: Orion Books, 1995), p. 312.

[16]. Graves in *The White Goddess* concentrates attention on "the apple-tree of the sacred thicket, the tree that is the harbourage of the hind. As Gwion writes: "I fled as a roe to the entangled thicket" …" (p. 246). Also he notes that "The Unicorn is the Roe

in the Thicket. It lodges under the apple-tree, the tree of immortality-through-wisdom" that Graves adds "can be captured only by a pure virgin—Wisdom herself." (p. 248) Graves then asks about the apple: "why should it have been given such mythic importance? The clue is to be found in the legend of Curoi's soul that was hidden in an apple; when the apple was cut across by Cuchulain's sword "night fell upon Curoi". For if an apple is halved cross-wise each half shows a pointed star in the centre, emblem of immortality, which represents the Goddess in her five stations from birth to death and back to birth again." (p. 250)

[17]. In *The White Goddess* Graves points out that: "The Goddess is herself a Queen bee about whom male drones swarm in midsummer, and as Cybele is often so pictured; the ecstatic self-castration of her priests was a type of the emasculation of the drone by the queen bee in the nuptial act. Venus fatally courted Anchises on a mountain to the hum of bees." (p. 188).

[18]. Cindy Lee, who was to supply the role recently vacated by Margot Callas.

[19]. "Had she not a secret passion for serpents, a delight in murder, a secret craving for corpse flesh, a need to spend seven months of the year consorting with the sly, the barren, the damned? She might cherish Orpheus while still on earth, even calling him beautiful—since his beauty reflected her own—mourn him when he was murdered.... Yet she could not be bound by his hopes for her perfectibility ... The Muse, in fact, alternates between the world of good and evil, plenty and lack; and her poet will have his head torn off and his limbs gnawn by greedy teeth if he attempts to change her.... "From "Intimations of the Black Goddess" from *Mammon and the Black Goddess*, p. 159-161.

[20]. "Intimations", p. 162.

[21]. "Intimations", p. 162.

[22]. "Intimations", p. 165. Another kind of "certitude" is offered to the poet in his commitment to the White Goddess, as in "The Personal Muse" from *Oxford Addresses on Poetry* (New York: Greenwood Publishers, 1968); in that commitment the Muse is also seen as offering the poet "a natural certitude of rightness" (p. 88), "her own certitude" (p. 89), but that certitude or "integrity" is in the end a function of her "ruthlessness" (p. 90)

[23]. I take both this phrase and the following from Michael Kirkham, *The Poetry of Robert Graves* (London: The Athlone Press, 1969), p. 244 and p. 257.

[24]. As Graves's nephew, Percival Graves, notes in *Robert Graves*: "[Cindy's] intuition enabled her to undertake the part of Robert's Black Goddess; and her understanding meant that she could sustain the role, so that after knowing her for more than a year Robert would still be praising her "fantastic delicacy of moral judgment". (p. 377)

In contrast with the Muse's full assumption of her role in the case of the Black Goddess's influence, it is in the nature of the Muse's connection to the White Goddess that "her eventual function and fate is to betray [the poet]; and thus forfeit the glory with which he enshrined her" ("Intimations", p. 156).

[25]. Kirkham, *The Poetry of Robert Graves*, p. 257

[26]. See note 22.

[27]. Most hauntingly conveyed in "Lion Lover":

> *You chose a lion to be your lover—*
> *Me, who in joy such doom greeting*
> *Dared jealously undertake*
> *Cruel ordeals long forseen and unknown,*
> *Springing a trap baited with flesh: my own.*
>
> *Nor would I now exchange this lion heart*
> *For a less furious other*
> *Though by the Moon possessed*

> *I gnaw at dry bones in a lost lair*
> *And, when, clouds cover her, roar my despair.*

[28]. It would overburden my presentation to enter more deeply into the long mythical lineage of the oak-tree, about which Graves is relatively mum in *The White Goddess*, perhaps because it is well known. It is perhaps enough to quote Ted Hughes "on that great tree" from "The Snake and the Oak", his Introduction to *A Choice of Coleridge's Verse*, (London: Faber and Faber, 1996) p. 11 and n.: "In almost all shamanic traditions, the tree is somehow central—as the spine common to both this world and the other ..." Nor is it necessarily a case of the Oak, for it can also be, as Hughes notes, a cosmic Ash Tree—or, indeed, the Elm, as in Sylvia Plath's poem of that name.

[29]. Kirkham, *The Poetry of Robert Graves*, p. 268. A similar view, seemingly with the endorsement of Ted Hughes, has been taken of Sylvia Plath's later work by Judith Kroll in *Chapters in a Mythology: The Poetry of Sylvia Plath* (New York: Harper and Row, 1976). Kroll speaks of Plath's "need to transcend personal history in a way more radical than that expressed in her poetry as mythic rebirth" (p. 210), a need that assumes at some point "a shedding of the mythic drama" (p. 182).

[30]. Cf. Ted Hughes's note in "The Snake and the Oak", p. 16 that begins "This Great Goddess incorporates fish and serpent ..."

[31]. That the pattern of the mythical fate involves reincarnation would seem to be incontestible:
> *Water to water, ark again to ark,*
> *From woman back to woman:*
> *So each new victim treads unfalteringly*
> *The never altered circuit of his fate,*
> *Bringing twelve peers as witness*
> *Both to his starry rise and starry fall.*

[32]. See *The White Goddess*:(pp. 472-475): "there seems no escape from our difficulties until the industrial system breaks down for some

reason or other, as it nearly did in Europe during the Second World War, and nature reasserts herself with grass and trees among the ruins.... I forsee no change for the better until everything gets far worse. Only after a period of complete political and religious disorganization can the suppressed desire of the Western races, which is for some practical form of Goddess-worship ... find satisfaction at last...."

[33].   *The White Goddess*, p. 472.

List of Works Covered

by Beckett
<u>Waiting for Godot</u>
<u>Endgame</u>

by Hemingway
A Clean Well-Lighted Place
Big Two-Hearted River
Fathers and Sons
A Way You'll Never Be
The Snows of Kilimanjaro

by Eliot
<u>The Waste Land</u>
<u>Ash-Wednesday</u>
Burnt Norton
East Coker
The Dry Salvages
Little Gidding

by Tennessee Williams
<u>The Glass Menagerie</u>

by Chekhov
<u>The Cherry Orchard</u>

by Arthur Miller
<u>Death of a Salesman</u>

by Brecht
<u>Mother Courage</u>

by Plath
The Colossus
Elm

The Birthday Present
Daddy
Lady Lazarus
Ariel
Edge

by Hughes
The Tender Place
The God
A Flayed Crow in the Hall of Judgment
The Executioner
Bedtime Anecdote
Crow Tyrannosauros
Crow on the Beach
The Scream
I know well/You are not infallible
Prospero and Sycorax
The swallow re-building/Collects the lot
Prometheus on the Crag, #2,#9
The Guide
The Risen
Chinese History of Colden Water
Salmon Eggs
October Salmon

by Graves
The Unnamed Spell (2)
The White Goddess (3)
The Gorge
A Restless Ghost
The Intrusion
Apple Island
The Hero (2)
In Her Praise
Deliverance
This Holy Month
Tomorrow's Envy of Today
Conjunction

To Juan
The Return of the Goddess

by Yeats
The Sorrow of Love
Reconciliation
A Prayer for My Daughter
The Second Coming
Nineteen Hundred and Nineteen
Demon and Beast
Meditations in Time of Civil War
Byzantium
Dialogue Between Self and Soul
Coole Park and Ballylee
Lapis Lazuli
A Long-Legged Fly
The Circus Animals' Desertion

PART TWO

MYTH, DEPRAVITY, IMPASSE

GRAVES, SHAKESPEARE, KEATS

John O'Meara

iUniverse, Inc.
Bloomington

MYTH, DEPRAVITY, IMPASSE

◆

Graves, Shakespeare, Keats

John O'Meara

iUniverse, Inc.
Bloomington

Contents

once again
for

ALINE

PREFACE

This book is a kind of compendium of thought about the mythical and what it represents as an idea of experience. Hence, my review of the various positions taken about myth by some of the more prominent modern theorists of myth, which I offer as a background to Graves in the book's first chapter. The questions I start from are the following: What are we to make of the astounding fact that Graves would appear to have successfully penetrated again into an objective mythical experience? And how far are we from any such prospect ourselves? To conceive of the Goddess appearing to us again with an actual pictoriality that arises out of the mythical world she inhabits, quite objectively, makes us profoundly uneasy and puts us in mind of how alien we are to such a projected experience. Graves blamed a long history of unreal rationalism for that sense of alienation, and Ted Hughes followed suit with an application of the same moral, basing himself on his own exhaustive study of Shakespeare's relationship to the Goddess in *Shakespeare and the Goddess of Complete Being*.

In this book I argue from the assumption that an objective mythical experience *should be* possible for us today, following the lead of Graves, but I proceed speculatively, accommodating our profound uneasiness about such an experience. However, I do not let the modern sceptic off easily. There is more than simply "a willing suspension of disbelief" in the approach I take to the idea of such an experience. In fact, I *commit* to it, taking exception to the easy conclusions of modern scepticism on the one side and the overly confident spirit of Hughes and of Graves on the other. Shakespeare's work I focus on as another way of assessing what it means for us to engage in a mythical experience today. For from Shakespeare we learn that there is far more to contend with in our inner make-up than what Graves or Hughes maintain, and that more will, therefore, have to be known about that make-up, before we can permit ourselves the kind of full engagement with our natures that the mythical experience requires of us.

The idea of such an experience remains, for all the commitment that is registered about it in one form or another, profoundly uncertain, and I also bring Keats in to show how our modern scepticism emerges in relation to it. However, I am just as bent on showing that, in our appreciation of Keats, we have thought *ourselves* into his position more than we are justified in doing. For Keats would appear to be no less committed to the idea of recovering mythical experience than are Graves and Shakespeare, and this in spite of his pronounced modern tendencies, which become for him, as I show, at a certain point a trap.

In my chapter on Graves, I stop to consider the views of Eliade, Cassirer, Jung, Barfield and Campbell. Thereafter, I build on a more modest range of primarily literary views of Shakespeare and of Keats, to suit my own emphasis. A special place is allotted in my presentation to the views on *Macbeth* as provided by James Calderwood and Harry Berger Jr. and to the views on Keats of W. Jackson Bate and John Middleton Murry. Far from being a comprehensive treatment, my chapters on those authors gradually slip away into a more direct presentation of my themes, as these seem to me to be illuminated by the literature itself. The effect, towards the end, will thus appear fragmentary, but that will seem appropriate to a book that reflects on our fundamental uncertainty in relation to the three questions that are raised:

- *Where do we stand in relation to the objective ground of myth?*
- *Where do we stand in relation to the depravity in our nature?*
- *What **do** we make of ourselves in supposing ourselves defined by a use of the Imagination developed in relation to ourselves alone?*

All three questions are brought forward here, what's more, inasmuch as three male poets, writing out of a basically male perspective, reflect to us our sense of what can come of these questions. I have attempted to bring these diverse matters together not with any notion that they have fully clarified in relation to each other—there would still be a need for the additional input that a woman's perspective would have to offer on these questions[1]; I bring these matters together here out of the view that for now they summarize *among themselves* the issue of what our relationship to mythical experience can be about. The common link among these three areas of focus is to a mythical unity that all three authors I treat of acknowledge as the ultimate goal of our experience. However, each of these authors assumes a relationship to this unity that is at once concrete and abstract, the element of abstraction in each author's relationship to unity being the measure of the unrealized portion of his involvement in it. We can only hope, therefore, that along will come another, a fourth, who will have the fuller resources needed, and the right audience, to begin to show us how, working out of all three areas, we can indeed make our way back to the mythical unity in which all will be resolved.

I

THE MYTHIC GROUND

I

In a public lecture[2] given at the Y.M.H.A. Centre in New York in 1957, Robert Graves directly addressed the ground of his mythical faith with the potentially explosive question:

> *Do I think that poets are literally inspired by the White Goddess?*

From the context of his address it is clear that Graves was not led to this question himself. It is prefaced by a remark that indicates it is being aired in response to signs of disbelief in his audience that he could be taking his claims so far. Graves's response to his question is a carefully crafted piece of evasive affirmation:

> *Some of you are looking queerly at me. Do I think that poets are literally inspired by the White Goddess? That is an improper question. What would you think, should I ask you if, in your opinion, the Hebrew prophets were literally inspired by God? Whether God is a metaphor or a fact cannot be reasonably argued; let us likewise be discreet on the subject of the Goddess.*

Rarely was Graves so circumspect in his proclamation of his great Theme. His confidence on this occasion is, in a somewhat unusual way, tempered by the doubt he is addressing in his immediate audience. His subdued tone reflects also the bafflement he appears to have felt about a critique that had been made of his presentation of the White Goddess, in a recent review by Randall Jarrell, the American poet.[3] Jarrell had argued that Graves's picture of the White Goddess was merely a projection of his own personal fantasy. Thus both Jarrell and Graves's audience combine to confront him with an image of the opposition he might expect to find to the *kind* of claims he was making, with their unquestioned assumption about the literal existence, in some sense, of the White Goddess. In the face of this opposition Graves momentarily dampens his claims in respect to how far they might be taken.

I linger over this episode because it points the issue of what someone who claims to have found a literal connection withthe mythical will face in his sceptical and uncomprehending audience. With that is raised the whole question of what the ground of a mythical faith can be. One may claim of Graves's lecture as a whole, in comparison with his many other pronouncements, a kind of retreat in the face of the enemy's display of its forces. Thus, for the most part here, he is content to reiterate that aspect of his Theme that is primarily historical. That approach is emphasized by way of making the point that

> *Mr. Jarrell cannot accuse me of* **inventing** *the White Goddess…*

Hence, also, his further statement that

> *It is enough for me to quote the myths and give them historical sense…*

And it is with this less-than-muted sense of being in the presence of the enemy that Graves proffers what is for him the comparatively reduced declaration, intended to set him on safe ground, that

> *I hold that critical notice should be taken of the Goddess.*

"Notice" of this kind is due because of the coherent "grammar of poetic myth" that Graves was known to have derived from his historical studies of the Goddess cult. Even Jarrell acknowledges that he is grateful for it, for on the basis of this "grammar" Graves was able to write poems that Jarrell describes as "some of the most beautiful poems of our time."[4] Especially is it a matter for Graves of taking notice of the "poetry which deeply affects readers", and how it comes to be. The answer is in "the persistent survival", among the "Muse-poets", of "faith" in the White Goddess—which may be conscious or unconscious. Their "imagery" can be proven to be "drawn" directly from Her cult, and the "magic" of their poems shown to be dependent on "its closeness to her mysteries."

Graves's account, bold as it is, still begs the question of what the ground of this "faith" might be, but, in this lecture at least, he is as sly as his enemy is unyielding. Primarily, he *reverts* (from the claim of literalness) to the view that

> *In scientific terms, no god at all can be proved to exist, but only beliefs in gods, and the effects of such beliefs on worshippers.*

Such a view, Graves maintains, applies as much to the Christian belief in a Father God as to the Jewish belief in the God of the prophets, and, therefore, can apply as much to a belief in the Goddess, whose religion can be attested to on the same grounds. Graves is as uncompromising about his own historical emphasis:

> *The most important single fact in the early history of Western religion and sociology was undoubtedly the gradual suppression of the Lunar Mother-goddess's inspiratory cult, and its supercession by…the busy, rational cult of the Solar God Apollo.*

Of the Goddess's presence in the religion of former times, and of its stubborn survival against the odds into modern times, there can be no doubt, and since poetic inspiration remains, in scientific terms, an undisclosed mystery:

> *…why not attribute inspiration to the Lunar Muse, the oldest and most convenient European term for the source in question?*

It is a triumphant gambit, because of the appeal, in "the *oldest…* European term", to priority in this case. However, Graves goes farther: he implies that, as "Protestant Doctors of Divinity…posit the literal existence of an all-powerful God"—claiming for themselves proofs of "supernatural happenings" in spite of these being "ill-attested" by science—adherents of the Goddess might do the same. There is also the argument from precedent and tradition (a very long tradition in this case), in which Graves deliberately milks the present perfect tense: "In fact, the Goddess has always been…The Muse-poets have always recognized" etc. And it is only *after* Graves has pursued this whole elaborate strategic disarming of the enemy, that we find him shifting back to a claim about the Goddess's literal role in the lives of poets:

> *By ancient religious theory the White Goddess becomes incarnate in her human representative—a priestess, a prophetess, a queen-mother. No Muse-poet can grow conscious of the Muse except by experience of some woman in whom the Muse-power is to some degree or other resident.*

From a claim from "ancient religious theory", Graves shifts here to a present *actuality*—"No Muse-poet *can*"—and this shift is now sustained. Finally, we hear from him again in the forthright mode in which his auditors had been accustomed to hearing from him before he came face to face with the opposition his claims provoked:

> *But the real, perpetually obsessed Muse-poet makes*
> *a distinction between the Goddess as revealed in the*
> *supreme power, glory, wisdom and love of woman, and*
> *the individual woman in whom the Goddess may take up*
> *residence for a month, a year, seven years, or even longer.*
> *The Goddess abides; and it may be that he will again have*
> *knowledge of her through his experience of another woman…*

    Graves's case is among the most extraordinary instances in modern times of a claim to literalness in the experience of myth, and it is for this reason that I choose to focus on him here. His case is the more extraordinary just because—in his comportment and in his whole manner of expressing himself—he is in every other respect the model of level-headedness, and is so to a fault (which has made him an easy object of caricature). I have also *begun* with the episode of the lecture because *it* represents, on the other side of the issue, a somewhat extreme instance of disobligingness when it comes to responding to a claim of literalness. Between these two extremes the issue of the *ground* of myth is thus raised. The encounter between the two here is not exactly what one would call fruitful; the issue degenerates into polemics, the appeal to "faith" appearing as the appeasing counter to be mutually appropriated by both sides. Perhaps in the case of Graves's audience nothing short of the grossest scientific "proof" would have satisfied the sense of "reality" that needed to be appeased, where only a more subtle order of metaphysical proof could be provided.

    The same could hardly be said of Jarrell, however, who is ready in his critique to credit Graves with "poems that almost deserve the literal *magical*"[5]. Only, Jarrell does not intend by "magical" the literal sense that Graves does, where for instance *he* writes, at the beginning of *The White Goddess*, "European poetic lore…is ultimately based on magical principles."[6] In his way of offering praise of Graves's poems—"*almost*…the *literal* magical"—Jarrell mischievously approaches Graves's sense while clearly intending another, very much more restricted one. Jarrell's use of "magical" intensifies the issue in yet another way, inasmuch as our use of the term allows us to draw on a literal connotation of the word where we do not in fact intend one—which we would scrupulously deny if ever held to account for it. Certainly we do not normally intend by it the literal rendering that Graves continues to proclaim, e.g., in his new Foreword to *The White Goddess*, written a few years after the critique by Jarrell:

> *My thesis is that the language of myth anciently current in the Mediterranean and Northern Europe was a magical language bound up with popular religious ceremonies in honour of the Moon-Goddess, or Muse…and that this* **remains** *the language of true poetry…*

And *because* it remains so, Graves was concerned that "poetry of a magical quality" should not continue merely as an incidental or haphazard achievement, the result of "an inspired, almost pathological, reversion to the original language", but should rather be strenuously researched and cultivated, on the clear basis of "a conscientious study of its grammar and vocabulary".

But it may be well to continue by looking at the poems by Graves that Jarrell himself describes as "magical"—what he calls the "mythical-archaic poems", among which are two of the best known, "The White Goddess" and "To Juan at the Winter Solstice". Thus we shall put off saying, for the moment, in what a mythical "faith" may be said to consist, or on what "ground" it may be said to be predicated, to consider first what *kind* of world it could be said to proclaim, or what world-view Graves can be said to have committed to on the basis of his experience of the ancient mythical material. We shall, in doing so, also be giving ourselves a chance to see precisely what kind of grammar and vocabulary we can expect to be dealing with.

Much of what Graves understood as to how the Goddess figures in our lives can be said to be contained in these two poems, which we may see as two parts of one whole, with "The White Goddess" (though second in composition) playing the first part to "To Juan". It is the forthrightness of his claims that impress themselves upon us in "The White Goddess". This forthrightness belies the strenuous effort that has been made first to disassociate from the main Western cultural attitudes that have obstructed a proper approach to the Goddess. These are gone into at great length in Graves's book, *The White Goddess*, but they may be summarized here as the 'ascetic' attitude associated with Christianity as well as Western Apollonian rational philosophy. The Goddess, among other things, demands one's engagement *with* the world; it could never be with Her a case of turning away from what the world has fully to offer, also to one's bodily experience and, from within that experience, to one's consciousness.

At the same time, the "journey" that the poem's speaker narrates, into "distant regions" in order to "find" Her, is less a journey across the world than it is a journey *into* Nature[7]:

> *Seeking her out at the volcano's head,*
> *Among pack ice, or where the track had faded*
> *Beyond the cavern of the seven sleepers:*

It is at this point, significantly, that the Goddess Herself arises:

> *Whose broad high brow was white as any leper's,*
> *Whose eyes were blue, with rowan-berried lips,*
> *With hair curled honey-coloured to white hips.*

The idea proposed as to how the Goddess is to be "found" has less to do with the typical mythical journey of the past than with a way of living into Nature that has much in common with latter-day Romantic experience. Thus Jarrell's term, "archaic", does not fit altogether. One need not go far either across the world or back into time to be able, in Graves's view, to "celebrate" the Goddess's presence; one need only be able to live one's "way" fully into Spring, as well as into all of the rest of the natural year.

Here is where the peculiar attitude involved in making the right approach to the Goddess makes itself felt. It must be, if one is to find Her, a matter of living fully into the *whole cycle* of the year, and so *quite as much* into Fall and Winter as into Spring and Summer. That thought defies one's imagination, as much as does the thought that one is to find Her "at the volcano's head" or "Among pack ice", or that, in aspiring to know Her *through* this kind of engagement, one risks, by one's unworthiness, being mentally struck down as by lightning ("the next bright bolt"). Graves reserves the certainty of being so much in tune with the essential Goddess Who lies behind Her natural manifestations—blessed, as he is, "with so huge a sense/Of her *nakedly* worn magnificence"—the possibility of being favored and supported in this venture seems within reach.

In "Juan" an extreme engagement with Nature constitutes again a first point of entry into the Goddess's world:

> *Is it of trees you tell, their months and virtues,*
> *Or strange beasts that beset you,*

Of birds that croak at you the Triple will?

But with "Triple will" we are already into the stuff of myth and very soon, with the further shift to the Zodiac, are suddenly plummeted into an Underworld-drama in which many of the elements of an assumed "faith" are being marshalled:

> *Or of the Zodiac and how slow it turns*
> *Below the Boreal crown,*
> *Prison of all true kings that ever reigned?*

We are asked to think that the Zodiac, as we know it in the outer world, continues in its existence and in its influence *in* this Underworld (though reduced to a slow turning there). This Underworld is also now seen as the

> *Prison of all true kings that ever reigned...*

And before we have had time to consider where we are with these references, we are precipitated through a tremendous drama in which we are asked to see a set of such "victims" given over to a destiny that involves repeated death and re-birth or re-incarnation:

> *Water to water, ark again to ark,*
> *From woman back to woman:*
> *So each new victim treads unfalteringly*
> *The never altered circuit of his fate,*
> *Bringing twelve peers as witness*
> *Both to his starry rise and starry fall.*

It might be thought that by "victims" Graves means every man and that men give *themselves*, like these "true kings", to the same destiny. *They* are "true" because given over to this destiny without reserve. *How* they are brought into the drama is then dramatized, the Goddess Herself appearing here as the main Agent in the "one story and one story only" that is "worth telling":

> *She in her left hand bears a leafy quince;*
> *When with her right she crooks a finger, smiling,*
> *How may the King hold back?*
> *Royally then he barters life for love.*

Summoned, as it were, to death by the Goddess—who assumes here a remarkable doubleness of form—this "King" now submits to what has all the marks of an ancient mythical Underworld-initiation:

> *Or of the undying snake from chaos hatched,*
> *Whose coils contain the ocean,*
> *Into whose chops with naked sword he springs,*
> *Then in black water, tangled by the reeds,*
> *Battles three days and nights,*
> *To be spewed up beside her scalloped shore...*

In the past this initiation was enacted *in some sense* literally[8]. Such initiation involved a microcosmic condensation of the whole experience of the cycle of death and re-birth, which was somehow lived out directly over the course of the "three days and nights" mentioned. The lines in their own terms are a tremendous evocation of the event described. Then Graves comes back, suddenly, to the *present* reality and the "fear" that he knows must lie in his own son's heart from having to submit to this forbidding destiny:

> *Much snow is falling, winds roar hollowly,*
> *The owl hoots from the elder,*
> *Fear in your heart cries to the loving-cup...*

"Fear" is to be countered by trust, in the dependability of the Goddess's "love"; this "love", from Her side, She bestows for the "life" given over to Her. In the meantime the sudden shift back to the present has the effect of emphasizing a man's individual-psychological "distance", in his own life, from the great realities of death and re-birth that have been "mythically" rendered and conceived.

A *literal* continuity between the two spheres is, nevertheless, assumed, and the medial ground is, once again, Nature. The "fear" Graves addresses in his son, and through him in every man, is the fear that haunts him from knowing that he must *go* to his death. Nature in its foreboding and destructive aspect speaks ultimately of the death he must endure. But the hope lies in the "love" that is tendered *out* of this prospect, which *returns* him from that great "ocean" or "sea" of death into which he plunges. He returns because he is *in* the Goddess, Who reserves to Herself the *power* to return, from the great "grapple" with death. And so She is presented at the end of the poem:

Her brow was creamy as the crested wave,
Her sea-grey eyes were wild,
But nothing promised that is not performed.[9]

✦   ✦   ✦

The cosmology in which Graves asks us to "believe" is especially marked by this emphasis on a literal connection, through Nature, to the great "sea" of death that the Underworld represents. In its darker, material aspect, Nature is seen as *continuous with* this Underworld. In "The Sea Horse" Graves directly applies himself in his consciousness of this cosmology. Things are still possible, the Goddess's order still accessible, if here only through the dark element that binds the poet to his beloved in an "unquiet love", the mark of their involvement in what makes Her Creation difficult. It is difficult because they share, through their physical nature, in the turmoil projected from the Underworld (from that same "ocean" or "sea" of death as presented in "To Juan"). This turmoil involves them problematically in "pain" along with the "love". The "pain" is connected also with their sexual nature, their sexual needs, which are not to be shied away from. "Renewal" or re-birth comes from the engagement with these needs. From the "blood-red" wound of the sexual encounter comes the "pain" of submission to the physical, which will always be a part of it, but through which "love" is affirmed.

Submission to the dark, material side of the Goddess's Creation *as mythically rendered* is the aspect of Graves's presentation that has met with the most extreme resistance. Resistance has come because of the literal emphasis Graves gives to this rendering. This reaction is especially strong in relation to his portrayal of the White Goddess or Mother of All-Living as "the ancient power of fright and lust—the female spider, the queen bee whose embrace is death."[10] She appears in this guise in the poem "She Is No Liar", where She is imagined "wiping away"

Honey from her lips, blood from her shadowy hand.

Graves's picture of the Goddess is of One Who *generally* submits her devotee to violent dispossession, but in "Lion Lover" Graves depicts himself as one who is only ready to accept his "doom":

Though by the Moon possessed
I gnaw at dry bones in a lost lair

Graves knows himself to be caught up in his physical nature and its confounding deprivation bearing on death. Yet in his submission to this doom he will often be re-paid, the sight of Her "love" appearing to him as a result of his strenuous refusal of any other more appealing life. Thus the Goddess finally appears "naked" to him, riding the lion of his beastly nature, as in one of those many artistic renderings of the Goddess out of the ancient and classical pasts[11]:

> *Your naked feet upon my scarred shoulders*
> *Your eyes naked with love,*
> *Are all the gifts my beasthood can approve.*

It is precisely this readiness, in the face of all deterrents, to *continue* to think himself in a relationship with His Creatress that explains Graves's great success, by moments, in thinking himself into the Goddess's order, however darkly problematic his expression of that order often appears to be. One may, indeed, speak in connection with his more successful efforts of an extraordinary *congruity* between his own consciousness and the mythical material he is proclaiming. In making his own individual approach to the Goddess's world, it almost seems at times as if the ancient material comes to meet Graves's efforts independently. Nowhere is this more dramatically so than where his efforts to reach out to the Goddess bring on *pictorial* manifestations: pictures of the Goddess that, as in "The White Goddess" and in "To Juan", suddenly appear out of their own inner Imaginative space—as if independent manifestations of a living Being:

> *Whose broad high brow was white as any leper's,*
> *Whose eyes were blue, with rowan-berried lips,*
> *With hair curled honey-coloured to white hips.*

> *She in her left hand bears a leafy quince;*
> *When with her right she crooks a finger, smiling,*
> *How may the King hold back?*

> *Her brow was creamy as the crested wave,*
> *Her sea-grey eyes were wild,*
> *But nothing promised that is not performed.*

As a poet certainly, Graves greatly challenges our readiness and ability to think ourselves into a cosmological otherworld, *in the first instance by virtue of his evocations of the Goddess's direct presence.* There are not only the instances from the centrepiece-poems—"To Juan" and "The White Goddess"—from which I have cited. In "The Intrusion", for example, the poet happens unexpectedly upon his beloved who, unaware of her beholding lover, betrays a form of absorption in herself that opens out on an extraordinary dimension. The poet is overcome—his "scalp crawls" and his "eyes prick at sight"[12]

> *Of her white motionless face and folded hands*
> *Framed in such thunderclouds of sorrow...*

The beloved is herself overcome by the influence that has taken hold of her; the emphatic touches in "motionless" and "thunderclouds" are enough to intimate the *otherworldly* influence under which she herself is struggling. This influence is then identified in terms of a *mythical* image, associated with the Goddess's freedom to define the limits of any effort that is made to partake in Her world:

> *This is the dark edge of her double-axe:*
> *Divine mourning for what cannot be.*

The lovers have been judged to be presently unworthy of any fuller stability in Her world, but they have nevertheless been directly marked by Her involvement in their effort. That effort has been, and is, at least successful to this point: that the Goddess *has* been directly involved. The poet will not pretend to alter this state of things, by aspiring to a more successful showing or by seeking to win his beloved over more securely to their mutually engaged faith, because it is presently how the Goddess has judged them, what *She* has made of their effort, while Her immediate involvement in expressing this judgment about them is, or should be, enough to convince *us* that what mutually engages the lovers does have the foundation in reality the poet has assumed.[13]

The shift to the mythical image in "Intrusion" follows *from* the experience of the Goddess's direct presence, which the poet and the beloved are sharing. This will alert us to the way Graves's images often operate where there is no such indication of a direct personal experience: for example where, crystallizing the Goddess in Her dark dreadful claim on him, he speaks of

> *Honey from her lips, blood from her shadowy hand*

or where, as Her bound servant, he appears in the image of the sea-horse with

> *Under his horny ribs a blood-red stain*

or as the lion whom the Goddess rides:

> *Your naked feet upon my scarred shoulders*

Here the personal and the mythical dimensions have merged; the images come to us implicitly *bound up with* Graves's direct personal experience of the Goddess; they are not just poetically or dramatically "worked up". So too, we may suppose, in the case of other images that seem to come without prompting from the immediate situation:

> *She in her left hand bears a leafy quince;*
> *When with her right she crooks a finger, smiling,*

> *Whose broad high brow was white as any leper's,*

> *Her sea-grey eyes were wild,*

I have called attention to the way these mythical images seem to come of their own accord and from their own dimension, as if independently of Graves's conscious intention, as if they had, that is, their own intrinsic value in relation to the personal experience he is having. If so, they are not then to be discounted as "merely" mythical, or metaphorical. They seem rather to represent the pictorial *equivalent* of that which is being projected *out* of that otherworldly order into which Graves has succeeded in personally penetrating.

II

Accounts of the mythical process contemporary with Graves, even in their most radical expressions, never go as far as to proclaim the immediate possibility of recovering the mythical world in the extraordinary form Graves's production attests to. This is so even in the case of Mircea Eliade, with whose accounts one may note the closest similarities in tendency. Eliade himself focuses on gods and the "Supernaturals" generally, rather than on the Goddess, but in Eliade also there is, seemingly, complete literalness in the approach to myth, so that we find in treatments of his work the very same rationally-justified, astounded critique as was levelled at Graves:

> *What sort of scholar would talk with apparent credulity*
> *about the Creation as if it really happened, about some*
> *myths 'participating' in others, about the gods as if they really*
> *worked **in illo tempore**, about myths as if they really arose*
> *in moments of actual release from history and sacramentally*
> *produced such moments for their devotees?*[14]

Eliade himself can attest to the experience, through myth, of "an encounter with a transhumant reality—which gives birth to the idea that something *really exists*"[15], and it is, moreover, in his view, "through the objects of this present world" that "one perceives traces of the Beings and powers of another world."[16] However, it is also clear that Eliade attributes that experience *strictly* to "[t]he man of the societies in which myth is a living thing"[17], or, as he puts it famously, "the man of the archaic societies"[18], who thrived in the remote past. Out of *that* context Eliade brings forward his ultimate view of a World that literally "'speaks' to man", and that "to understand [that World's] language [man] needs only to know the myths and decipher the symbols."[19] All of these descriptions *could* apply to Graves's own experience, except that nowhere does Eliade assume the possibility of such an experience in the modern present. On the contrary, that present is defined by Eliade as, uniquely, a time of deep historical subjection, cut off as it is from all the advantages of transcendence that derive from mythical experience, as these were formerly available to archaic man.

For Eliade—as indeed for all of the great artists and thinkers of his time[20], the modern present involves us in a world that, in its very nature, is metaphysically inconsequential, defined (to quote his own Camusian turn of phrase) principally by that temporal rhythm "in which we are condemned to live and work".[21] Misfortune and death in that context become themselves "absurd"[22], and Eliade has been seen as resorting, in his response to that condition, to the classic attitude of his own Mioritic hero of folk tradition. He imposes a meaning on the absurd by viewing the tragedy of the modern age not "as a personal historical event but as a sacramental mystery"[23], a low-point, as it were, of "Chaos" that *must* be "followed by a new Creation", of a sort that can eventually be "homologized with a cosmogony".[24] Eliade is already pointing the way to that cosmogony through his own "nostalgia" for the archaic.[25] In the meantime, he could recognize, especially in the area of modern literature, "a revolt against historical time",[26] and especially against what he alludes to as "certain contemporary philosophies of despair".[27] That revolt is achieved paradoxically through the creation of closed, hermetic universes—Eliade cites the pre-eminent case of *Finnegan's Wake* by Joyce. These "cannot be entered except by overcoming immense difficulties, like the initiatory ordeals of the archaic and traditional societies."[28] In this way the opportunity for a new "initiatory gnosis" is created that is built up from the "ruins and enigmas" of modern existence—the Waste Land, so to speak—that Eliade sees as the first phase in the return to cosmogony. No doubt he would have seen in Graves's own work some "initiatory gnosis" of the sort, especially in the case of Graves's monumental prose work, *The White Goddess*, which T.S. Eliot described as a "monstrous, stupefying, indescribable book"—echoing his earlier comments on *Finnegan's Wake* as "a monstrous masterpiece". What Eliade would *not* have allowed, however, is a possibility of recovering the mythical experience of archaic man immediately and directly in the modern present, as Graves was also claiming to do.

In fact, the modern theory of myth is almost uniformly based on an *acceptance* of our separation from the mythical experience, even where that experience *seems* to be fully grasped as a radical alternative. In the case of Ernst Cassirer, for instance, an account is offered of the nature of mythic thinking especially powerful for the way it brings out the radical kind of metaphorical *identification* mythic thinking involves. Cassirer could see very clearly that

> *for mythic thinking there is much more in metaphor than
> a bare "substitution", a mere rhetorical figure of speech;
> that what seems to our subsequent reflection as a sheer
> transcription is mythically conceived as a genuine and direct
> identification.* [29]

Were we to assume a recovery of mythic thinking in our own time, one could refer this account to the metaphors Graves himself applies to the Goddess in speaking of *the dark edge of her double-axe* or *blood from her shadowy hand*. However, like Eliade, Cassirer was elaborating on what he saw as an *archaic* mode of thinking, very distant from our own time. In contrast with that former mode, modern thinking thrives on its unique *separation* from "the hard realistic powers"[30] of the mythic image. In the modern-day production of Holderling and of Keats particularly, "the mythic power of insight breaks forth again in its full intensity and objectifying power"[31], but it does so in "the world of poetry...as a world of illusion and fantasy".[32] Cassirer sees this ultimately as "liberation", since word and mythic image are now used by the mind as "organs of its own, and [the mind] thereby recognizes them *for what they really are*: forms of its own self-revelation."[33]

From this last remark, one sees where Cassirer finally stands. It had always been for him, as he insinuates elsewhere, a matter of "the direction of the subject's interest"[34], even where it *looks* like objectivity has been conferred on the mythic process, as where he says of it:

> *all spontaneity is **felt as** receptivity, all creativity as being, and every product of subjectivity **as so much** substantiality...*[35]

One needs to bring out the emphasis that is implicitly made here. It was for Cassirer a necessity for humankind, in its archaic experience, to *assume* an objective presence behind its mythical invention, for only in that way could an idealization of spiritual reality be conceived that would justify all future expression of the human spirit and its ever-progressive elaboration; thus

> *the Word **has** to be conceived, in the mythic mode, as a substantive being and power, before it can be comprehended as an ideal instrument, an organon of the mind, and as a fundamental function in the construction and development of spiritual reality.*[36]

In this way mythic thinking is finally rationalized to fit in fully with our modern experience, and it is in the spirit ultimately of a *modern* teleology, in diametric contrast with Eliade's direction, that Cassirer involves us in his extraordinary accounts of the power of mythic identification, paradoxically among the most aesthetically satisfying formulations we have.[37] The effect is ambiguous to the point where we can speak of a philosophical *tour de force*. Cassirer continues to the end to insist on the radical uniqueness of mythic thinking, but from a point of view that, paradoxically, affirms his and our hard-earned separation and freedom from its peculiarly captive mode of operating.

Like Cassirer, Owen Barfield also welcomed our necessary freedom from the phenomenal experience with which archaic man originally identified both at the level of the mythic image and of the word. It was part of *his* view, however, that what archaic man was about was not just mythical invention:

> *Men do not invent those mysterious relations between*
> *separate external objects, and between objects and feelings or*
> *ideas…The language of primitive man reports them as direct*
> *perceptual experience.*[38]

It was Barfield's special purpose (at a time contemporary with Cassirer) to claim that *originally* an objective presence does indeed lie behind the mythic image. This view is at the basis of his statement that "Mythology is the ghost of concrete meaning."[39] Barfield grounded this view on an elaborate etymological approach to the history of words, from which we gather that archaic man *must* have been involved in the phenomena, and in the representation of the phenomena, in the direct way Barfield describes:

> *you may imply, if you choose…that the earliest words in use*
> *were 'the names of sensible, material objects' and nothing*
> *more; only, in that case, you must suppose the 'sensible objects'*
> *themselves to have been something more; you must suppose*
> *that they were not, as they appear to be at present, isolated or*
> *detached from thinking and feeling.*[40]

Archaic representation involves, in fact, a whole *different* figuration, one that reflects "an awareness which we no longer have, of *an extra-sensory link* between the percipient and the representations."[41] Such a link (referred to 'mana' or 'waken') is "anterior to the individuality of [both] persons and objects"[42]—it presupposes originally "experiencing the phenomena [themselves] as representations"[43]. On that basis Barfield fills out the corollary understanding, that "This extra-sensory participation of the percipient in the representation involves a similar link between the representations themselves and of course between one percipient and another."[44] Barfield, quoting Durkheim, takes it still farther back to

collective mental states of extreme emotional intensity, in
which representation is as yet undifferentiated from the
movements and actions which make the communion towards
which it tends a reality to the group. Their participation in it
is so effectively lived that it is not yet properly imagined.[45]

Like Cassirer, Barfield sees a long progression in freedom from these phenomenally captive origins. We have, in the meantime, separated out from this experience, and a concomitant of the process has been that the phenomena themselves have detached from the original element in which both humankind and the phenomena were at one time involved. Thus,

As consciousness develops into self-consciousness, the [now]
remembered phenomena become detached and liberated from
their originals and so, as images, are in some measure at
man's disposal.[46]

From here Barfield plots out two courses. On the one hand, there is the direction of modern-day science, which today dictates experiencing the phenomena "non-representationally, as objects in their own right, existing independently of human consciousness".[47] This leads to the idea of the manipulation of nature as just so many objects, to be tossed about at will, and to what Barfield calls "idolatry", "involving in the end the elimination of those last vestiges of original participation, which...survive [even] in our language".[48] There is, however, another direction that follows, from understanding that, as humankind was *once* involved (without its will) in the phenomena, so (on the basis of freedom) it can be *again*. This leads to the equally extraordinary idea—at the other extreme from scientific manipulation—of a new Creation in which "man himself now stands in a 'directionally creator relation'"[49] to the phenomena.

Something of *this* direction is already suggested, Barfield claims, in a "high" or "prophetic" art, in those instances where "a real analogy" is pursued "between metaphorical usage and original participation".[50] However, one is only able to *build* on this analogy

if, but only if, we admit that in the course of the earth's
history, something like a Divine Word has been gradually
clothing itself with the humanity it first gradually created—
so that what was first spoken by God may eventually be
respoken by man.[51]

And for this to be the case, Nature, and not my own fancy, must be my representation, for then,

> *I know that what so stands is not my poor temporal*
> *personality, but the Divine Name in the unfathomable*
> *depths behind it. And if I strive to produce a work of art, I*
> *cannot then do otherwise than strive humbly to create more*
> *nearly as that creates.*[52]

Barfield thus brings us back, ultimately, to a cosmogony that would open the door for someone like Graves to find acceptance for the relationship to Nature that *he* claimed, except that what Barfield had in mind was a creative direction that was but "rudimentary as yet" and "mainly impulsive so far".[53] It is unlikely that he would have seen even in Graves's extraordinary output evidence of the "final" participation Barfield could look forward to. In the meantime, the creation of poetry, though implicitly *involved* in such a prospect, would seem to continue to import our present distance from it:

> *For it is the peculiarity of metaphorical language that, at*
> *first sight, it does often resemble very closely the language of*
> *participation; though upon closer examination its existence is*
> *seen to depend precisely on the absence of participation.*[54]

It was as far as the modern theory of myth would go to support Graves in his claim.

There was, what's more, to be direct *opposition* to Graves's claim, from another area of the modern theory of myth, where the science of psychoanalysis comes into it. That Graves's poetic creation was centred in the Goddess made complete sense in the natural-cosmological terms of myth, but all that had, in turn, been fully rationalized by the psychoanalysis that confidently proclaimed these terms mere projections of the unconscious. In the natural-cosmological terms in which Graves pursues his production, as we have seen, to embrace death, as the Solar King embraces death, is to embrace the power to return from death: a goal that psychoanalysis could easily refer to the need in every man to sublimate an unconscious desire for incest with the Mother. As Jung explains:

sun myths and rebirth myths devise every conceivable kind of
mother-analogy for the purpose of canalizing the libido into
new forms and effectively preventing it from regressing to
actual incest.[55]

Freud and Jung could also explain Graves's emphasis on the darker
problematic aspect of the Goddess and Her Creation and why it *must* figure
in his representation, for the Mother has the power both to give and to take
away, as Randall Jarrell was especially intent on pointing out:

> *That all affect, libido, mana should be concentrated in this*
> *one figure of the Mother-Muse; that love and sexuality*
> *should be inseparably intermingled with fear, violence,*
> *destruction in this "female spider"—that the loved one should*
> *be, necessarily, the Bad Mother who, necessarily, deserts and*
> *destroys the child; that the child should permit against her*
> *no conscious aggression of any kind, and intend his* **cruel,**
> **capricious, incontinent,** *his* **bitch, vixen, hag,** *to be neither*
> *condemnation nor invective, but only fascinated description*
> *of the loved and worshiped Mother and Goddess, She-Who-*
> *Must-be-Obeyed—all this is very interesting and very*
> *unoriginal. One encounters a rigorous, profound, and quite*
> *unparalleled understanding of such cases as Graves's in the*
> *many volumes of Freud...[and]...in Volume VII of Jung's*
> **Collected Works,** *in the second part of the essay entitled "The*
> *Relations between the Ego and the Unconscious".*[56]

Even the 'objectivity' that could be claimed for the independent power
of Graves's images, seeming as they do to come from an otherworld of their
own accord, is accounted for, in the psychoanalytic view, by the nature
of the "archetypes" that offer themselves as "analogies" to the instinctual
processes, for

> *The archetypes are the numinous, structural elements of the*
> *psyche* **and possess a certain autonomy** *and specific energy*
> *which enables them to attract out of the conscious mind those*
> *contents which are best suited to themselves.*[57]

The *individual* archetypal symbol—whether sea-horse, or subjected lion, or
even the bloody hand of Graves's Goddess—according to Jung

*carries conviction and at the same time expresses the content
of that conviction. It is able to do this because of the numen,
the specific energy stored up in the archetype.*[58]

Not that the creation of these analogies does not constitute

*a serious problem because, as we have said, they must be ideas
which attract the libido.*[59]

Hence, the tremendous significance Jung attaches to the creative fantasy,
which

*is continually engaged in producing analogies to instinctual
processes in order to free the libido from sheer instinctuality
by guiding it towards analogical ideas.*[60]

In the end such creation, according to Jung, will also *necessarily* produce
faith, for

*Experience of the archetype is not only impressive, it
seizes and possesses the whole personality, and is naturally
productive of faith.*[61]

No less than Jung was Joseph Campbell ready to allow for the psychic
inevitability of the initiatory images that were formerly supplied from
myth. So much so that without the supports from myth, these images must
be reproduced in dream, for the same reason that Jung cites, that otherwise
there could only be instinctual regression:

*Apparently there is something in these initiatory images
so necessary to the psyche that if they are not supplied from
without, through myth and ritual, they will have to be
announced again, through dream from within—lest our
energies should remain locked in a banal, long-outmoded
toyroom, at the bottom of the sea...the ageless initiation
symbolism is produced spontaneously by the patient himself at
the moment of the release.*[62]

It was *also* Campbell's view, however, that a crucial distinction would have to be introduced between the *sources* of dream and those of myth (a view that is paralleled in the distinction Graves introduces between poems and dreams[63]):

> But if we are to grasp the full value of the materials, we must note that myths are not exactly comparable to dream...
>
> we are in the presence rather of immense consciousness than of darkness...
>
> And so, to grasp the full value of the mythological figures that have come down to us, we must understand that they are not only the symptoms of the unconscious (as indeed are all human thoughts and acts) but also **controlled and intended statements** of certain spiritual principles...[64]

On the basis of his own vast research into these mythological figures and materials, Campbell could bring himself to the point of formulating the one great principle that underlies them all:

> Briefly formulated, the universal doctrine teaches that all the visible structures of the world—all **things** and beings—are the effects of a ubiquitous **power** out of which they rise, which supports and fills them during the period of their manifestation, and back into which they must ultimately dissolve.[65]

One notes of Campbell's emphasis in this passage the focus on "all *things* and beings" that are "the effects" of this "ubiquitous power". *Objectivity* is, in this way, restored to the mythical process. And it is in this spirit that Campbell throws himself into his own engagement with the mythical experience. It takes a form here that might lead one to suppose it was Graves himself who is speaking:

> the meeting with the goddess (who is incarnate in every woman) is the final test of the talent of the hero to win the boon of love (charity: **amor fati**), which is life itself enjoyed as the encasement of eternity...[66]...the goddess is red with the fire of life; the earth, the solar system, the galaxies of far-existing space, all swell within her womb. For she is the world creatrix, ever-mother, ever-virgin. She encompasses

*the encompassing, nourishes the nourishing, and is the life
of everything that lives. She is also the death of everything
that dies. The whole round of existence is accomplished within
her sway, from birth, through adolescence, maturity, and
senescence, to the grave. She is the womb and the tomb: the
sow that eats her farrow. Thus she unites the "good" and
the "bad", exhibiting the two modes of the remembered
mother,* **not as personal only, but as universal.** *The devotee
is expected to contemplate the two with equal equanimity.
Through this exercise his spirit is purged of its infantile,
inappropriate sentimentalities and resentments, and his
mind opened to the inscrutable presence which exists, not
primarily as "good" and "bad" with respect to his childlike
human convenience, his weal and woe, but as the law and
image of the nature of being.*[67]

At another point, Campbell will describe it as a passage

*from the infantile illusions of "good" and "evil" to an
experience of the majesty of cosmic law, purged of hope and
fear, and at peace in the understanding of the revelation of
being.*[68]

Here, we will feel, is all the confirming support Graves would have
needed, for like him Campbell assumes that is it both possible and
imperative to recover the mythical experience now. Campbell was pursuing
his own view at this time altogether independently of Graves, who had
published *The White Goddess* only a year before Campbell brought out
Hero with a Thousand Faces (from which these excerpts are taken.) The
concurrence is extraordinary and might have given pause to Jarrell when he
brought forward his critique of Graves some seven or eight years later. An
entirely independent case had been made for the objectivity of the process
that Jarrell, following Jung, had preconcluded to be purely subjective.
In fact, with Campbell, as with Graves, it is precisely the point that the
psychoanalytic patient must learn to transcend his own personal situation
by entering fully into the universal process. (For Graves it is the poet's task
to lead him there.) Then he would see that the "good" and the "bad" that so
obsess and tie down his mind, and that are the basis of his "hope" and "fear",
arise as the principles upon which the order of Nature itself is founded.
Unity, if anywhere, will be found there. This was already understood in the
Romantic context out of which Graves was writing: "fear" (in "To Juan")

is ultimately subsumed in "love". It is how Wordsworth himself presents it, who also saw it as a case of refusing the regression back to death; only in Wordsworth, it is the universal forms of Nature that assure his passage through:

> [I] *rather did with jealousy shrink back*
> *From every combination that might aid*
> *The tendency, too potent in itself,*
> *Of habit to enslave the mind, I mean*
> *Oppress it by the laws of vulgar sense,*
> *And substitute a universe of death,*
> *The falsest of all worlds, in place of that*
> *Which is divine and true. To fear and love,*
> *To love, as first and chief, for there fear ends,*
> *Be this ascribed; to early intercourse,*
> *In presence of sublime and lovely Forms,*
> *With the adverse principles of pain and joy,*
> *Evil, as one is rashly named by those*
> *Who know not what they say. From love, for here*
> *Do we begin and end, all grandeur comes,*
> *All truth and beauty, from pervading love,*
> *That gone, we are as dust.*[69]

Campbell himself assumes an ultimate peace from the unity of the two experiences as these come together in the Mothering Goddess:

> *She was Cosmic Power, the totality of the universe, the*
> *harmonization of all the pairs of opposites, combining*
> *wonderfully the terror of absolute destruction with an*
> *impersonal yet motherly reassurance.*[70]

Likewise, in "To Juan" as we have seen, Graves assumes an ultimate unity, but in him the duality persists, if only because *he* was working this experience out immediately and directly through the form of being he saw himself as having at that moment. Hence the persistence in *his* representations of the Goddess of the dual aspect of Her involvement with him. It was in any case Graves's view (at least for the longest time; there would be a further evolution in his view towards the end of his career[71]) that man had always been and would have to remain in a dualistic relationship with his Creatress, for

Man is a demi-god: he always has either one foot or the other in the grave; woman is divine because she can keep both her feet always in the same place, whether in the sky, in the underworld, or on this earth. Man envies her and tells himself lies about his own completeness, and thereby makes himself miserable; because if he is divine she is not even a demi-goddess—she is mere nymph and his love for her turns to scorn and hate.[72]

III

What are we to make, then, of the insistent efforts of Campbell and Graves to announce the prospect of a new mythical experience in the modern world, one founded on the basis of Nature, in defiance of the rigidly qualifying strictures of the many acknowledged modern theorists of myth? In Graves's view, inability, or unwillingness, to recognize that the time was ripe for a fresh breakthrough into mythical experience has a clear historical explanation. It is the end-result of an intellectual pretension to resolve the almost intolerable duality in which man is naturally placed, by which he has, over centuries, rationalized himself outside the sphere of Nature, and so outside the Goddess's order.[73] Referring himself directly to the mythical record, Graves put it as follows:

> [man] *is divine not in his single person but in his twinhood.*
> *As Osiris, the Spirit of the Waxing Year, he is always*
> *jealous of the weird, Set, the Spirit of the Waning Year, and*
> *vice-versa; he cannot be both of them at once except by an*
> *intellectual effort that destroys his humanity, and this is the*
> *fundamental defect of the Apollonian or Jehovistic cult.*[74]

By this "cult" Graves had in mind the longstanding effects of the decisive intervention over the course of the 1st millennium B.C. of patriarchal influences that had been slowly seeping into both the Hellenic and Hebraic cultures, from which our own Western experience derives. War had been declared in Heaven with the conflict between Jehovah and the Great Goddess of 7th century B.C. Jerusalem, which led to Her displacement by this Universal God, and

> [t]*he result of envisaging this God of pure meditation, the*
> *Universal Mind still premised by the most reputable modern*
> *philosophers, and enthroning him above Nature as essential*
> *Truth and Goodness was not an altogether happy one.*[75]

> *Then came the early Greek philosophers who were strongly*
> *opposed to magical poetry as threatening their new religion*
> *of logic, and under their influence a rational poetic language*
> *(now called the Classical) was elaborated in honour of their*

patron Apollo and imposed on the world as the last word in
spiritual illumination.[76]

Not that the elaborate, withering indictment of Western tradition that we get from Graves in *The White Goddess* does not still leave him with the challenge of effectively harnessing the energy associated with his engagement with the Goddess. For without a deliberate, conscious reining of this energy, the need for which Graves himself acknowledges, there is the real danger of being destroyed by it, as Graves's poems themselves bear witness.[77] The purpose of the post-Exilic religious reformation that substituted Jehovah for the Goddess had been precisely to disassociate man from the destructive influence of his commitment to the 'darker' side of the Goddess's claims on him. Thus a recent reader of Graves, considering the challenge of this crucial opposition, between the "voracious life-giving energy" on the one hand and "the rationalizing element" on the other, concludes:

> *the issue is how successfully the two key elements can be*
> *accommodated without the energy being destroyed.*[78]

One keeps this universal energy of Nature under control, according to this reader, "through mythic or religious ritual".[79] Ted Hughes, a modern poet whom one should be linking with Graves, is further recruited on behalf of this view.[80] However, it is truer to say that this force of mythic or religious ritual, if it is effective, must *by its own operation* control the energy. We have an especially powerful instance of the operation of this force (of mythic ritual) in Graves's poem, "She Is No Liar":

> *She is no liar, yet she will wash away*
> *Honey from her lips, blood from her shadowy hand,*
> *And, dressed at dawn in clean white robes will say,*
> *Trusting the ignorant world to understand:*
> *'Such things no longer are; this is today.'*

✦   ✦   ✦

"Such things no longer are;"—Graves's view was that modern man had come into a new age in which all that had formerly obstructed the Goddess's power to direct his life had been left behind. Graves's faith that this was so was categorical, and the situation could not be reversed for him.

With a characteristic freedom from the effects of history, he could say with complete assurance and with a complete finality, in "The End of Play":

> *We have reached the end of pastime...*
> ....
> *We have at last ceased idling...*
> ....
> *We tell no lies now, at last cannot be*
> *The rogues we were—so evilly linked in sense*
> *With what we scrutinized...*[81]

One is astounded by the unitary view Graves takes of history, which allowed him to affirm this faith and to install himself, very simply, without any further sense of any conflict that might subvert or continue to wear away at his vision.[82] It is the measure of a formidable single-mindedness in Graves that in this view he stands perhaps alone.[83] All had been for him a matter of the suppression merely of the Goddess-culture, which had remained inexpungeable and irrepressible, so that it was only a matter of time before that culture would openly affirm itself again. Hence the account of his purposes as Graves shared this with his audience in his 1957 Y.M.H.A. lecture:

> *It is enough for me to quote the myths and give them*
> *historical sense: tracing a certain faith through its historical*
> *vicissitudes—from where it was paramount, to when it*
> *has been driven underground and preserved by witches,*
> *travelling minstrels, remote country-folk and a few secret*
> *heretics to the newly established religion.*[84]

This faith had been restored again in the twentieth century principally through Graves himself, though Graves further cites, as indirect evidence, the fact that the Virgin Mary could now in the established religions "legitimately be saluted as 'the Queen of Heaven'—the very title borne by Rahab (the Goddess Astarte), against whom the prophet Jeremiah declaimed in the name of his monotheistic Father-god Jehovah."[85]

Graves's assurance in proclaiming this faith is in large part a feature of its surviving power as he saw this operating especially in British culture. Thus he emphasizes that "the Queen of Heaven with her retinue of female saints had a far greater hold in the popular imagination between the Crusades and the Civil War than either the Father or the Son."[86] This Thunder-God, as Graves presents Him, did get re-instated at the time of the Puritan Revolution in England, but it is characteristic of Graves that he sees this God's triumph as "short-lived"; it could never have withstood "the stubborn conviction" among the British that Britain was "a Mother Country, not a Father-land".[87] Writing out of this view as well as the power of his own experience, Graves has simply no inclination to consider that perhaps Western civilization as a whole had been through a deeper conflict and a deeper agony. However, Ted Hughes, who was (up to a point) a professed disciple of Graves, took a very different view of the matter in his book, *Shakespeare and the Goddess of Complete Being*. There it is Hughes's special insistence that man *continues* in conflict with himself over the Goddess, and no one saw that this would be so with greater clarity than did Shakespeare, whose case *about* the conflict, according to Hughes, has still to be heard—through his plays.[88] It is the conflict of the Reformation itself, behind which Hughes, like Graves, sees the conflict of Jehovah and the great Goddess of 7th century B.C. Jerusalem.[89] It is, according to Hughes, the *one* conflict in which Shakespeare is engaged from the beginning of his career to its end.

Macbeth, for Hughes, is the play in which this conflict comes to fullest expression, being also the turning point in Shakespeare's own dealings with it. In his earlier tragedies, including *Hamlet* and *King Lear*, Shakespeare had already dramatized the process by which his heroes suddenly succumb to the "delusion"[90] of thinking their beloved ones unholy. In this they pretend to do *without* the Goddess's all-supporting life by charging *Her*, as it were, with dark and unholy motives. Now, in *Macbeth*, the nature of this charge is fully exposed, for the erroneous "Tarquinian" madness that it represents, for which the hero must be destroyed. It is the hero's rational "Adonis" world of "Puritan-style ideals"[91]—which underlies that madness—that must be destroyed, by the irrepressible life of the Goddess. Macbeth's real crime in this respect precedes his appearance in the play and is the measure of his value as a representation of the more recent Shakespearean tragic heroes who precede him. Macbeth must be set right by being driven to destroy his Adonis-nature, murdering Duncan and seeking to murder Banquo in the process, only because all are guilty of rejecting the Goddess. However, up to that point Shakespeare's heroes have *thought* themselves justified in their charge, and it is the power that this thought exercises over them that so impresses Hughes and (so Hughes supposes) Shakespeare:

> *Even after it has been capsized in spectacular fashion by that irrational secret-sharer [Tarquin] rising from beneath it, that point of view, of the Adonis ego, though it no longer has any*

*control over its actions, always retains the ability, like a ship's gimbal, to think itself rational (at least, it does so up to the point at which the ego is destroyed, and a new self, neither Adonis nor Tarquin, emerges—as begins to happen in **King Lear**).*

It is Hughes's argument that Western man continues to lie somewhere in the general area in which Shakespeare's tragic heroes find themselves before *Macbeth* comes through to set right all delusion. The challenge for Hughes lies in the fact that rational man must learn to see him*self* in Macbeth and indeed in every Shakespearean tragic hero who comes before him. Shakespeare had given direct and complete expression to Western man's judgment of the Goddess, only to bring out, in fact, the *tragedy* in that judgment:

> *What Shakespeare **goes on** to reveal is that in destroying her* [the Goddess] *he destroys himself and brings down Heaven and Earth in ruins.*[92]

But this is, for Hughes in any case

> *the inevitable crime of Civilization, or even the inevitable crime of consciousness.*[93] *Certainly the crime of the Reformation—the "offense/From Luther until now/That has driven a culture mad" as Auden phrased it.*[94]

But what if this sudden shift in consciousness in the hero, into judgment, turned out *not* to be some misguided "offense" stemming from a "delusion", whether this is seen as criminal or tragic (which is to say, in the latter case, stemming from "error"), but a new *objective* development, which Shakespeare took that seriously because it seemed to him it *had* become the reality. Everything *had*, disastrously, fallen apart, and all because the kind of "love" Shakespeare's tragic hero had known with his beloved *had* failed and a new perception of the extent of human depravity come into view. If this is so, the story would not then be (as it appears to be on the surface) about "rejection of the Female" or "the Puritan fear of female sexuality", but about some still *deeper* failure or change, something still *more* to reckon with than either Graves or Hughes seemed ready to acknowledge: a matter of coming to terms with a deeper degree of depravity than we had supposed ourselves subject to and that could, therefore, potentially only confound us the more. This is to shift the focus I have been pursuing thus far into a still more problematic depth—"fear", as in the case of Macbeth, originating, in this conception, from a deeper instability and a deeper derangement. I shall thereby be raising a still *further* issue that would seem to arise from the course Western experience has taken, which throws into doubt whether Graves's (and Hughes's) conception of "love" and of the "Female" or Goddess takes us far enough or as far as we need to take ourselves, if we are to avoid any deeper subversion than what Hughes claimed has characterized Western experience thus far.[95]

II

THE WORST OF DEPRAVITY

For, what shall we say *is* Macbeth's "fear" and *what* the violence of conception that takes him over, to the point where, it would seem, he has *no choice but* to yield?

> *why* do I yield to that suggestion
> *Whose horrid image doth unfix my hair*
> *And make my seated heart knock at my ribs*
> *Against the use of nature?*

Hughes and Graves would have us believe that this is the Goddess taking Macbeth over, possessing him in order to avenge Herself against him for the crime he has committed against Her. [96] Macbeth's crime lies in rejecting the Goddess by turning away from Her sensual creation, for which *he* has judged Her unholy. But does Macbeth, when viewed more closely, represent the *judgment* of sensuality, or does he not rather represent the complete *indulgence* of it, along with Lady Macbeth, and indeed all the characters in this play, with whom he is united in a complete sensual ambition? To what extent all are immersed in the darkest sensuality in *Macbeth* can be gleaned from what James Calderwood has to say about the opening battle scene in which a universal ambition is drastically played out:

> *As priestly leaders of the royal forces Macbeth and Banquo*
> *preside over a ceremony in which the Scots are purged and*
> *exalted by the shedding of sacred blood in the King's cause*
> *even as mankind was once purged by the shedding of Christ's*
> *sacred blood on Golgotha. Only men in battle who bathe in*
> *their own and their enemies' blood, are able to partake bodily*
> *and symbolically in the divinity of the state. As Christ's*
> *blood streaming in the firmament offers everlasting life to the*
> *worshiper, so the sacred blood of battle yields immortality to*
> *Macbeth and Banquo as Bellona's deathless bridegrooms and*
> *as participants in the greater life of the state (Macbeth will be*
> *king, Banquo will beget kings).*[97]

We are, with *Macbeth*, in a world that, in its original situation—before the tragic breakdown—is, in fact, complete as perhaps no other is in Shakespeare. It is a complete world because of the *grounds* of its justification, archaic as those grounds certainly are, involving human nature as they do in the complete depth of its violent sensuality. From *this* starting position (in itself an extraordinary feat of cultural anamnesis on Shakespeare's part) Shakespeare had a point to make, as we shall see. As Calderwood explains, war is intrinsic to this archaic world, being literally its means of divination and of sanctification, for,

> *It enables kings to look into the entrails of violence and see if*
> *they are still sacred to the gods*[98]

The Challenger in this world is thus the King's necessary and welcome counterpart, since *he* raises, by his own daring rebellion, the issue of the king's sacredness, which must be continually justified anew, and in this sense

> *each fight with a challenger who would kill him is a test of*
> *the king's sacredness: will the golden bough remain on its*
> *branch? Will the god's strange heart still beat within him?*[99]

The seemingly complete extent of the violence, as we have it in *Macbeth*, represents the fullest measure of that justification. In fact, so complete is the violence at a certain point we are *un*able to distinguish the king's challenger from his defender. As Calderwood puts it, "it is a scene of undifferentiated brutality" for "all are bloodily one in battle".[100] But this is as it ideally should be, for only out of the deepest engagement in these terms—the deepest violence and the deepest effort of will on both sides, will justification come. Thus in the context of this battle

> *violence erodes cultural distinctions, even the fundamental*
> *distinction between "us" and "them", yet its function is*
> *to reaffirm and recreate distinctions by singling out, not*
> *scapegoat victims, but heroic survivors.*[101]

For in this context, "surviving is a sacred achievement".[102]

It is the chief value of the warrior in this world that he can survive this scene of battle, as Macbeth and Banquo survive it, and in doing so justify himself. The king's justification thus follows from the warrior's own. If the warrior is happy to serve his king, this is because, as Harry Berger Jr. points out, it is the king who provides him with the "bloody occasions"—and so "the reputation and honors" that follow from success on those "occasions"—by which the warrior seeks to prove and to justify himself.[103] It is easy to see, at the same time, the constant threat that might be posed to the king by the pride of the warrior on whose extreme prowess the king must rely for his justification.[104] We can see how ideas of service and love would then enter into this context, to safeguard against overweening pride, and as it were to sublimate the threat of violence. It was the view of Johannes Huizinga that these ideas come into play in the time of the Middle Ages (in which Shakespeare's action is set) as a purely formal code of conventions, deliberately constructed and imposed on a tendency to ferocious passion that is everywhere present at that time because of its reigning quality of pride.[105] Thus

> *Love has to be elevated to the height of a rite. The overflowing violence of passion demands it. Only by constructing a system of forms and rules for the violent emotions can barbarity be escaped.*[106]

> *The passionate and violent soul of the age…could not dispense with the severest rules and the strictest formalism. All emotions required a rigid system of conventional forms, for without them passion and ferocity would have made havoc of life.*[107]

And so we may approach those extraordinary moments in Shakespeare's play when Macbeth and Lady Macbeth formally express their obeisance to Duncan in spite of the extreme achievement that Macbeth has displayed in battle that seems to redound more to his own honor:

> Duncan. *O worthiest cousin!*
> *The sin of my ingratitude even now*
> *Was heavy upon me: thou art so far before,*
> *That swiftest wing of recompense is slow*
> *To overtake thee. Would thou hadst less deserved,*
> *That the proportion both of thanks and payment*
> *Might have been mine! only I have left to say,*
> *More is thy due than more than all can pay.*

> Macbeth. *The service and the loyalty I owe,*
> *In doing it, pays itself. Your highness' part*
> *Is to receive our duties: and our duties*
> *Are to your throne and state children and servants;*
> *Which do but what they should, by doing every thing*

Safe toward your love and honour.

Duncan.   *Welcome hither:*
I have begun to plant thee, and will labour
To make thee full of growing.

*   *   *

Duncan. *See, see, our honoured hostess!*
The love that follows us sometime is our trouble,
Which still we thank as love…

Lady Macbeth.   *All our service*
In every point twice done, and then done double,
Were poor and single business to contend
Against those honours deep and broad wherewith
Your majesty loads our house: for those of old,
And the late dignities heaped up to them,
We rest your hermits.

We are setting aside for the present the effect on these moments (in the way *we* actually see them) of the "evil" intention in Macbeth and in Lady Macbeth that has *also* disturbingly penetrated this world. Here I wish to propose that the play's original experience transcends Huizinga's notion of a deliberately constructed culture, as if sentiments of love and service were for the most part, as he argues, only put on, only moving *towards* being essential, if no *less* crucial for all that.[108] On the contrary, there seems a case for saying that service and love are themselves an intrinsic part of the unified whole of the original *Macbeth*-world—as *much* a feature of what holds that world together and makes it complete, as the extreme violence on which that world is predicated. It is a logical predication, for if it *is* the extreme violence that makes the *Macbeth*-world complete—because only such violence creates the necessary basis for a complete justification—so too must the love that finally supports that justification be complete.

We are to imagine an *original* condition of culture in which utmost sensual depths of dark violence are perfectly expressed and perfectly contained by the love and service that support and motivate that violence. It is what we glimpse in those moments of obeisance that unite Macbeth and Lady Macbeth in the same expression of will. These moments present the characters in the image of what they *were* until now, borne up by love and service. Only, the characters have now separated out from the reality and so give us merely the image. So too was Macbeth in battle at one time borne up by love and service, until things changed, though we are only given insight into Macbeth's love in hypocritical fashion later, in the words he uses to justify slaying Duncan's guards *after* he has murdered Duncan:

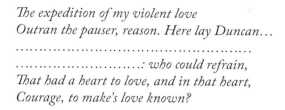

> *The expedition of my violent love*
> *Outran the pauser, reason. Here lay Duncan...*
> ....
> ....: *who could refrain,*
> *That had a heart to love, and in that heart,*
> *Courage, to make's love known?*

Here is our glimpse into the principal original motive of this world, now gone preternaturally awry. All *was* formerly a unity—the violence and the love quite *one*, until the supporting love goes out of it. Macbeth finds himself in battle immersed in an extreme violence, fighting the King's cause suddenly *without* the love that had borne him up in his will to that point. That fact is momentously registered through the contrast with Banquo *who himself has battled no less fiercely or completely* but who comes away from his engagement as Macbeth could have expected to—supported still by love.[109] Herein lies the horror of the separation of "foul" from "fair" from the former unity in which they lay; what was "fair" and should have remained "fair", and does remain "fair" for Banquo (the "foul" being incorporated into *it* for him) has become simply "foul" for Macbeth. His complete violence of will has been released from the supporting reality of love, with the effect that, without its support and without its defense, he is now overwhelmed by the violence of his will. In this complete world, Macbeth's will has identified with the King in fighting his cause; stripped now of any further underlying motive of love, Macbeth *becomes* in his will the very King with whom he is identified in his defense. His very identity has gone over to *being* King, and he meets the recognition from the Witches that this is so with fear because in that moment for the first time he consciously recognizes that this is so. His displacement of Duncan as King has already taken place and so *must* lead to murder.

What Calderwood's account overlooks is that the situation in *Macbeth* has altered—preternaturally so, so that we view all that we are given in the beginning of the play as it were in double form. We see on the one hand what the *Macbeth*-world is originally constituted of and at the same time measure a seismic alteration in it, which has everything, in fact, different and looking different. That effect extends to the imagery of Golgotha that the Sergeant elaborates in his account of the battle, which does *seem* to positively identify the blood of the battling warriors with that of Christ, but *in fact* registers an effect wildly inappropriate. Calderwood himself acknowledges the association as a "grotesque collusion".[110] This is generally the case with all that is presented in the play's opening scenes. A new *difference* has come into it and to some extent come into the consciousness of all the characters who have witnessed Macbeth's action on the battlefield, though, being unused to any other world, none are in the position to recognize what that difference imports. Nevertheless, it is clearly present in the consciousness of the *effect* of Macbeth's deeds, which project him as bearing the very identity of the Rebel or Challenger with whom he has literally united in battle, and who, by this perverted route, through Macbeth, has *become* King:

> Ross. *The king hath happily received, Macbeth,*
> *The news of **thy** success: and when he reads*
> ***Thy personal venture in the rebels' fight,***
> *His wonders and his praises do contend*
> ***Which should be thine or his:** silenced with that,*
> *In viewing o'er the rest o' the selfsame day,*
> *He finds thee in the stout Norweyan ranks,*
> *Nothing afeard of what thyself didst make,*
> ***Strange images** of death. As thick as hail*
> *Came post with post, and every one did bear*
> ***Thy** praises in his kingdom's great defence,*
> *And poured them down before him.*

Macbeth is originally identified with a form of extreme expression in violent will that has been the supporting power of his society until now while the substance of love also motivated it. The sudden *withdrawal* of this substance of love now leaves the will to operate on its own. Macbeth is suddenly left without any defense against that will, which being as extreme as the love that contained it, cannot be resisted. The human will has come free in its essential depravity, and no defense in human nature is able to protect against it. Thus the horror and the fear that overcome Macbeth who is left grappling helplessly with himself, for the utmost violence of his will is bound to overpower him. It is the measure Shakespeare has taken of the depths of human depravity; he has traced it back to this original situation when love had all in check. Then, dramatizing the moment in which the primal human will separates out from love, he shows with a perfect horror how little power human nature on its own can have over this will. To make the point with an even greater effect of horror, he then brings into his exposition diachronically the power that the *ideal* of love might still be thought to have over the will—for love has now *become* an ideal, is no longer the governing reality. This is where Macbeth imagines the angels judging his murderous intentions before he gets down to the murder. Here Shakespeare brings love back into it, with all the power it could exercise over the mind *as* an ideal, and bringing it back he demonstrates how the ideal in this case can have no power over that will. Macbeth's most evolved Imaginations of that ideal, by which his projected deed is judged, do have the effect of rousing his conscience but can have no effect in keeping him from seeing the deed through.[111]

What can Shakespeare's purpose have been in depicting this primal scene if not to cite, as evidence, the sheer extent of violent sensuality that is there deep down in the human make-up, if only as an atavistic survival today? Starting from an archaic world, which Shakespeare in his own way recovers, he shows how sensuality in this degree would *have* to be restrained by a power of love that is there originally in the same degree. He assumes, as his own mythographer of the archaic, that formerly this was so, and then deliberately takes us back, to that fateful moment when separation from love is brought about. The sensuality that had until then been kept in check now subverts disastrously from the sheer extent of its expression, its completeness. Having once subserved the "mana" of love, it is now exposed for the horrible depravity it constitutes when left to its own purposes and acts in its own right. It has the power of a pure unchecked somatic *disturbance* that can only take Macbeth away with itself in his mind.[112] This is what absorbs him in fear from the start, and what keeps him in fear throughout. And so his famous visions, which only have the *content* of moral imagination when in *substance* they are woven out of his disturbance, so that the imagination of Duncan in his virtues *must* give way to those of the daggers that rush him into the murder without impediment. Those visions continue, of course, beyond the murder, and are continually at play in Macbeth[113], until, by the sheer force of his destructive will, he manages in a sense to kill them, destroying his whole human nature in the process. In comparison with Macbeth, Lady Macbeth one might say has only "played" at being possessed, is not as fully engaged, is herself in dismay at the diabolic visions that continue in her husband.[114] She goes mad ultimately less from the influence of demonic possession than from her horror of Macbeth's complete separation from her, the only person with whom, in this world of violent debacle, she could have retained *any* form of hopeful human complicity.

II

The action in *Macbeth* is only the most extreme and the most horrid case of a tragic pattern in Shakespeare that is typical of this phase. We feel the connection back to the other tragedies especially where Macbeth and Lady Macbeth are suddenly presented to us, at the scene of the murder, in their fundamental innocence. It is the effect that so impressed John Middleton Murry:

> *That a man and woman should, in the very act of heinous*
> *and diabolical murder, reveal themselves as naïve and*
> *innocent, convulses our morality and awakens in us thoughts*
> *beyond the reaches of our souls.*[115]

Innocence is the fundamental condition of Shakespeare's tragic characters, when one compares them to the villains via whom their destinies are galvanized. Villains though they have *become*, Macbeth and Lady Macbeth are still innocent, and so tragic, and the lesson they dramatize is therefore the more horrifying because of that. Their fate is typical of the Shakespearean tragic action: innocent as they are, they are now subverted by their own sensuality, which they had *thought* love, and which was indeed love until their condition altered. The reality of sensual life has suddenly become pretension, and we see now that they are *composed* of sensuality and are judged for it. Sensuality, separated from love, turns into depravity.

The moment when this alteration takes place is the moment of evil, which strikes like lightning, immediately and with an overwhelming violence, because, at any and every cost, the separation from sensuality must now take place—for whatever evolutionary reasons we may divine. The Shakespearean villain, from this perspective, is merely party to the process, a mechanism merely who adds to the effect of the process that must now go forward. Shakespeare's tragic characters remaining, as they do, profoundly attached to the sensuality and to the love that they have known, which is the only love they *can* know, the effect of separation is world-altering; but it is now what *has* to be borne, for human sensuality can only subvert now.[116] How dismal a process this is the plays bear witness to, for Shakespeare's tragic characters remain profoundly implicated. And in this they are the image of what *we* might be if we thought ourselves into, or pretended to live out, our own sensuality, in the complete and unthinking way we might wish to.

Lear is only slightly less horrid as presentation in this respect than is *Macbeth*. Lightning strikes here in the same way—the scene altering instantaneously, and with a complete irreversibility. A love that was until then supported in its sensuality now converts, disastrously—into hate, from the influence of a sensuality now become depravity:

> *For by the sacred radiance of the sun*
> *The mysteries of Hecate, and the night;*
> *By all the operation of the orbs*
> *From whom we do exist and cease to be;*
> *Here I disclaim all my paternal care,*
> *Propinquity and property of blood,*
> *And as a stranger to my heart and me*
> *Hold thee from this forever. The barbarous Scythian*
> *Or he that makes his generation messes*
> *To gorge his appetite, shall to my bosom*
> *Be as well neighboured, pitied, and relieved,*
> *As thou my sometime daughter.*

No villain is required to help subvert things here, unless that villain might be Cordelia. It will seem outlandish to say so, but this is nevertheless in a certain sense the case. Of the perversely sensual basis of Lear's love of Cordelia there is no doubt, but to the extent that Cordelia is involved in this love, who can say that she herself does not *share* in that sensuality or express *herself* in it? Cordelia balking at the profession of her love for Lear in the ritual, from this point of view, can be seen as a deliberate effort to repress her own involvement in that sensuality, which she finds she cannot openly express herself in, from a reticence she cannot control, which itself converts to pride.[117] Evil has entered the *Lear*-world as it were through this back route. Pride of this kind can easily be seen as hate; and so Lear sees it; he sees, also, the evil at work through it, and on that basis must react in his turn, for he can only reject Cordelia for it. That reaction is repeated later when Lear sees it in Goneril:

> *Darkness and devils!*

Only, by comparison of course, Cordelia is relatively far more innocent. It is principally through Lear that the subversion by sensuality takes place and depravity is exposed. As the passage quoted above shows, the breakdown is as great, and as profoundly sensual in its turn, as the borne-up experience of love that had sustained it until this moment. But what can we imagine

Cordelia's perception of Lear to be at this moment, or of her own love shared with him up to now? As far as I know, no commentary exists on what we may suppose Cordelia is experiencing through the extensive silence that marks her response to Lear's outburst at this point. But we can surely imagine that, among other feelings, Cordelia would be wondering about the basis of the love shared with him until now, and feeling some guiltiness about it. Not in the sense that she wonders how she could love this man, but that she wonders on what grounds she herself has been having this love, since it was love partaken of *with* him. When she and Lear meet again later in the play, after much suffering, both have by then been largely purged of the sensual basis of the love that they once shared.[118]

No one is spared the judgement; I have elsewhere[119] gone in some depth into the basis of guilt also in Desdemona, after Othello himself breaks down. The sensuality that absorbs *them* from the beginning needs no elucidation, and it becomes the doorway into a view of the depravity that is thought to lurk in these characters as an essential condition— tragically so in light of how they otherwise appear to us on the surface, as perhaps Shakespeare's greatest romantic lovers. The breakdown from sensuality into depravity is overwhelmingly clear in the case of Othello, but Shakespeare's vision of fundamental depravity extends in the play, as I show, to Desdemona herself. It is a measure of the universal import of what we may call the Shakespearean doubt at this time; it is a doubt that Shakespeare had carried over to *Othello* from *Hamlet*. Human nature is seen in *Hamlet* as *determined* by lust, this being the reigning view of human nature on which Shakespeare was then acting, which he had derived from Luther.[120] Even if we feel that Shakespeare stands finally for something else, something ultimately beyond this pessimism, it would seem that he assumed this view of human nature to be fundamentally true, and it is how his characters are shown to us, after falling from their formerly protected sphere in a world where lust and a general sensuality are originally absorbed in a certain order of love. Love in the tragedies is presented by Shakespeare in those terms, and it is *this* original ordering love that now goes; when it does, the subversion by sensuality is overwhelming—virtually everyone will and must die from it, in one elaborate way or another.[121]

Hamlet's subversion by sensuality is in his mind, but the subversion is no less real for that. The picture of lust that presents itself to him from his world derives not only from what he sees in the relationship between Claudius and his mother, but also from the relationship between his mother and his father:

why, she would hang on him,
As if increase of appetite had grown
By what it fed on:

Originally, Hamlet's picture incorporates this sensuality of his parents into an idea of their love, in keeping with the fundamental pattern of experience in Shakespeare's tragedies, and Hamlet's own love of his father is bound up with this picture. But with the Ghost's revelation about his condition in the afterlife, the lust (typically) separates out from that picture as its own force, for which his father is now suffering punishment in the otherworld.[122] His father's murder at Claudius's hands is in this respect but the image of the former's condemnation of himself, as if in his own lustful relationship to his wife lay the seeds of her further relationship to his murderer Claudius, who *is* the demonic image of himself.

Soon Hamlet is bitterly generalizing this condition of lust about everyone. If what his mother has made of herself with Claudius, or what Claudius himself represents of the grossest sensuality, so subverts Hamlet's mind, it is because they have become the images of a universal human condition that Hamlet can now see also touches him, and he is now himself subverted:

for virtue cannot so inoculate our old stock but we shall relish
of it

for the power of beauty will sooner transform honesty from
what it is to a bawd than the force of honesty can translate
beauty into his likeness: this was sometime a paradox, but
now the time gives it proof.

It is the same view of a now *altered* condition of love that Iago expounds upon at length in *Othello*, that condition being (appallingly) the natural ground for his own introduction onto this scene. Addressing a love *thus altered*, Iago can now confidently proclaim of *it*:

It is merely a lust of the blood and a permission of the will.[123]

III

To return to the model put forward by Graves and by Hughes—I see a very different picture emerging from Shakespeare's presentation. An *original* picture presents itself—an original archaic world—in which love in various forms does indeed reign over all and have all in hand, and we can certainly conceive of *this* totality as expressing the Goddess's primal hold over Her indulged creation. Lust and a *general* sensuality that makes room for self-indulgence, ferocious character, and even violence—all this may be said to have had at one time an assigned place within an order principally directed by love. But then this indulgent and supporting love withdraws, and all is as if poured out, in a way that seems to confirm directly all that Luther had said[124] was true about human nature: that it is fundamentally, grossly and hopelessly depraved:

> *A serving-man, proud in heart and mind; that curled my hair; wore gloves in my cap; served the lust of my mistress' heart and did the act of darkness with her...one that slept in the contriving of lust and waked to do it...false of heart, light of ear, bloody of hand; hog in sloth, fox in stealth, wolf in greediness, dog in madness, lion in prey.*

Edgar's speech, as Poor Tom, catalogues it all. Humankind has been left to itself alone, subject to almost any subversion by its own sensuality, and with no further defense against itself, save for what it might find of support from whatever might come of this situation. If we are to speak of any further *return* to the Goddess, surely it would have to be with reference ultimately to *all* that we may suppose human nature to be composed of, as Shakespeare saw it. And, coming away from Shakespeare, it will boggle our minds to imagine the kind of confidence that would allow us the total leap in human experience that Graves for one proposed.

We may suppose that what Shakespeare thought of human nature would have some bearing on what we consider Imaginatively possible today, and Ted Hughes certainly assumed this, though I would propose a different lesson to be derived from what Shakespeare presents. The problem of our re-uniting with the Goddess necessitates for Hughes a complex evolution *with* Shakespeare, through the whole of the rest of the work that follows from his great tragedies. It is therefore in no simple sense that Hughes wishes to propose our extrication from the consequences that have followed from Man's historical rejection of the Female, as he sees the problem.[125]

Only, the fear in Shakespeare, the pity and the terror, would seem to stem from a deeper source than simply the fear of female sexuality. It is fear of an actual and a complete depravity reigning potentially in us all, to which even woman in her relative innocence is subject. That is the full extent of the Shakespearean despair: all are overwhelmed, and moreover with a violence that does not appear to have limits, except that Shakespeare's characters bear it all in their deaths. From the Shakespearean account, there would seem to be far more in human nature to contend with that would need watching over, some still deeper influence or threat in the blood than what either Graves or Hughes seems ready to acknowledge—some graver menace that Shakespeare would have thought should concern us from our continued embroilment in a fundamental sensuality that defines us all.

Of all the ways in which human nature may be threatened, the experience of subverted love may well be the worst. In Shakespeare the experience is conceived in the absolute terms of our separation from an original, archaic condition of love that has left us utterly vulnerable. Thus Shakespeare could not see any hope *in the immediate term* except directly through our suffering of that separation, or our suffering through it. All the best characters of his imagination are sacrificed to this idea, in the literal sense that all die from it, and that *would* have to drive him further to wonder if this could be all. His coming through beyond this point, as it were back to unity in the Goddess, was as hard a route as any could take, and hardly how we would wish to imagine our way through. Shakespeare's route represents how we would have to come through if we were to act on our hope for ourselves immediately, in our total psychological condition at present, and the cost of that immediate venture is consequently as great as it can be. The tremendously arduous route Shakespeare took from here must for that reason stand *also* in the nature of a warning, as to what we might wish to pretend to from a misplaced idea of our capacities at present.

In comparison with the Shakespearean venture, Graves's venture builds on a peculiar *acceptance* of his immediate condition, and that is Graves's strength. One could hardly deny to him, as we have seen, a profound power to mediate the Goddess's order. He himself involves us in the total reaches of that order, in which the whole range of human experience is accounted for. But it seems that it is enough for him that he has seen that order and that he can fitfully and every so often see it again, and in the meantime is content to think himself very simply into a proper alignment with the Goddess's purposes. This is at the cost, however, of facing more *directly* the greater range of passions with which a man can yet imagine himself contending, it might seem to him hopelessly.[126] Recovering the totality of experience is recognized by Graves as the end goal, but with an *acceptance* of the way things are at present, so long as a proper alignment with this goal is maintained. This perfectly nice, if perfectly profound, adaptation to his situation is what led Hughes to bewail Graves's too strict limitations as a poet, as one critic has pointed out:

> *For all the excitement of the chase, there is something*
> *distancing and detached in Graves's evocation of the Goddess.*
> *Take, for example, the first line of the dedicatory poem with*
> *which the book (**The White Goddess**) opens: "All saints revile*
> *her, and all sober men." This is measured, cool, and polished,*
> *and virtually lacks any pulse at all. It is as if this control*
> *of the verse and the emotion behind it was part of Graves's*
> *defense mechanism—a means of controlling the threat of*
> *the energy. This may be what Hughes has in mind when he*
> *writes of Graves's poetry operating at "some kind of witty,*
> *dry distance,"*[127]

There is more of careful rationality in Graves than one might have expected of one who was otherwise so critical of Western rationalism. Hughes seems to have felt that *he* took on more, was more aware also (after Reformation man) of his own potential for rejection of the Goddess, was also more aware, as Shakespeare was, that approach to the end-goal would have to involve a greater and more immediate reckoning with those deeper passions that Graves cavalierly puts away. I have quibbled with Hughes, however, for his own relative degree of superficiality, when one refers him to Shakespeare, because Hughes supposes that such passions as a man has to deal with are merely the result of a mistaken perception of the corruption of his beloved or his fear of the Female only.

Any illuminating process which might come to Shakespeare out of humankind's immediate situation, as he understood it, could only come to him by a process of self-growth that few will be able to manage for now. That is because he took *on* more, far more than we are in any position to do ourselves. He was unable to abandon his humankind to their experience, could only see their tragedies through with every one of his ill-fated characters and so, seeing these through, could re-emerge eventually with a far greater perception of the restored mythical totality than even Hughes was able to imagine of him. The corruption by evil is suffered totally, but it is merely suffered; it is not to be understood in terms of any mistaken psychology, hubris, or hamartia, however inevitable, or even as a simple affront to the Goddess. A universal corruption is suffered through totally; it has been the only means for bringing humankind as a whole out of its former condition of sensual embroilment. The consequence of that embroilment has been the extreme violent death of the beloved, marked as this is also by the extreme despair of the hero through whom a prevailing evil has come. The death of Desdemona, the death of Cordelia, as the final consequence of evil: these are challenge enough for now. They are enough of a measure of the tragic tendencies in human nature with which, according to Shakespeare's presentation, we would have to reckon, before we could begin to work our way back into any unity such as would compare with what was formerly ours in the archaic sphere.

Even so, Shakespeare could not *foresee* his re-emergence from tragedy. It was not as if he was conscious of any illuminating power of vision which was his *before* he undertook the plunge into the totality of human errancy. The illuminating process came to him, in fact, from without, from an illuminating power that, at any given moment and at every given stage, remained always fully outside and beyond him, streaming into him and through him strictly from without. He could not have predicted how things would develop, or even that they would. He had been overwhelmed himself, as could only be the case, with the series of deaths that had come from his imagination: Ophelia, Desdemona, Cordelia. From there, for many months it would seem, he lived with the death of the beloved as the symbolic end-consequence of the human tragedy.—Until, with *Pericles*, the light begins, faintly at first, to shine through again, though not without a drastic re-living, a necessary re-surfacing, of the quintessential tragedy—as this takes shape in the death of Thaisa. We have the rest of Shakespeare's progression from here by way of symbolical allegory. At the center of that progression is the experience of the death of the beloved that continually accompanies Shakespeare through the whole series of events that are dramatized right through to the end of *The Tempest*. That death Shakespeare can never leave sight of again, for it represents the outcome of human tragedy itself. Without the continued Imagination of it, there could no longer be for him any further genuine progression. Hence, beyond the death of Thaisa in *Pericles*, there is the death of Hermione in *The Winter's Tale* and the (much overlooked) death of Prospero's wife, each of which symbolizes the fundamental experience of human tragedy Shakespeare could no longer let go of. Out of this *then* comes the further, great experience of the recovery of unity to which Shakespeare's last plays bear witness as a whole. This unity Shakespeare would appear to have been returned to in the most immediate terms only because, having exposed himself fully to the human tragedy, he was now without fear of any further subversion by human nature.

◆   ◆   ◆

It is a long process, however, by which Shakespeare is brought back to unity. The whole range of tragic experience he had seen through would have to be distributed over all of the last plays in order for that experience to be properly seen and dealt with.[128] That effort involves Shakespeare in a production over years. Thus *Pericles* re-visits the effects of tragedy from the point of view of the hero's fundamental innocence of it; *The Winter's Tale* from the point of view of a complete guiltiness: together they are the combined aspects of Shakespeare's perception of how tragedy has operated in the fates of his tragic characters. Beyond these profound analytical ventures back into the heart of tragic experience, Shakespeare then gives us the fully bodied drama of *The Tempest*. In this play Shakespeare brings the many aspects of the *resolution* of tragedy in turn to bear on the life of Prospero. It is thus Prospero who finally embodies the complete integration in mind and soul that Shakespeare ultimately inherits precisely from the completeness of his progression through tragedy.[129]

One only has to think of what the death of Thaisa in *Pericles*, the death of Hermione in *The Winter's Tale*, and the death of Prospero's wife in *The Tempest* continue to represent symbolically in the way of an experience of human anguish. The experience of human tragedy *continues* in Shakespeare's mind, and when the mythical world finally does break in again on Shakespeare it does so within the terms of this experience. It breaks in on him for the first time when Thaisa recovers, or rather is recovered, from death—*with all that that symbolically implies* of a re-emergence for Shakespeare. In her very first words, as she returns to consciousness, Thaisa calls upon Diana, the Goddess as Virgin, as the ruling Spirit Who underlies this whole action. The Goddess Herself will later appear to Pericles in a dream, to exhort him to make his way to Her temple where Thaisa has lain for as many years as it has taken their lost daughter to come of age. The final reunion of these three in the closing scene of the play represents, in fact, a first significant stage of integration after tragedy for Shakespeare. [130]

The appearance of the Goddess Diana points to a deeper movement of mind and Imagination in Shakespeare that lies well beneath the surface detail. There is an experience of being supported again from being *through* tragedy. That experience is represented as lying at first well outside and beyond where the tragic psyche is at present, as given in the condition of Pericles. The new experience originates in the sphere where Thaisa lies when she is first recovered, well beyond the immediate experience of tragedy through which Pericles continues to live. Fourteen years must go by, a prolonged period of spiritual gestation, before re-integration can begin, during which time the human psyche would seem to be adapting to the tragedy still further, a time in which there is a further, one might say a complete, absorption of the tragedy. Finally the support comes through again. A daughter had sprung in the meantime between the hero and his beloved—a daughter named Marina, and it is she who, having come of age, now appears to Pericles to lift him up again. Who is this daughter but the image of Pericles's own suffering—Shakespeare's own suffering—somehow bearing fruit as a power that now lifts the tragic psyche beyond itself? She is the image of *its* suffering, but now made good:

> *she speaks,*
> *My lord, that, may be, hath endured a grief*
> *Might equal yours, if both were justly weighed.*

How else shall we characterize this daughter but as the enduring self *become* the higher self through which transcendence has come?[131] The tragic psyche or self/Pericles, which in enduring transcends itself, makes itself worthy of uniting with a higher aspect of itself/Marina, and it is this new *integration* in the self that opens the door again to the objective mythical world mediated through Diana. Only *after* this integration in the self does the inspirational dream then come to Pericles that exhorts him to visit Diana's temple, a dream in which Diana Herself appears to him. At this temple he is to rehearse the tragic story that has been his—as if to say that that has been the only way to come to this point and is to continue to be borne in mind. Only thus is Pericles further reunited with his beloved, Thaisa, who is by now a high priestess of Diana—we can only imagine in *what* sphere of higher life together. The reunion takes place in a sphere where the engrossment in sensuality has been virtually abandoned.[132] The process of separation has been drastic and complete. And there is now the return to an experience of mutual support on every hand, with no tragedy subverting: indeed the tragedy has been fully taken up into the new experience.

With *The Winter's Tale* we enter a second stage of re-integration for Shakespeare after tragedy, the *whole* tragedy being re-created again here, through the symbolic death of Hermione, but from the point of view of the tragic hero's complete guiltiness rather than his innocence. A correspondingly deeper suffering is thus enacted in Leontes, which calls for a complete penance, beyond endurance, as befits reckoning with a complete guilt. As in *Pericles*, tragedy is again re-lived but with the birth of a daughter built into it; there is not the death of the beloved alone.

Then follows the same union of the tragic self/Leontes with its higher aspect/Perdita, and from this the still grander re-union with the beloved/Hermione that completes all. Between *Pericles* and *The Winter's Tale*, the self/Shakespeare's own is thus restored from tragedy—by the end of *The Winter's Tale* to a complete integrity again, beyond both innocence and guilt.

As Shakespeare is in progression, more and more of the evolutionary pattern is filled out, with every opportunity given along the way. Thus there is *less* in *The Winter's Tale* of the drama of union between the tragic and higher selves/Leontes and Perdita, because the drama of union in those terms has already been given in *Pericles*. We assume it and fill it out further for ourselves in this second stage. In *The Winter's Tale* the focus is more on the re-union with the beloved/mother/Hermione, which is only imperfectly given in *Pericles*. There is also in *The Winter's Tale* more focus on the relationship to the higher power/Perdita of a *suitor* to that power/Florizel, a relationship that had yet to find any real development in *Pericles* in the relationship between Marina and Lysimachus. A more *direct* relationship is now in development between the daughter and this suitor, which suggests a kind of passing on of the inheritance from the tragic past, as if one might now come into the higher development directly, beyond the error-ridden ways of that past—a form of life projected for the future. But there is the further danger that what is given as an immediate opportunity will itself founder, *without* the connection in consciousness back to the tragic humanity through whose suffering it was brought into being. Hence Camillo's role in this play, who dissuades the young lovers from simply going their own way, directing them back towards Leontes and alerting Polixenes about it so that he follows after them. Camillo in this way brings the young couple back into the circuit of the whole human destiny of which they are the crowning expression or else nothing at all:

> *A course more promising*
> *Than a wild dedication of yourselves*
> *To unpathed waters, undreamed shores, most certain*
> *To miseries enough...*

◆   ◆   ◆

One cannot overstate the achievement that *The Winter's Tale* represents as a perfect harmonizing of the whole tragedy for Shakespeare, one effect of harmonization building successively upon another until we reach the very last scene in which Hermione is restored to Leontes. But the tragedy is never forgotten, and it is built upon still further in *The Tempest*. Here it appears in the form of the death of Prospero's wife, which is accompanied by the events of treachery that follow upon Prospero's choice of devoting himself to this death. We may imagine Shakespeare in the completeness of his evolution having reached a point where the higher development has grown out still further, as represented in the daughter Miranda, herself a progressive advancement on Perdita—the development, as it were, in yet a third stage. Continuing to read allegorically, the higher self/Miranda is in this case perfectly assimilated by the hero/Prospero, from whom, in spite of the tragedy, she is never separated. The whole inner process has thus been absorbed in Prospero, in whom a certain completeness of development may be assumed. As much is then made of the suitor/Ferdinand's relationship to the daughter/Miranda as in *The Winter's Tale*, and indeed far more, for this now represents Shakespeare's fullest and grandest projection of what our future hope can look like. In this consummate play's dream of a still fuller and fuller harmony spreading over everything, the whole of the outer world is then brought into conjunction with all that is bodied forth in Miranda and Ferdinand as the image of our ideal, restored humanity. Wonder at Miranda is reflected *back* to all, from her who is the very spirit of the *higher* wonder that resides in the mankind she now extols:

> O brave new world,
> That has such people in't![133]

Nor has Shakespeare omitted to consider the whole as an *objective* development, ruled over by "the gods" on whom Gonzalo calls to bless this scene: for it is the unitary forces which *they* control that have brought this whole development into being:

> Look down, you gods,
> And on this couple drop a blessed crown!
> For it is you that have chalked forth the way
> Which brought us hither.

◆   ◆   ◆

The mythical unity is thus restored in Shakespeare to that point, and on quite another level from when the fierce nature of the primal sensual forces was a part of it. All ferocious sensuality has been removed from the picture that arises out of the world he presents in the end. Here then is another measure of where we stand in relation to the mythical forces about which

Graves has challenged us in modern times. In comparison with Graves Shakespeare offers a more complete picture of what we can understand to be at stake. From Shakespeare's point of view, there would appear to be far more of human nature to contend with, far more of a struggle with this nature to anticipate, and consequently more of a prospect following from our ultimate success with this struggle. It is a view that looks more boldly to the future on the basis of a far more courageous consideration of our whole nature as inherited from our archaic past. Contrastingly, Graves's view is of our situation in relation to the basic prospect, looking out from a standpoint somewhere between before and after, as it were out of our *present* embroilment in our sensual nature, to the limited extent that we may speak of our coming to terms with it.

We will now consider yet another approach to the mythical forces— in the case of Keats, whom I have chosen as a kind of spokesman for another range of effort. *His* effort lies somewhere in between Shakespeare's involvement in all that is inwardly at stake in relation to those forces, and Graves's more fitful Imaginative engagement, which, if psychologically reckless, yet took him to the brink of an objective image-making, or pictoriality, that would also appear to be intrinsic to the mythical experience. Looking at Keats will allow us to see also where the *Romantic* sensibility might be said to lie in relation to this experience. And so with that we shall have covered still more of the range of the *historical* effort that has engaged Western man in his desire to think himself again into the fullness of the world in which the Goddess, it has been thought, continues to rule.

III

IMPASSE OF THE IMAGINATION

I

I t is well-known that Keats envisioned his *own* connection back into the Goddess's order and to the fullness of the mythical creation with which She is directly associated also by him. The prospect of an ultimate union with the Goddess is allegorically projected in "Endymion"; an eventual "happiness" is conceived in these terms. But Endymion must live, for now, through the tragic frustration of separation from his Beloved. He lives in a form of dispossession the inverse of that experienced by Venus with Adonis in their classic story. There are, however, many intimations of the final union with his Goddess that is to come. He is already endowed by Her with the power to penetrate the underworld. Here he attends directly on Adonis's blissful re-awakening to Venus after his usual winter's sleep. Venus Herself inspires Endymion to hope, by foretelling his own reunion with his beloved Goddess. And so he continues to think happiness in spite of being returned at this moment to his solitary self, cut off once again in his earthly condition from the super-earthly vision with which he has momentarily been blessed.

Endymion witnessing the moment of Adonis's revival prefigures the power over death that Keats could project for himself from an Imaginative connection to *his* Goddess. The vision of that power is extended in the later episode with Glaucus. Here Endymion assumes a role of savior for *all* lovers who have been severed by tragic fortune in a world hostile to their union. Soon his heart is itself captured by an Indian maid of flesh and blood, but he feels he has, in this merely temporal love, in the meantime compromised his passion for his Goddess. He is thrown into a state of utter lassitude and dejected resignation from his now conflicted condition.[134] In the Cave of Quietude that he then reaches, all speaks to him of his readiness to abide in the mystery of his own uncertainty, removed at once from his ideal goal and his earthly object. It is not hard to see in this situation an anticipation of the more highly evolved rendering, in the "Ode to a Nightingale", of that same suspended open-ness to fate that we associate with Keats's idea of "negative capability". The episode in the Cave has been seen as the problematic climax to "Endymion" and its *actual* end, in contrast with the poem's formal ending, which seems to *force* a union between the ideal and the earthly, simply to complete the pattern predicted for its action.

Somewhere over the course of revising "Endymion", it would appear that Keats conceived of a new major poem, the epic "Hyperion".[135] With this poem Keats stepped still *further* back into the archaic world he had already been presenting, taking himself back to the time when Saturn and his fellow Titans had just been dethroned, by the lesser gods of Olympus. However, this focus marks a significant alteration in Keats's approach, for he had now conceived the idea of an *evolution* through worlds. Evolution, in some form or other, had come *from* the separation from the archaic unity—tragic though that separation is also. Apollo, as the god who is to supercede Hyperion—the last of the older gods from Saturn's reign to retain power—points to the possibility of a fuller experience of the world *in knowledge*. Keats is clearly suspended now between his primal commitment to the archaic unity, which the former reign of Saturn represents, and his understanding that the experience of the world that has been had since will also have to receive his commitment. Apollo cannot rest until he has known all about the world he is helping to bring into being. Through this focus on the moment of Apollo's instalment, Keats is allegorically envisaging the possibility also of exploring his own state of knowledge as a poet in his present condition, separated from, yet continuing in a relationship to, the archaic unity.

But the thought of where he stood with his own present condition would appear to have driven Keats, in a further development, to consider his older epic approach to his theme outmoded, so that he soon felt forced to abandon the "Hyperion". Not long before he undertook the writing of "Hyperion" Keats had met Fanny Brawne. The meeting inspired him to take up the poetic cause he had set for himself with a renewed sense of all that he felt he could accomplish. But then the realization set in that he had more to make of his own experience in the present, and "Hyperion" was abandoned. That understanding coincided with a development in passion in his relationship to Fanny. In "The Eve of St. Agnes" Keats's ideal ambitions now give way to a forthright affirmation of the predominant value of his earthly love for Fanny. In the poem, Porphyry, the male lover, is intent on persuading his beloved Madeline to accept that, steeped as they may be in an ideal dream of love, it is finally the *reality* of love that matters. What matters is that they have each other now, in flesh and blood. And Keats's characters *will* escape in the dead of night, defying all conventions, into a new world that is now theirs in reality, if still hedged round with the deep mystery of love. So Porphyry and Madeline disappear together at the end into the storm that bears at least some marks of the world of archaic mystery of that poem.

The turning point in the poem is when Porphyry succeeds in rousing Madeline from her visionary dream of the love of him (brought on by a potion she has taken) by singing into her ears the story of "La Belle Dame Sans Merci". The singing of that song seems to be intended (by Porphyry) to suggest that there is something of the unreal cruelty of that Dame in Madeline while she continues to lie in a mere swoon of love, more content with the idea of it than the reality. However that may be, within a few months Keats had indeed written his famous poem on that subject, as if he had been made aware, in the meantime, of a power in Fanny to dispossess him of any hope of love in the real world. She had reverted in this poem to being the cruel and elusive Dame, possessed of an otherworldly power of love that could only leave Keats, as her lover and knight errant, at the complete mercy of her influence over him. The two poles of earthly and ideal destiny are thus brought again into seemingly impossible opposition to each other. Here was the very situation in real terms that Keats had allegorically prophesized for himself in "Endymion". Only, the opposition had polarized even further.

In "La Belle Dame" one might think Keats had found his way directly to the Goddess on whom he had attended since "Endymion". "La Belle Dame" Graves saw as one of the central expressions of the Goddess's influence in English poetry.[136] But in this poem the Goddess appears as the *counterpole* to the all-harmonizing entity Keats had made of her in "Endymion". She *was* that entity until the tension between earthly and ideal commitments drives Endymion into that intense area of uncertainty that would only seem to make him ready to accept any outcome. Keats would appear to have entered in this later period, between "St. Agnes" and "La Belle Dame", into roughly the same condition Endymion is in when worn out by his own impasse. That Keats could not rest content with a relationship to the Goddess such as he presents in "La Belle Dame" is a significant measure of his complex distance from Graves's own indulgent aesthetic about Her—Keats demanding more, by way of a total satisfaction.

The further transformation Keats undergoes at this point is extraordinary, for it suddenly points a direction the *opposite* of that on which he seemed bent until now in referring himself to the archaic unity. His case represents, in fact, the complete counterpole to the concern with the mythical-archaic that has occupied *us* thus far. Keats would appear in this period to have found himself acting on the idea of the necessity of a *modern* production opposed to the archaic: a new project that he had been turning over in his mind for over a year. It appears that he saw in

Wordsworth his model in this direction: his model in renunciation. In the previous April he had turned

> to the large question…whether Wordsworth has indeed a
> potential epic sweep, and has thus "martyred himself to the
> human heart"—martyred the freer, older uses of poetry to the
> inevitably pressing needs of the modern age.[137]

Keats's original ambition, in conceiving of "Hyperion", had been to set his account of the evolution of consciousness into the greater framework of archaic origins and ultimate ends, and so his idea of a major poem that might rival any of the ancients (from the Greeks to Milton):

> a poem in which, however much he would try to follow out
> what he felt to be the great modern challenge to poetry, he
> also naturally wanted to catch what he could of the amplitude
> and vigor that we honor in earlier works while fearing to do
> other than imitate our contemporaries.[138]

> Apollo's painful evolution into growing consciousness would
> tap, perhaps closely parallel, personal experiences of his
> own.[139]

But, as we have seen, knowledge would mean, sooner than Keats had planned, knowledge of his own condition in the present, especially as

> now Keats began to think of history as a process in which
> the changes that take place are fundamental. Men and their
> achievements must be seen in relation to the age in which
> they live.[140]

However, Keats had not anticipated being plunged into a new mode of poetic uncertainty, at the opposite end from that older mode in which the results had seemed foretold:

> the situation would involve an additional loneliness that he
> had not anticipated, and it certainly emphasized the distance
> still to be travelled.[141]

> With every further step in knowledge, to be sure, the

inscrutable mystery of things seems only to deepen, and the uncertainty of human judgements to become more obvious.[142]

But

In this protective labyrinth, still to be explored, there will be a "sanctuary" with all that a "working brain" may find or construct

Naturally there will be uncertainty…there is the possibility of mere illusion as well as creativity.

thought will inevitably be "shadowy"…[143]

Yet if, at the moment, "We see not the balance…" and "are in a mist," that only means that the life of thinking man must be a search…[144]

✦   ✦   ✦

The immediate first result of this new poetic life, on which Keats embarked at this time was the "Ode to Psyche". On first appearance this poem will strike us as a simple carry-over from the archaic mode of Keats's mythic ambitions. There is the direct apostrophe to the Goddess in the poem's first line, as if Keats might be settled elsewhere than in his modern present, and there is also the poem's basic fictional drama, which sets us in the immediate company of Cupid and his beloved Psyche. Do we assume that Keats projects himself in their company as they were of old? Or are we not more likely to see this as, quite self-consciously, fiction? Yet Keats in this poem is claiming 'actually' to see them immediately in his Imagination in the present moment. It is his boast that *he* is the one, in this late age, to have discovered Psyche as the "latest born and loveliest far/Of all Olympus's faded hierarchy", whom no ancient religion had ever formally recognized.[145] And he is now to be Her priest and poet.

It is true that Keats laments that there can be no form of religious expression in his day to compare with the way his discovered Goddess would have been honored in the past, had She been known then. This also suggests a throwback to the archaic setting in which Keats's Imagination had been immersed to this point. Some consciousness remains of his tragic distance from the full-fledged directness with which he imagines the transcendent realities of Nature to have been celebrated then. But he feels the momentousness of his own role as priest to his Goddess all the more, precisely from knowing that a new venture must consequently arise out of the present, and it is *as a comparative metaphor* that Keats is here drawing on the effective power projected of archaic religious practice. That the archaic detail has turned into comparative metaphor we might have deduced from the explicit subject of Keats's poem—Psyche, that is the Mind itself, and so by deduction his own mind in relation to that greater Mind's Imaginative promptings *as these can be known in the present*. His own mind, or Imagination, had now become the object of Keats's devotion, to draw on at will for the further exploration of reality, which might now take almost any direction. That his focus has turned inward is made explicit in the poem's last stanza, where the poet speaks of building a temple

> *In some untrodden region of my mind,*
> *Where branched thoughts, new grown with pleasant pain,*
> *Instead of pines shall murmur in the wind:*

It is also significant that Keats should *continue* with the natural imagery from this point, which has now converted into metaphors for the Mind's own experience, its own infinite depths of subtle variety and invention:

> *Far, far around shall those dark-clustered trees*
> *Fledge the wild-ridged mountains steep by steep;*
> *And there by zephyrs, streams, and birds, and bees,*
> *The moss-lain Dryads shall be lull'd to sleep;*

With the reference to Dryads here, some part of the archaic world has been internalized, but in this new sanctuary of his own mind, the Imagination, combining Mind with Love (Cupid), will be free to search out and to create at will, to forecast and to conclude as *it* deems right. Here Keats had reached the point he had projected for himself when a year earlier he had spoken of "the Chamber of Maiden Thought" into which one comes out of a first "infant or thoughtless Chamber"—this last being the Chamber he had been in while given to his automatic allegiance to the epic-archaic ideal he had derived from Milton. Beyond the second Chamber, of Maiden Thought, lies still *another* that Keats was now poised to enter:

> *Well—I compare human life to a large Mansion of Many*
> *apartments, two of which I can only describe, the doors of*
> *the rest being as yet shut upon me—The first we step into*

we call the infant or thoughtless Chamber, in which we remain as long as we do not think—We remain there a long while, and notwithstanding the doors of the second Chamber remain wide open, showing a bright appearance, we care not to hasten to it; but are at length imperceptibly impelled by the awakening of the thinking principle within us—we no sooner get into the second Chamber, which I shall call the Chamber of Maiden-Thought, than we become intoxicated with the light and the atmosphere, we see nothing but pleasant wonders, and think of delaying there forever in delight. However, among the effects this breathing is father of is that tremendous one of sharpening one's vision into the heart and the nature of Man—of convincing one's nerves that the world is full of Misery and Heartbreak, Pain, Sickness and Oppression—whereby this Chamber of Maiden Thought becomes gradually darken'd and at the same time on all sides of it many doors are set open—but all dark—all leading to dark passages—We see not the balance of good and evil. We are in a Mist—We are now in that state—We feel the "burden of the Mystery,"[146]

Keats had for the first time reached this third Chamber, which he leaves unnamed, with his "Ode to a Nightingale" and his "Ode on a Grecian Urn". With the illuminating consciousness he had broken into, as the "Ode to Psyche" presents this, identical with his inward-turning Imagination, Keats was now set to take on whatever of human suffering he could manage to draw within the scope of that Imagination.[147] This Imagination is *immediately* conceived in relation to human suffering, and human suffering to the Imagination, so that in "Nightingale" Keats can *begin* in the very midst of this suffering:

> *My heart aches, and a drowsy numbness pains my sense...*

From this suffering, however, Keats is drawn up into his Imagination as the immediate counterbalance to it, although no sooner has he found wings for flight than he is brought back, in another remarkable inversion, to the seemingly irrepressible condition of suffering—

> *Where but to think is to be full of sorrow*
> *And leaden-eyed despairs*

A significant distinction is thus drawn between the terrible human suffering that is our lot, and the beautiful ideal, at the other extreme, of the aspiring Imagination, which the world of our suffering is bound to wear away at:

> *Where Beauty cannot keep her lustrous eyes*
> *Or new Love pine at them beyond to-morrow.*

Characteristic of his situation now, the opposition of suffering only drives Keats to seek *more* of the Imagination, to penetrate more deeply into it:

> *Away, away! For I will fly to thee*

it might seem only in order to escape from his suffering, except that his suffering remains bound up with his Imagination. It is more to the point that in penetrating more deeply into the world of Imagination Keats comes more fully into a power that *transmutes* his suffering, or that at least affirms the ideal ever more strongly against it. It is a world that offers an inexhaustible potential for re-orientation and renewal, immediately supported as Keats is in the tenderness and in the complete richness of the Imagination's influence, which incorporates only the beautiful in Nature and the terrible into the beautiful. That we have here entered a purely inward world is broadcast to us in the language distinctive of Keats's effort in this stage:

> *But here there is no light*
> *Save what from heaven is with the breezes blown*
> *Through verdurous glooms and winding mossy ways.*

> *I cannot see...*
> *.....................*

> *But, in embalmed darkness, guess each sweet...*

Keats gives himself to his Imagination, in fact, as his own voice, which is now creating *out* of the world that he has penetrated, taking us up along with him. He is inspired by the *supreme* voice of the Nightingale, which, out of this world, apotheosizes the Imaginative power in its seemingly infinite resourcefulness. In a further supreme twist, this seems to Keats then the finest moment in which to die, while he is utterly given to the beauty-making power of his Imagination, which can make a beautiful thing also of the moment of death:

> *Now more than ever seems it rich to die,*
> *To cease upon the midnight with no pain,*
> *While thou art pouring forth thy soul abroad*
> *In such an ecstasy!*

But this triumphant moment immediately prompts the further thought that in the meantime *he* will have turned to dust,

> *Still wouldst thou sing, and I have ears in vain—*
> *To thy high requiem become a sod.*

The Imaginative power, for its part, will have remained behind and beyond him, intact as it always has been through the generations. That he has now become concerned with what becomes of us individually does not stop him from speculating more about the Imagination itself, and he is finally left wondering how real his life is in comparison with *its* reality. But even so his concern has *become* the individual death—his own death, as an instance of the death of each one of us. And it could only have been a natural thing for him to proceed from here to the "Grecian Urn" as his next object of focus.

The title of this poem, "Ode on a Grecian Urn", immediately sets us in relation to death, and to the ashes that this urn contained, or was meant to contain, at one time. We imagine the owner commissioning the sculpting of an elaborate scene onto the urn intended *for* him, or perhaps sculpting it onto this urn himself. Set all around its solid frame is a scene depicting the effects of human passion as at some ancient orgiastic religious festival. Men in this scene merge with gods, in pursuit of maidens who are loath to be caught but are otherwise themselves caught up in the "wild ecstasy" of this celebration. At this scene there is also a playing of pipes and of timbrels, and soon the poet has immersed himself in the action, conscious of the fact that it captures an effect of life lived in the moment of the happiest passion, preserved in this artistic expression as if forever. Trees and their boughs, the piper himself, as the "happy melodist" of the poem, piping his song, the lovers in pursuit of each other—all have remained as they are, intact from the ravages of time, preserved in this moment of the happiest passion. The best of human life has in this way been saved from death, the Imagination of the sculptor having exercised itself in a supreme temporal expression of its power. No greater possibility could be conceived.

Like Keats, applying himself in his own Imaginative power to this scene[148], the sculptor/owner has brought his Imagination to bear to the fullest possible extent on the physical fact of death as represented by the ashes in the urn. How sublime the effect when we imagine Keats imagining his own ashes in that urn! Clearly he had brought his idea of the opposing claims of death and of the Imagination into the greatest possible tension here. The terrible effects of passion over time—

> *That leaves a heart high-sorrowful and cloy'd*
> *A burning forehead and a parching tongue.*

are in this scene pre-empted as if forever. But in the meantime our attention is brought back to the actuality of the desolation that lies everywhere beyond the scene depicted on the urn. There is the account of the also forever silent streets that have been emptied of the folk that have flocked to this triumphant festival:

> *And, little town, thy streets for evermore*
> *Will silent be; and not a soul to tell*
> *Why thou art desolate, can e'er return.*

The frame of reference extends here surely also to us as *we* gather around Keats while reading this poem.

We have thus in the end been merely "*teased* out of [the] thought" of death, though we are left possessed at the same time of perhaps the finest form of consolatory expression art can devise, within the scope of the possibilities available to the Imagination. This becomes our way of understanding what the urn is finally said to proclaim out of itself:

> "*Beauty is truth, truth beauty, that is all*
> *Ye know on earth, and all ye need to know.*"

Art, by its power to absorb us totally *in* the beautiful, beyond the terrible reality of our mortality, expresses all that it is possible to express of the truth of the Imagination. Beyond that expression, however, lies another truth—the truth of the desolation of reality of which we are a part when we are returned to dust. But it has sufficed in the meantime that we are and will have been consoled while we are alive, and for that the Imagination is there—for that art has been there.

It is, however, as far as Keats could go with the beauty-making power of his Imagination. He had far more to say *about* it in his illustrious Letters. He had been, for over a year, through an intense if quiet period of preparation, and it is clear that he had then profited immensely from the inspiration of Fanny's immediate presence in the house which he now shared with her along with her mother and his friend Brown. But Brown's house would have to be rented for the summer, and the separation from Fanny that ensued would cut him off from his inspiration. He had in any case reached with "Urn" an extraordinary end-point beyond which he could not go and could never have gone. He had taken the claims of the Imagination, upon which he had alighted so momentously, as far as they *could* go. And how, one might ask, could he not then do as he did do, which is return to the old production with which he had long been identified, before his sudden plunge into his modern present?

Thus followed "Lamia" and a return to "Hyperion", which had now become "The Fall of Hyperion", in both of which we may divine a new despair and a more serious falling away from himself. His perception of the influences of love had taken a still more drastic turn (from "La Belle Dame") in "Lamia". Suddenly the beloved has become, at the other extreme from La Dame, a figure of hopeless demonic import (in opposition to the figure of hopeless heavenly import of La Dame)—embodying Keats's condition of frustrated passion at this time.[149] The final formal judgment of Lamia in the poem expresses no settled position in Keats but is itself part of the hopeless dialectic of Keats's problem in his frustration.[150] As for "The Fall", this poem Keats would eventually, as in the case of its earlier version as "Hyperion", likewise abandon. He was all the more likely to abandon it after the Odes, which makes Keats's choice of returning to this subject seem like a desperate one. His immersion in his own modern present, complete as this had been, and indeed extreme, would have dispossessed him of any connection back to this outworn form of production. And yet it is clear that the idea of the epic-archaic project had not left Keats. Indeed, how could it, seeing as this was, for him also, and would have to be, the primordial concern of the poetic-Imaginative life in one form or another?

In one respect at least "The Fall" represents a kind of advancement on the "Urn"—in the case of the so-called "Induction" to the poem, which represents a new stage of vision for Keats. But it is still so much in an earlier outworn mode (for all its remarkable graces, derived from Dante) that surely Keats could see there was no future in it for him. In content, if not in form, it represents an advancement.[151] After envisioning his own death in "Urn", and surviving the deprivations that had come from separation from Fanny, it is easy to conceive Keats in the condition that is noted of the poet in the "Induction":

> *Thou hast felt*
> *What 'tis to die and live again before*
> *Thy fated hour*

The poet is suddenly projected into the typical world of the medieval dream-vision, but before he comes into his vision of Moneta, he pledges himself to

> *all the mortals of the world,*
> *And all the dead whose names are on our lips,*

The phrasing is a throwback to the episode in "Endymion" when Keats saw himself as the savior of all lovers who had died separated from each other. It appeared now as if he had indeed come to the verge of that role in his life. The air that greets him in this new world of vision is said to be filled

> *with so much pleasant health*
> *That even the dying man forgets his shroud*

Keats, it would appear, could now think himself into a still further sphere in which, like Shakespeare, the world's tragedies can no longer leave him, a sphere in which he can only occupy himself with these tragedies, and it is precisely this choice of life that has won him his unique audience with the envisioned Moneta. But this apparent advance in vision can only lead Keats back to his epic-archaic project, specifically to "Hyperion" (now re-named "The Fall"). And so this Moneta Keats presents predictably as the last surviving Power out of the Golden Age over which Saturn formerly ruled before this world was overturned by the Olympians. It is She who since that time has been

> *left supreme,*
> *Sole priestess of this desolation*

And the poet is the one who, by his extreme commitment to human suffering has worked his way to Her (he is valued less as a poet than as a dreamer or visionary of this kind). Scenes of that "high tragedy" are now to unfold in vision before the poet out of Moneta's "globed brain" where they lie stored up in memory.

It is not difficult to see that Keats had always had the idea of epically referring the particulars of human destiny back to a primordial unitary life which he associates with the reign of Saturn before his Fall. Human suffering was for him an expression of that Fall, and Keats could feel that, in the completeness of his own commitment to human suffering, he had reached the stage of identifying himself with that Fall. One can only imagine what he would have wished to do from here. One could see him pursuing the tragedy farther along in time, at least (for now) to the point of the Fall of Hyperion, the last God from that earlier Age to give up his primal power. Apollo was to be his successor, he Whom Keats in the earlier "Hyperion" had addressed as "the Father of all verse." A first stage in the evolutionary development of the world would have thus been reached. It would be the poet's role to transmute suffering, but there was now the role, beyond the poet, of the dreamer or visionary, who in a further development can bring humankind back to the primal unity, beyond suffering and death, an act that would correspond to a restoration of Saturn's former reign.

This was quite the epic project, but only the kind of thing the poets of the Romantic Age, to which Keats belonged, imagined for themselves as the end-goal of their visionary-poetic striving.[152] But as a *form*, or mode of production, the older style could hardly have done the job any longer of convincingly embodying the quality of human suffering and of human expression of Keats's own time. The already prescribed externality of the older style could never have left room for an appropriate expression of present inner development. And yet, how far could the plunge towards modernity, into the strictly present moment of the Imagination, have taken Keats? Having confined himself so strictly to the present moment, he had gone with the Imagination as far as it could go, for the pure inwardness of *this* mode could never have converted into any further external development. It leaves him in the end with no further possible power over his destiny than what he depicts in "Urn".

He had, it is true, made a further advance in experience, as expressed in the Induction to "The Fall", but as we have seen is immediately claimed again by the outworn style. That it was an advance in experience from the point he had reached in "Urn", and as such extraordinary, who can doubt, but one can only feel that Keats would have done better to begin with a completely new poem, and with a more direct approach, perhaps along the lines of the one Coleridge had made in "Kubla Khan".[153] If we are to believe

Middleton Murry, it would appear that Keats *misconceived* of his role as an epic poet, in the comparison with Wordsworth. Wordsworth never had given himself to the modern at the expense of the "older uses of poetry":

> *Wordsworth is not claiming[154] that he has 'epic passion' and that he 'martyrs this to the human heart'; but that his poem is to be more than the equivalent of Milton's epic, and is (so to speak) to be the veritable epic of the human soul.[155]*

> *If Milton's work were to be emulated, it could only be emulated as Wordsworth emulated it, by attempting to create an epic of the rediscovery of vital religion in the experience of prophetic man.[156]*

There could only have been for Wordsworth a form of epic poetry that arose "prophetically", that is to say anterior to outer forms, from the human soul itself, for which Keats in his own way might have been eminently suitable if he had not been from early on so obsessed by those "older uses" of poetry to which he had adhered, following Milton. In the reactionary turn towards the modern, Keats had then *also* gone too far. With him the human soul then became its own end, to the point where he stood without any further relation to an objective otherworld that might counterbalance it from the other side. Keats had thus *generally* reached impasse, in relation to which he does not appear to have made any further headway. And it will seem fitting, if sad, that his last great poem should be his "Ode To Autumn". Keats had inevitably turned his attention back to the scene of outer nature, on all that stands in full harvest but is also at the point of death, which is just where Keats found himself, before the final decline.

Some external inward would have to be grabbed hold of once again, if the mythic unity *were* to be recovered, and this the Romantic Imagination, for all the extension of experience one finds in it, was finally unable to do. The Romantics found themselves caught between the old and the new, and in Keats's case it finally led to too much of the new: to an *over*-valuation of the human soul, at the expense of any further relation to an objective otherworld. One would be able to cite innumerable critics and readers who have over the years made an ideal of the modern scepticism of Keats: his ultimate regard for the earthly above the ethereal or the super-earthly, the natural above the visionary etc.[157] But that way of appreciating Keats has really been our own modern way; it has expressed our own fundamental bias, for it overlooks the fact that Keats found himself, as a result of his going in that direction, ultimately alienated from the mythical destiny that, like all of his fellow Romantics, still concerned him very much.

At the same time, as we have seen, an archaic style out of the past had *over*claimed his attention, with the result that he had dispossessed himself of any authentic relation to the mythical sphere from that side also. He was more aware of being mistaken in this respect than were Shelley or Byron, for example.[158] Graves's efforts to re-connect with the mythical, though they may seem to revert to something much older[159], in fact make the very old new again. In contrast with the Romantics, however, no account of a process of inner growth, in his case, testifies to the path that led him to his amazing breakthrough. Graves had claimed, in fact, some form of *immediate* transposition of the poet into the frenzied visionary condition that allows him to re-connect again. The poet was, indeed, for him,

> *a deutero-potmos: a second-fated one who has, as it were,*
> **already** *died, and conversed with the oracular dead*[160]

Perhaps in this context we should not be making light of the fact that Graves *had* passed through a form of death, literally on the battlefield, and had in fact at one point been declared dead.

Death will surely come into it at some point. Shakespeare had had the relative leisure to imagine himself, over many years, into the suffering and death of his characters, and thereby *drove* himself into a new mythical world. Keats, with the Odes, stands in his newly conceived power of Imagination, as we have seen, over and against death, which *he* brings into focus as our final destiny impervious to all further scrutiny. He was then cut off from further production when his fatal illness set in, not long after the period we have covered. He had, just before that, progressed to a state in which it seemed to him he literally knew what it was like " to die, and live again before/ [His] fated hour." He was now living with death in a new way, and from this condition came his extraordinary imagination of Moneta, which *might* have issued out into a new relation to the mythical.[161] For any one of various reasons that prospect was not to be, but I have noted how along the way Keats had seriously bipolarized himself, separating himself radically from the mythical quest by indulging in our own modern bias of immersion in the strictly present moment of the Imagination. When, inevitably, he came back to the mythical quest, he had no more developed a form of his own for coming to terms with that quest than when he had opted to retreat from it—ending up as sadly baffled as when he had left off...

ENDNOTES

1. A matter that I began to address myself with my chapter on Sylvia Plath in *The Modern Debacle*, New York: IUniverse, 2007.
2. See Appendix B in *The White Goddess*, ed., Grevel Lindop, London: Faber, 1999, 489-504.
3. The review is directly brought up in Graves's lecture. It first appeared in *The Yale Review* in the 1956 Winter and Spring issues, and was later collected in Randall Jarrell's *The Third Book of Criticism*, Farrar, Straus & Giroux, 1965, 75-112.
4. *The Third Book*, 112.
5. *The Third Book*, 90.
6. *The White Goddess*, 13.
7. All references to *The Complete Poems*, ed., Dunstan Ward and Beryl Graves, London: Penguin, 2003.
8. See, for example, Mircea Eliade who speaks (in connection with another kind of initiation having to do with a return to the womb) of "the adventures of Heroes or of shamans and magicians…in their flesh-and-blood bodies, not symbolically." *Myth and Reality*, New York: Harper and Row, 1963, 81.
9. The further question will be raised, of course, how *woman* undergoes this grandiose destiny. As we shall see, as the one in whom the Goddess directly reflects something of Herself, the Goddess being up to a point in fact "incarnate in every woman", woman must necessarily experience the whole cycle of death and rebirth in her own way, though this matter is not gone into anywhere in Graves, as far as I know. As a male poet, clearly Graves narrates his "story" largely from his male perspective, although given his orientation towards the Goddess,

73

he is necessarily involved in offering some highly subtle views of woman's own role and experience in this picture. For a more complete picture of these views than can be offered here, see my chapter on Graves in my book, *The Modern Debacle*.

10. *The White Goddess*, 20.

11. As in the Indian mythology, for one. See, for example, the illustration provided by Joseph Campbell in his *Hero With a Thousand Faces*, Princeton: Princeton Univ. Press, 1973; orig. pub., 1949, between 228 and 229. Italian Renaissance art, drawing directly on ancient Roman models, bears further, abundant testimony to this graphic mythical subject. See Edith Balas, *The Mother Goddess in Italian Renaissance Art*, Pittsburgh: Carnegie Mellon University Press, 2002, 6 and 120 *passim*. **The lion**, as a constant attribute of the Goddess, represented, generally, the savagery of the earth and the wildness of the brute—in Graves's own terms human beastliness as well: all tamed by, or brought under the controlling power of, the Goddess originally (see Balas, 22-23 and 59n.26.) However, at a certain point, as we shall see when we turn to Shakespeare, humankind becomes fully responsible for itself, which is the occasion of great despair in the first place.

12. Terms that draw on Graves's idea of the effectiveness of what he calls a "true" poem, in *The White Goddess*, 20: "The reason why the hairs stand on end, the eyes water, the throat is constricted, the skin crawls and a shiver runs down the spine when one writes or reads a true poem is that a true poem is necessarily an invocation of the White Goddess..."

13. Readers who wish to follow the complex, evolving fortunes of the poet and his beloved, beyond what is only hinted at in this study, should be referred my chapter on Graves in *The Modern Debacle*. See also below for Keats's own presentation of an evolving relationship between poet and his beloved.

14. See Ivan Stenski, *Four Theories of Myth in Twentieth Century History*, Bassingstoke, Macmillan, 1987, 75.

15. *Myth and Reality*, 139.

16. *Myth and Reality*, 142.

17. *Myth and Reality*, 141.

18. *Myth and Reality*, 12.

19. *Myth and Reality*, 141.

20. See my study, *The Modern Debacle*.

21. *Myth and Reality*, 192-193.

22. Stenski, 128.

23. Stenski, 128.

24. *Myth and Reality*, 190: "Everything leads us to believe that the reduction of "artistic universes" to the primordial state of *materia prima* is only a phase in a more complex process, just as, in the cyclic conceptions of the archaic and traditional societies, "Chaos", the regression of all forms to the indistinction of the *materia prima*, is followed by a new Creation, which can be homologized with a cosmogony."

25. Stenski, 102. Nostalgia, incidentally, was an intrinsic feature of Camus's philosophy, as in *The Myth of Sisyphus*.

26. *Myth and Reality*, 192.

27. *Myth and Reality*, 189.

28. *Myth and Reality*, 188.

29. Ernst Cassirer, *Language and Myth*, New York: Dover, 1953, 94.

30. *Language and Myth*, 99.

31. *Language and Myth*, 99.

32. *Language and Myth*, 99.

33. *Language and Myth*, 99.

34. *Language and Myth*, 37.

35. *Language and Myth*, 62.

36. Cassirer (*Language and Myth*, 45) expands upon this matter as follows: "some indirect relationship must obtain, which covers everything from the most primitive gropings of mythico-religious thought to those highest products in which such thought seems to have already gone over into a realm of pure speculation."

37. Among these one might put together the following synopsis: "Mythical thinking…is captivated and enthralled by the intuition which suddenly confronts it. The ego is spending all its energy on this single object, lives in it, loses itself in it. Only when this intense individuation has been consummated, when the immediate intuition has been focused and, one might say, reduced to a single point, does the mythic or linguistic form emerge, and the word or the momentary god is created. At this point, the word which denotes that thought content is not a mere conventional symbol, but is merged with its object in an indissoluble unity. What significance the part in question may have in the structure and coherence of the whole, what function it fulfils, is relatively unimportant—the mere fact that it is or has been a part, that it has been connected with the whole, no matter

how casually, is enough to lend it the full significance and power of that greater unity. Whoever has brought any part of a whole into his power has thereby acquired power, in the magical sense, over the whole itself." (*Language and Myth*, 32, 57, 58, 92.) That "whole", that "greater unity", Graves might be thought to have himself brought forward in that great centre-piece of his poetic oeuvre, "To Juan at the Winter Solstice".

38. Owen Barfield, *Poetic Diction* , London: Faber, 1962, 86.

39. *Poetic Diction* , 92.

40. *Poetic Diction*, 85.

41. *Poetic Diction*, 34.

42. *Poetic Diction*, 32.

43. Owen Barfield, *Saving the Appearances*, London: Faber, 1957, 142.

44. *Poetic Diction*, 32.

45. *Poetic Diction*, 32. Durkheim is quoted from *The Elementary Forms of the Religious Life*.

46. *Saving the Appearances*, 126. In my section on Barfield I am, of course, bound to reproduce his own homocentric terms, although it is clear that while "man" or "archaic man", as terms, will be accepted of a cultural past largely fashioned by men, they are hardly suitable for a future in which women, no doubt from quite another perspective, will also be doing much of that cultural-artistic fashioning or "creation" Barfield anticipates happening. I have myself offered a brief treatment of Sylvia Plath's unique production from this point of view, in *The Modern Debacle*.

47. *Appearances*, 142.

48. *Appearances*, 144.

49. *Appearances*, 144.

50. *Appearances*, 127.

51. *Appearances*, 127.

52. *Appearances*, 131-132.

53. *Appearances*, 144.

54. *Appearances*, 121.

55. See *Symbols of Transformation*, New York: Harper, 1962, 224.

56. "Graves and the White Goddess" from *The Third Book of Criticism*, 107.

57. *Symbols of Transformation*, 232.

58. *Symbols*, 232.

59. *Symbols*, 227.

60. *Symbols*, 227.

61. *Symbols*, 232.
62. *Hero With a Thousand Faces*, 10. Clearly the male point of view on this issue is assumed by Campbell here, as indeed also by Jung in the section of *his* work I have quoted.
63. Cf. *The White Goddess*, 334: "an obvious difference between poems and dreams is that in poems one is (or should be) in critical control of the situation; in dreams one is a paranoiac, a mere spectator of the mythographic event".
64. *Hero*, 256-257.
65. *Hero*, 257.
66. *Hero*, 118.
67. *Hero*, 114.
68. *Hero*, 137.
69. Cf. Barfield on Jung: "the traditional myths and the archetypes which he tells us are the representations of the collective unconscious, are assumed by him to be, and always to have been, neatly insulated from the world of nature with which , according to their own account, they were mingled or united... The psychological interpretation of mythology...when it actually comes up against the nature-content of the myths...still relies on the old anthropological assumption of 'projection.' (*Appearances*, 134-135)
70. *Hero*,115.
71. In "Conjunction", for example, Graves intuits the final unity for himself.
72. *The White Goddess*, 476. Campbell himself assumes the possibility of progression, but could allow for much relativity along the way: "As [a man] progresses in the slow initiation which is life, the form of the goddess undergoes for him a series of transfigurations: she can never be greater than himself, though she can always promise him more than he is yet capable of comprehending. She lures, she guides, she bids him burst his fetters. And if he can match her import, the two, the knower and the known, will be released from every limitation. Woman is the guide to the sublime acme of sensuous adventure. By deficient eyes she is reduced to inferior states; by the evil eye of ignorance she is spell-bound to banality and ugliness. But she is redeemed by the eyes of understanding. The hero can take her as she is, without undue commotion, but with the kindness and assurance she requires, is potentially the King, the incarnate god, of her created world." *Hero*, 116 "[T]he whole sense of the ubiquitous myth of the hero's passage is that

77

it shall serve as a general pattern for men and women, wherever they may stand along the scale." *Hero*, 121.

73. How far this rationalizing element dictates to the modern theory of myth may be gathered from the extreme views of Levi-Strauss who, in insisting on "the unique cognitive status of myth", went so far as to see myth as possessed of "its own entelechy" and so "explained by nothing except "myth"". Thus myth is, in the end, its own "meta-language…as fully rational as any other communication", though, according to Levi-Strauss, it took the "super-rationalism" of Freud to allow us to see the possibility of reaching such "knowledge". See Stenski, *Four Theories*, 152-158. This insistent rationalizing of mythical consciousness has carried over also into the literary criticism on Graves, especially in more recent years, even among those who otherwise profess an intense admiration of his work. Thus we have watched Graves's life-long poetic effort to express himself in his relationship to the Goddess reduced to a matter of the deliberate cultivation of "ineffability"; his effort to present the Goddess in his book, *The White Goddess*, to a need to create "fixity", while his apparent renunciation of "the high mythopoeic mode" in his late poetry has been seen as a deliberate "effacement" and "erasure" intended to overcome a sort of Sisyphean repetition to which Graves must have felt condemned in continually re-stating the "one story":

> "the force of the accumulation of similes, metaphors, traces, marks, black and white of Graves's writings, is that it obliges readers to interpret the ineffability of the Triple Muse as a meaningful function within a larger semiotic system."

> "Graves was certainly perceptive enough to know that the link between words and things can never be fixed, that poetry and truth make two—yet he chose to fix it, and to write within that fixity. *The White Goddess* is a monument to that fixity…"

> "the advent of the Black Goddess is marked in the verse by a deliberate effacement of the language of the high mythopoeic mode in favor of a discourse which strips away many of the outward trappings

of myth…[It] spells possible release from the life-long obligation to write a muse-poetry *which is condemned to do little more than generate restatements* of the recurring monomyth. The Black Goddess exists, therefore, as in one sense the end of myth, the simultaneous completion and erasure of the single poetic theme,…" [Italics mine.]

In the case of the first and third quotations, see Robert A. Davis "The Black Goddess" from *Graves and the Goddess*, ed., Ian Firla and Grevel Lindop, Selinsgrove, Susquehanna Univ. Press, 2003, 109-111. In the case of the second quotation, Andrew Painter, "How and Why Graves Proceeded in Poetry", also from *Graves and the Goddess*, 149.

For my critique of the easy view of late Graves as voiced by Davis here, see my *Debacle*, 71-75.

74. *Goddess*, 476.
75. *Goddess*, 455.
76. *Goddess*, 6.
77. See, for example, "This Holy Month". The need to counterbalance the energy with some form of right consciousness is implied in Graves's qualification above concerning the Western disposition to rationalism: cf. "not *altogether* happy."
78. See Nick Gammage "The Nature of the Goddess: Ted Hughes and Robert Graves" from *New Perspectives on Robert Graves*, ed. Patrick J. Quinn, Selinsgrove: Susquehanna Univ. Press, 1999, 151.
79. Gammage, 151.
80. Gammage (151) quotes Hughes from his "Interview with Ekbert Fass" from *The London Magazine*, January, 1971: "If you accept the energy, it destroys you. What is the alternative? To accept the energy and find methods of turning it to good, or keeping it under control—rituals, the machinery of religion. The old method is the only one."
81. See, along with "The End of Play", "No More Ghosts" and "To the Sovereign Muse".
82. "To the Sovereign Muse":
    This was to praise you, Sovereign muse,
    And to your love our pride devote,
83. How much alone see *The Modern Debacle*.

84. *Goddess*, 496.
85. *Goddess*, 499.
86. *Goddess*, 398.
87. *Goddess*, 399.
88. According to Hughes we need to see our way beyond the conflict (for the moment theoretically) by embracing Shakespeare's projection of how it finally resolves: "Since this great Court case is, as it were, still unfinished, the reader (like Shakespeare, and like my book, I trust) will have to make efforts to surmount the quarrel, and embrace Shakespeare's final judgement." *Shakespeare and the Goddess of Complete Being*, London: Faber, 1992, 44.
89. *Shakespeare and the Goddess*, 15.
90. *Shakespeare and the Goddess*, 15.
91. *Shakespeare and the Goddess*, 50.
92. See also Gammage (156-157): "Hughes…describes how… rejection of the diabolic—part of the Goddess of total unconditional love—is actually the rejection of [the hero's] own soul…The hero, Hughes argues, cannot separate the two aspects of the goddess—the creative and the destructive—and so ends up rejecting both…"
93. Suggesting that there was no other way to see it for what it is than to live through the consequences of it.
94. *Shakespeare and the Goddess*, 43.
95. With this shift in my argument, following Shakespeare's lead, I now embark on a more radical view of our *general* implication in guilt, man's *and* woman's, even if the human tragedy, as Shakespeare saw this, is brought to our view by man. It is also clear, as we shall see, that for Shakespeare only woman can finally bring us out of this human tragedy as we have inherited it.
96. It is typical of Graves's already advanced view of this situation that he does not even credit Macbeth with murdering Duncan. In his view it is Lady Macbeth who commits the murder under the influence of an avenging Goddess who is showing Herself again against the pretentious dominance of rational man and very naturally disposing of him: "for it is her spirit that takes possession of Lady Macbeth and inspires her to murder King Duncan". *The White Goddess*, 417. Hughes has it literally the same way but is himself anxious to bring out the whole process by which man has gotten himself into that condition. He speaks "of Lady Macbeth as Queen of Hell. Possessed by the powers of the Goddess (who was

rejected before the play began), her avenging fury has already marked down the rational 'ruler' of the Adonis world that rejected her…[N]ot only will Macbeth's Adonis persona have to die, but Duncan and Banquo too." *Shakespeare and the Goddess*, 246.

97. *Shakespeare and the Goddess,* 84.

98. See *If It Were Done: 'Macbeth' and Tragic Action,* Amherst: University of Massachusetts Press, 1986, 81.
   "Sacred to the gods", and, one must add, to the Goddess: her association with war is a staple of the lore about her. See Balas, 169*passim.*

99. *If It Were Done,* 82.

100. *If It Were Done* 79, 77.

101. *If It Were Done* 84. Clearly a point on which Calderwood distinguishes himself from another great theorist of sacrificial ritual, Rene Girard, whose focus is precisely on the ritual value of "scapegoat victims". See his *Violence and the Sacred,* Baltimore: Johns Hopkins University Press, 1977.

102. *If It Were Done,* 89.

103. See "The Early Scenes of 'Macbeth': Preface to a New Interpretation", *English Literary History,* 47, 1980, 26: "Among the benefits that flow from the king to his subjects are bloody occasions. His vassals are under obligation to him for the chance to fight and kill, to die nobly, to show valor and loyalty, to contend with others in manliness, to compete for reputation and honors by which valor is rewarded…Bloodshed is the proof of manliness and the source of honor and reputation. Bloodshed, bloodiness, bloody-mindedness quicken the pulse of the social order and sharpen its edge."

104. Thus Berger says of the role of the king in *Macbeth*: "The more his subjects do for him, the more he must do for them; the more he does for them, feeding their ambition and their power, the less secure can he be of his mastery." (24-25) "All seem aware of the precariousness of the symbiotic relation to the king…" (28)

105. See Johannes Huizinga, *The Waning of the Middle Ages,* London: Edward Arnold, 1955 (orig.pub., 1924) 18: "Pride…the sin of the feudal and hierarchic age…" See also *Homo Ludens,* Boston: Beacon Press, 1955, 111-112 : " pride and vainglory, the desire for prestige and all the pomp of superiority."

106. *The Waning of the Middle Ages,* 96. Cf. Jung, *Symbols*: "symbol-formation…has no meaning whatever unless it strives against the

resistance of instinct, just as undisciplined instincts would bring nothing but ruin to man if the symbol did not give them form." (228); "the old brutality returns in force..." (230)

107. *The Waning of the Middle Ages*, 40.

108. "That reality has constantly given the lie to these high illusions of a pure and noble social life, who would deny? But where should we be, if our thoughts had never transcended the exact limits of the feasible?" *The Waning of the Middle Ages*, 94. "For the history of civilization the perennial dream of a sublime life has the value of a very important reality." (82)

109. Cf. I.iv: "There if I grow, / The harvest is your own." It is significant in this respect that both in Holinshed/Boece and in Buchanan, the immediate sources on which Shakespeare drew for *Macbeth*, the murder of Duncan *involves* Banquo as an accomplice. Shakespeare clearly had his own emphasis to make.

110. *If It Were Done*, 84.

111. Thus, to adapt a phrase from Bradley, "the despair of a man who [has] knowingly made war on his own soul": A.C. Bradley, *Shakespearean Tragedy*, New York: St. Martin's Press, 1978, orig. pub. 1904, 359.

112. See J.I.M. Stewart, *Character and Motive in Shakespeare*, Longmans, 1949, 93: "The thought of murdering Duncan, first or new glimpsed in the recesses of his mind at the prompting of the witches, produces violent somatic disturbance, as the prospect of a ritual act of cannibalism may do in a Kwakiutl Indian."

113. As in the banquet scene where the Ghost of Banquo appears to him. Cf., also, III.ii: "these terrible dreams/That shake us nightly."

114. Cf. III.iv.

115. See *Shakespeare*, London: Jonathan Cape, 1959, orig. pub. 1936, 325. The scene in question is II.ii, when Macbeth enters having just murdered Duncan.

116. For a fuller exposition of this dominant process in Shakespeare, see my *Othello's Sacrifice* (Toronto: Guernica, 1996), Part Three, 77*passim*.

117. I elaborate further on this viewpoint in *Shakespeare, the Goddess, and Modernity*, which is to appear under the IUniverse imprint concurrently with this second edition of *Impasse*: see the chapter "On King Lear".

118. Ferocity, a sensual quality, is a definite aspect of Cordelia's character which she shares with the whole of the Lear-family,

qualified though the ferocity is in her case by a more deep-set goodness. Cf. V.iii: "Shall we not see these daughters and these sisters?"

119. See my *Shakespeare's Muse*, New York: IUniverse, 2007, 22-23.

120. See *Shakespeare's Muse*, 8-9, also my "Preface on *Hamlet* and Luther" in *Otherworldly Hamlet*, Montreal: Guernica, 1991, 15ff.

121. Another kind of love, of the spirit, will have to emerge from human nature. This is the ultimate end of the tragic process in Shakespeare, as I show in Part Three of *Othello's Sacrifice*, 87*passim*.

122. See my chapter on "Sexuality" in *Otherworldly Hamlet*, 50ff.

123. More on this in *Shakespeare's Muse*, 22ff, and in my monograph, *On Luther*, Ottawa: Heart's Core Publications, 2009 (see the section on *Othello*), 44ff.

124. For an elaborate discussion of Shakespeare's complex relation to Luther see *Shakespeare's Muse*, 8-11;27-28. See also *Othello's Sacrifice*, 80-81.

Clearly, Shakespeare goes on to deal with the fall into human nature in his own highly characteristic way, being his own tragic visionary.

125. One needs to see for oneself how Hughes perceives Shakespeare's experience taking shape with every play that came from his hand from *Hamlet* onwards.

126. How the conflict of feelings between Graves and his beloved is handled in "Eurydice" is a case in point. In this poem Graves appears to be almost reached by the influence of passion as experienced by the Shakespearean (and the general Elizabethan) hero. At some point the poet expresses himself in the same bitter contempt and hatred of the beloved, for her betrayal of their shared ideals:

> *Look where she shines with a borrowed blaze of light*
> *Among the cowardly, faceless, lost, unright*
>
> ....
>
> *She has gnawn at corpse-flesh till her breath stank,*
> *Paired with a jackal, grown distraught and lank*

The beloved has *wandered* from them, disloyal to their cause, and the poet has come to the limits of his endurance in watching their love betrayed. Even so, Graves cannot let himself be taken away with his feelings, abiding in the simplicity of his unshakeable allegiance to his Goddess, whom he will not allow to be forsworn—no matter what the cost, even should this be, metaphorically-speaking, his own head (as Orpheus lost his to the frenzied Bachannals who here represent the beloved's own power to destroy him by persisting in her betrayal; in that case he will be left then to his singing, for *later* generations to understand):

> *My own dear heart, dare you so war on me*
> *As to strangle love in a mad perversity?*
> *Is ours a fate can ever be forsworn*
> *Though my lopped head sing to the yet unborn?*

Graves is so persuaded that it is man who, even in such circumstances, fails to understand the beloved, is so given up to the idea that man must refuse his own demands on the Goddess, that he must see to it that himself is strangled in his own passion of revolt, as another poem, "Myrrhina" clarifies:

> *O, why judge Myrrhina*
> *As though she were a man?*
> *She obeys a dark wisdom*
> *(As Eve did before her)*
> *Which never can fail,*
> *Being bound by no pride*
> *Of armorial bearings*
> *Bequeathed in tail male.*
> *And though your blood brother*
> *Who dared to do you wrong*
> *In his greed of Myrrhina*
> *Might plead a like wisdom*
> *The fault to excuse,*
> *Myrrhina is just:*
> *She has hanged the poor rogue*
> *By the neck from her noose.*

But there is much ambiguity in "Eurydice". The poet speaks of a 'scene' of violent passion between himself and the beloved:

> *In a mirror I watch blood trickling down the wall—*

confronted by which, the poet asks:

> *Is it mine?*

This might read, and was probably intended to be read, as suggesting that the poet remains superciliously unaffected by the beloved's violence and beyond its power to destroy his faith, as the rest of the line seems to clarify:

> *Yet still I stand here, proud and tall.*

The destructive import of this passion is thus simply put away by Graves, as an affront to the incontrovertible will of the Goddess (to which the beloved's passion is thus referred).

But has Graves not in this but denied a passion that might otherwise as validly have claimed his attention as evidence of a hopeless reality—which, we may suppose, has not gone away only because it has been thought away? Might the poem not even be thought to suggest that the poet himself has indulged in vengeful passion? I must confess that initially I read the poem as confessing as much, though the poet does turn away from the passion in the end, one way or the other. For why ask "Is it mine?", as if to suggest that perhaps it may not be, being in that case her blood, which *he* has spilled? The poet might simply have said: "It is mine." There would have been no ambiguity then. Can we see in this ambiguous effect, in fact, some form of implied confession of violence in himself?

127. Gammage, 151.
128. Many of the earlier plays are echoed in passages from the last plays: e.g., *Macbeth* in the scene between Cleon and Dionyza in *Pericles*; *King Lear* in the scene of recognition between Pericles and Marina; *Othello*, of course, in *The Winter's Tale*; *Hamlet* and *Macbeth* in *The Tempest*.
129. See *Othello's Sacrifice*, 88ff. for a full treatment of this whole evolution, which I can only outline here.
130. In Her medieval and Renaissance manifestations, the Goddess appears typically in the form of a Virgin, reflecting the purifying process with which She is by then also connected, apart from the more material (sometimes perversely material) forms She takes in Graves's history. Diana, especially as Diana of Ephesus, is in this respect a classical prototype of Her later form. Such developments substantiate that additional evolution of the Goddess *into* the Sophia as Erich Neumann once pictured this:

> *The dual Great Goddess as mother and daughter can so far transform her original bond with the elementary character as to become a pure feminine spirit, a kind of Sophia, a spiritual whole in which all heaviness and materiality are transcended. Then she not only forms the earth and heaven of the retort that we call life, and is not only the whirling wheel revolving within it, but is also the supreme essence and distillation to which life in this world can be transformed.*

All this is, what's more, also relative to what mankind can make of itself:

The Archetypal Feminine in man unfolds like mankind itself. At the beginning stands the primeval goddess, resting in the materiality of her elementary character...at the end is Tara[-Sophia]...an eternal image of the redeeming female spirit. Both together form the unity of the Great Goddess who, in the totality of her unfolding, fills the world from its lowest elementary phase to its supreme spiritual transformation.

The Great Mother, Princeton:
Princeton Univ. Press, 1955, 334-335.

Goddess lore as a whole will confirm that chastity alone is the quality that ever allowed direct access to the Goddess. See Balas, 177*passim*.

131. See *Othello's Sacrifice*, 97ff for more on this.

132. See *Othello's Sacrifice*, 96, for an elaboration on this.

133. Even Antonio, the worst of the conspirators, is drawn into this impression. However, I do not pretend to claim that Shakespeare feels that literally all can be set right again. It is clear that in the end Antonio and perhaps also Sebastian (Stephano, and Trinculo) do *not* come along: there is an aspect of the human will that finally resists reformation. However, this Shakespeare recognizes as the ultimate human problem only the more clearly now that his has become the will to ultimate harmony.

134. The conflict between the ideal and the earthly, as well as their potential mutual impenetrability one by the other, all in connection with an attainable Goddess who engages the poet on these issues, is a staple of the Romantic Imagination generally. In this respect Endymion's quest for his Goddess may be fruitfully compared, e.g., with Heinrich's quest in Novalis's *Heinrich von Ofterdingen*, or that of the hero in Shelley's *Epipsychidion*. Behind this extensive presentation in Romantic literature lies the story of the Goddess as summarized, e.g., by Cartari in his *Images of the Gods of the Ancients* (see Balas, 190):

The story goes...that the goddess possessed a pure and chaste love for [a] young man [Attis], and gave this to him along with the charge of caring for all her sacred things, on the condition that he preserve his virginity and modesty for all time. And this he promised to do and swore to uphold the obligation. But the poor wretch did not observe his vow, but instead fell in love with a beautiful nymph, daughter of the river Sangarius in that country. He remembered the promise made to the goddess, but nevertheless took pleasure in his new love.

135. See Walter Jackson Bate, *John Keats*, Cambridge, Massachusetts: Harvard University Press, 1964, 390.

136. See *The White Goddess*, 418ff.

137. *John Keats*, 333.

138. *John Keats*, 374.

139. *John Keats*, 391.

140. *John Keats*, 322.

141. *John Keats*, 324.

142. *John Keats*, 322.

143. *John Keats*, 494.

144. *John Keats*, 322.

145. In this aspect, at least, Keats had convincingly filled in the evolutionary story on which he was epically bent originally.

146. "To this point Wordsworth had come...when he wrote "Tintern Abbey" and it seems to me his genius is explorative of those dark Passages." (Letter of 3 May, 1818.)

147. Keats's approach is in this the *opposite* of Shakespeare's for whom the illuminating consciousness is provided from without, from a point that is always, at any given moment, finally outside his own immediate inner life, as we have seen above, 49.

148. It is very possible that Keats invented this "Grecian" urn.

149. Coleridge reflects a similar experience to us in his "Christabel", which must have served as one source of inspiration for Keats when writing his poem.

150. Unable to marry for lack of a proper profession at this time, Keats had conceived of "Lamia" as a way of establishing himself with a wider reading public and so achieving some financial independence.

151. For the influence of Keats's ideas in this poem on later 19th century aesthetics, see Frank Kermode, *Romantic Image*, London: Routledge, 1957.

152. One thinks, pre-eminently, of Shelley's *Prometheus Unbound*.

153. Keats was generally under Coleridge's influence at this time. See Beth Lau, *Keats's Reading of the Romantic Poets*, Ann Arbor: University of Michigan Press, 1991, 85-86. See, also, Jack

Stillinger, "Keats and Coleridge" from *Coleridge, Keats and the Imagination*, ed., J. Robert Barth, S.J., and John L. Mahoney, Columbia: University of Missouri Press, 1990.

154. In "The Excursion".

155. *Keats*, London: Jonathan Cape, 1955, 279.

156. *Keats*, 283.

157. See. e.g., Glen O. Allen, "The Fall of Endymion: A Study in Keats's Intellectual Growth" from the *Keats-Shelley Journal*, Vol. VI, Winter, 1957, 57: "Keats exchanged his ethereal attachments for his earthly ones…" Or Jack Stillinger, "Keats and Coleridge", 27: "his scepticism toward the visionary in practically all his major narrative and lyrics of 1819 is tantamount to an acceptance of the naturalized imagination central in the poetry and theories of Coleridge and Wordsworth rather than with the more transcendental and visionary schemes of Blake and Shelley." Yet cf. Allen Tate, "On the Limits of Poetry" from *Collected Literary Essays*, Denver: Colorado, 1959, 163-164, who only wished Keats had been more capable in this direction: "His goddess, insofar as she is more than a decorative symbol in Keats, was all Uranian… His pictorial and sculpturesque effects, which arrest time into space, tend to remove from experience the dramatic agitation of Aphrodite Pandemos, whose favors are granted and whose woes are counted in the actuality of time." "In Keats's mind… there was, to put it in the simplest language, a strong compulsion towards the realization of physical love, but he could not reconcile it with his idealization of the beloved." 163-164.

158. Both of whom were much taken with "Hyperion" (i.e., its first version, the only one to be published in Keats's lifetime). Byron compared some of its passages to Aeschylus.

159. Back to pre-Minoan times, in comparison with Keats who was drawing on Classical lore.

160. See Graves, *Poetic Craft and Principle*, London: Cassell, 1967, 135.

161. See Kermode, *Romantic Image*, 8; "Moneta, I take it, represents the survival of the archaic way of thought—imaginative rather than discursive ("the large utterance of the early gods"), *undissociated*, mythopoeic; more profound, though certainly, to use the word in a limiting sense, less *human* than the discourse of 'philosophy' which Keats, with his tentative evolutionism, was trying to accept as a necessary human development."

PART THREE

THIS *Life,* THIS Death:
WORDSWORTH'S POETIC DESTINY

JOHN O'MEARA

iUniverse, Inc.
Bloomington

THIS LIFE, THIS DEATH

Wordsworth's Poetic Destiny

THIS LIFE, THIS DEATH

Wordsworth's Poetic Destiny

JOHN O'MEARA

iUniverse, Inc.
Bloomington

A Note on References, and Acknowledgments

Wordsworth's great epic poem, *The Prelude*, was only thus named (at the suggestion of his wife, Mary) posthumously, in 1850 when the poem came out for the first time. Until then, Wordsworth had spoken of his poem simply as "The Poem to Coleridge". However, for convenience I have referred to the poem as *The Prelude* from its very inception in 1798. Over the years the poem assumed several forms: (what have come to be known as) the *Two-Part Prelude* of 1799, the *Five-Book Prelude* of 1804, the 1805 *Prelude* and the 1850 *Prelude*.

All quotations from *The Prelude* are from *The Prelude 1799, 1805, 1850* ed. Jonathan Wordsworth, M.H. Abrams, and Stephen Gill (New York: Norton, 1979). References are to the 1805 text—unless the context requires otherwise. Line numbers have been given only as it seemed necessary to facilitate reference for the reader. For comparative reference, indispensible also has been *The Five-Book Prelude*, ed. Duncan Wu (Oxford: Blackwell, 1997). Without these highly useful editorial productions, work on the present book would have been greatly prolonged.

Contents

Foreword

Looking ahead to the 250th anniversary of William Wordsworth's birth, it seemed fitting to be coming forward, even if some time before that occasion, with this modest booklet on the great hopes and eventual destiny of one of our most highly revered poets. A culturally-alert reader will have noticed that the title quotes from William Butler Yeats.[1] There was no intention of implying a comparison between the two poets, ironic or otherwise, although the allusion could fruitfully open up a whole area of broad study on the way the themes of life and death have been lived out among our poets generally. I do not enter into any such comparative view in this study, but as an analogy between Yeats and Wordsworth is suggested, I do well to state here that the latter's experience has little to do with the notion of having everything in hand and in perfect balance that Yeats's phrase implies in *its* context. On the contrary, far too much was at stake for Wordsworth in the case of life and in the case of death for him to feel that they would not rather inevitably polarize and stand radically opposed to each other, so long as the forces of life remained fundamentally untapped and death a dark enigma. In many ways the following study dares to present itself as a necessary corrective to many of the easy views we have taken as to where this sublimely creative poet stood on this score. Inevitably, *this* intention, quite deliberately conceived, will be judged to arise from a personal view of the pattern of Wordsworth's poetic production, and with this assessment I am ready to concur, so long as my readers will feel that the adventure they have taken with me was worthwhile and they have been enlivened by it.

JOM

---

[1] From "An Irishman Forsees His Death"

For

Aline

who re-visited

Wordsworth

with me

on a long holiday spent in the Lake District

in the summer of 2010.

Who can forget that bend where the Derwent River

meets Cockermouth Castle,

on a sombre day?

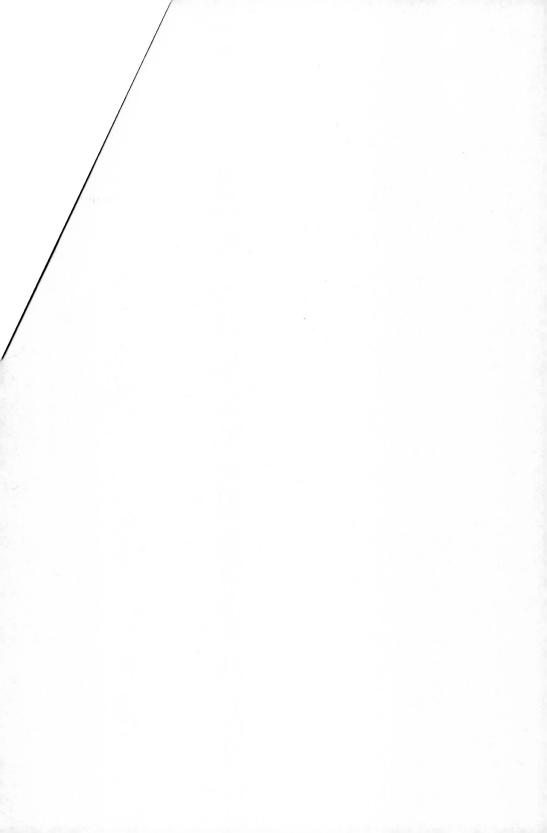

He had lost the path that should have
kept leading more confidently and
deeply inward . . .

—Seamus Heaney

(i)
From *The Recluse* and *The Prelude* to *Intimations*

A Hopeful Beginning

Already months before his troubled sojourn in Germany in late 1798/early 1799, the idea had been sown in Wordsworth that he should commit to a long philosophical poem, tentatively entitled *The Recluse*—the sort of grand, representative project Coleridge saw as appropriate to him as the outstanding poet of his time and the successor to Shakespeare and to Milton. This idea for a poem, which was largely of Coleridge's conception, constituted for Wordsworth at once a source of deep inspiration and a burdensome challenge the inhibiting effects of which in the long term do not fully begin to show (or at least they do not become fully understandable to us) until years later when he took up with his *Prelude* once again in 1804. During his time in Germany, Wordsworth responded to Coleridge's challenge with what became initially the first part of the *Two-Part Prelude*, which Wordsworth saw as a complete form of the poem by the time he extended it to that length in late 1799. One can imagine how Wordsworth felt while in Germany, isolated as he was in a rather extreme way by impossibly cold weather which virtually confined his movements to a single room for weeks. He was again radically cut off from the world of Nature that had, not too lately, literally saved him in mind and soul.[1] In the meantime, the idea of the philosophical poem that he especially ought to be getting down to write but which he had not yet attempted, must have pressed hard on him, greatly adding, by its own pressure, to the distress he was feeling in his unpromising isolation. In what must be regarded as among the most thrilling moments in English literature, Wordsworth then heroically set down the first few words of the forthcoming *Prelude*, beginning, disconcertingly, in mid-line:

> *Was it for this*
> *That one, the fairest of all rivers, loved*
> *To blend his murmurs with my nurse's song . . .*

In his isolation Wordsworth had decided to call back for himself the Nature from which he was at this moment so distressingly separated and that had so profoundly determined his existence from the time he was born, as if to ask the fateful question: 'Can this deep impasse into which I am plunged at this moment be any proper consequence for all that went into making me?'[2] Thus began Wordsworth's work on *The Prelude*, on which he was to lavish his attention for many years to come. He was at this moment fighting back, but instead of getting down to *The Recluse*, as was expected of him, suddenly he immersed in a long series of reminiscences that were soon to absorb him in and for themselves. He would throw an appearance of justification over his new project by maintaining that he was only going back into his life to see for himself how Nature had shaped him for the outstanding task Coleridge had assigned him. At the end of the first part, he claims that it has been his hope that, by returning to the sources of what went into making him, he might find the proper impetus to engage in the greater work assigned to him. But it is clear that Wordsworth feels pulled in two different directions: on the one hand, there is the call to write a great philosophical poem, *The Recluse*, as a work befitting him as the outstanding poet of his time, and on the other, there are his own poetic impulses that are driving him to look back deep into his past for insights into all that his extraordinary life in Nature had bred in him as though these insights might be an end in themselves. As it is, it is somewhat surprising on the surface, though as we shall see in keeping with the deep dilemma that would continue to plague Wordsworth, that he would *not* return to his own project until many months later, even after his welcome release from Germany and his happy return to England.

In fact, he would not take up with *The Prelude* again until the end of 1799, and even then only after a long walk through the Lake District had roused his creative instincts in a rather extraordinary way. Coleridge was on the verge of leaving the District for work in London, and that occasion of leave-taking would also seem to have inspired Wordsworth to take up with his poem again. *The Prelude* remained, on the surface, a kind of link to the other poem, and he was undertaking it again on this occasion, it would seem, out of a desire to grace Coleridge's departure with a further show of his determination to understand how his unique experience of Nature had benefited him in his projected task. Not even for Wordsworth was this early version of *The Prelude* the poem that he felt he should be writing. At the same time it is clear that it was, even then, already shaping up as a great poem in its own right and a fully worthy end in itself. This one can see from the superior quality, the great wealth and depth of the detail Wordsworth was bringing forward. There is an extraordinary, patched-up effort to immediately round it out into a whole and to bring this subordinate account to a swift close, but at the same time clearly an extraordinary excess in Wordsworth's account as if he were trying to bring it all together too soon. In time he could only feel that there was all that wealth of experience to get back to. And yet he did *not* get back to it—not for another four years, so great was the concern in the depths with satisfying, in the meantime, the responsibility of grand achievement that had been thrust upon him with the *Recluse*-project.

Discouragement, or the Inhibiting Power of *The Recluse*

Not until he gets back to *The Prelude* four years later are the deep contradictions into which the *Recluse*-project had plunged Wordsworth faced openly and directly. Once again this occurs in the few months before Coleridge was slated to depart, this time for Malta for a period of convalescence that would last two years. Wordsworth's great skills as an editor of his work are very much in evidence when he takes up with the poem again in January of 1804. Returning to an independent piece he had written in late 1799, proudly referred to in a later book as his "glad preamble" (Bk.VII.4), he makes it now into the opening of his poem. With this piece he re-invokes that great sense of unadulterated promise that had taken him over four years earlier, when, returned to England, it seemed to him that everything had become possible again, and the *Recluse*-project itself stood within sight.[3] Taking up from here four years later, he narrates this earlier moment further, expanding once again on the sense of hope portended.

But already there was a premonitory sign, even at that moment, of the failure to come, or to see it from another viewpoint, evidence of an irruption of that alienation from himself that was already at work in Wordsworth as the effect of the inhibiting power which the *Recluse*-idea had exercised in him:

> *but the harp*
> *Was soon defrauded, and the banded host*
> *Of harmony dispersed in straggling sounds*
> *And lastly utter silence.*

> (Bk.I.104)

Wordsworth carried on, ignoring this momentary irruption, which in any case he could not have understood at that time; he is immediately returned to his seemingly unbounded joy and hopefulness. His mind had, in this access of great feeling, at some point turned again to the great project he was called on to realize. But he remained foiled and, in a dramatic conflation of the whole intervening period since then (right up to the time he takes up with *The Prelude* again in 1804), now confesses to extended failure:

> *But I have been discouraged . . .*

> *. . . .If my mind,*
> *Remembering the sweet promise of the past,*
> *Would gladly grapple with some noble theme,*
> *Vain is her wish—where'er she turns she finds*
> *Impediments from day to day renewed.*

> (Bk.I.134)

This failure is seen in direct relation to the *Recluse*-project, but it is not, strictly-speaking, restricted to it. In addition to the failure he confesses to here, other more obscure feelings have emerged that have plagued him to the point where he has not been able to give himself even to lesser work—as he had, for instance, back in 1802, when he composed his Sonnets[4]. The mysterious inhibiting "trouble" of which he speaks in this section (I.144-156), and which has kept him from undertaking poetic work, very much suggests the "thought of grief" and the "dim sadness" which he had entered into some few months before he turned to the Sonnets, respectively in his *Intimations* and *Resolution and Independence* (on which more below). In this section of *The Prelude*, he implies that his feelings of baffled "trouble" have been general *over this whole intervening period.*

From here Wordsworth proceeds to account for the whole series of deliberations into which he was led in his attempt to find a proper form for his epic project. None of these were thought to have been suitable, and even when he turns to something in tune with his more immediate concerns—

> *Some tale from my own heart—*
>
> (I.221)

he is likewise baffled, feeling the influence of what he refers to as "deadening admonitions" (225). Embracing still more directly the possibility of "some philosophic song/Of truth" (230), of the sort that he and Coleridge have been contemplating, he finds that he can only put off "this awful burthen"; he cannot face up to it, and the lingering effect of this general impasse has been to leave him radically uncertain of his creative motives. By then it is clear enough that the idea of the philosophic poem it was thought he was meant to write is having a great inhibiting effect on him rather than offering an incentive to create, and in his turmoil over his dilemma, Wordsworth begins to evoke the figure of Hamlet languishing under the burden of some higher injunction:

> *. . . Thus from day to day*
> *I live a mockery . . .*
> *. . . .with no skill to part*
> *Vague longing . . .*
> *From paramount impulse . . .*

A timorous capacity, from prudence;
From circumspection, infinite delay.

(238)

Contrasting so dramatically with this continuous state of unrelieved frustration is the extraordinary life of freedom Wordsworth can alternatively conceive for himself as one so capable of giving himself to Nature for its own sake—precisely along the lines of the extraordinary celebration of freedom he offers us in the opening section of his poem—his "glad preamble". Four years earlier it had seemed to him that "The earth [was] all before [him]" (I.15) and he could undertake anything. A radical opposition is thus set up between the direct call to some higher duty and an equally high-minded open potentiality that might be leading Wordsworth in any creative direction and become, at a certain point, its own end. In the latter case this is an ideal potentiality for realizing the unrealized that might take any form at any time and that Wordsworth will celebrate more than once over the course of his *Prelude* when he gets down to it (see below p.19; also endnote 25). This radical contrast, as Wordsworth becomes aware of it, suddenly links him in his anguish also with the figure of Milton in *Lycidas*, although the main point of reference remains, throughout the following passage, his association with Hamlet:

—Ah, better far than this to stray about
Voluptuously through fields and rural walks,
And ask no record of the hours given up
To vacant musing, unreproved neglect
Of all things, and deliberate holiday.
Far better never to have heard the name
Of zeal and just ambition, than to live
Thus baffled by a mind that every hour
Turns recreant to her task, takes heart again
Then feels immediately some hollow thought
Hang like an interdict upon her hopes.[5]

(I.252)

It is equally significant, and for our purposes here when we will turn to Wordsworth's *Intimations* Ode still more significant, that in focusing his distress over this creative impasse in his life, Wordsworth should see himself as going empty-handed to his grave:

> *Unprofitably travelling towards the grave*

(I.269)

The thought of an alien death triumphing over his impoverished imagination was at this time already raising its ugly head.

Choosing His Own Direction

It is at this intensely dramatic juncture in his re-working of *The Prelude* that Wordsworth's great editorial skills are again displayed, for he *re-introduces* into his poem at this point the opening section of his initial version of *The Prelude* as composed in Germany in late 1798:

> *Was it for this*
> *That one, the fairest of all rivers, loved*
> *To blend his murmurs with my nurse's song . . .*

(I.272)

With this wonderful maneuver and sudden *re*-affirmation of himself, Wordsworth once again brings Nature back into it. He brings the whole course of that extraordinary experience of Nature that he had known over years to bear directly on his anguish and his dilemma. Among other things, an entirely appropriate antecedent for his mysterious earlier "this" is now supplied. It is the same dilemma that he finds himself addressing years later; only it is now more greatly evolved: 'Can this deep impasse into which I am plunged be any proper consequence for all that went into making me?' At the same time, one has the sense that among Wordsworth's concerns is how he could now be in such "perplexity" (I.268) when Nature's whole way with him until now would appear to have served no other goal than to create in him the unity of a "calm existence" (I.360) out of every episode of distress he had known.[6]

Wordsworth returns to his research into the course of his ongoing experience with Nature still under the guise of a relation to the epic project that has been assigned to him. The questions that he had put to himself earlier, as to whether Nature can have been entertaining "a vulgar hope" (I.493), when she singled him out for Her attention, or whether he could possibly be "uselessly employed" (501) in so scupulously researching Her work in him—these questions, appropriated to the present context, are clearly referred to the larger commitment to *The Recluse*, which he appears still to be honoring. However, his questions also point in another independent[7] direction, as if Nature might have had another purpose in mind, connected with his insistent need to return to the experiences that went into shaping him. Thus Wordsworth re-affirms his "weakness . . . for days/Disowned by memory" (642), and his 'loath'-ness "to quit/Those recollected hours that have the charm/Of visionary things" (658).[8] This was the second time he was having this thought, coming back to it in 1804, and while he is still hopeful, as he says, that the exercise of researching his past will "spur [him] on" (652) to the greater project, he is ready to think that the exercise of researching "visionary things" will be of significance in itself. He has, in any case, reached a point of impasse in his life which makes it necessary for him to choose to continue in that direction in which he had set out years earlier. And so, as he says,

> *I chuse it rather at this time than work*
> *Of ampler or more varied argument,*

(670)

He does so, he says, only because movement in this direction has "revived" his creative "mind" (665), by giving him a purpose. Coming to this decision some four years later, however, one can only wonder what effect a long period of bafflement and thwarted impulse would have had in the meantime on Wordsworth's creative possibilities.

Revolt, and More Bafflement

The further issue is raised as to how he was managing his relationship to Coleridge over this whole period. After all, it was the latter's uncompromising expectation, from the time the idea was first proposed five years earlier, that Wordsworth would soon be launching into the only poem that would do full justice to himself, and one imagines (vicariously) to him, Coleridge, also.[9] But at this late point Wordsworth had not come through, and now he was conveying decisively his intention of committing himself to his own large project, at least for now. The intensity of the anguish Wordsworth expresses in his conflict with himself over this matter, bearing, as we have seen, directly on the fortunes of his creative life, is enough to persuade us of a deep struggle with Coleridge's influence, which he certainly felt, at this level, as a bane. Coleridge had himself, by then, grown powerless to envision the kind of creative accomplishment which he had thought was the one that promised especially to distinguish them as poets. Two years earlier, he had himself responded to Wordsworth's lament over blighted powers of Imagination (as expressed in the first part of his *Intimations* Ode) with a confirmation (in *Dejection*) that things had come to the same for him. In the meantime, Wordsworth had not accepted as readily as Coleridge had those limitations on his creative impulses that appeared to have obstructed his further development as a poet, and one must speak of a kind of revolt against Coleridge, in however qualified a form this may have been put, in his renewed determination to pursue his own way with *The Prelude*.[10]

But four long years of bafflement about his purposes had intervened, and having asserted himself again in his revolt in 1804, none too strangely perhaps, after his initial revisionary work and the composition of a third Book, there would be a further, if brief, interruption of over a month before he would finally begin to compose more.[11] But by then Wordsworth's basic purpose and orientation had altered, and the more sense one has of how, and to what extent, he *had* been baffled, in that long period of procrastination over four years, when his creative impulse seemed in a certain peculiar way stifled, the more clearly do we penetrate to the actual organizing structure of this new work as he now conceived of it.

For in returning to *The Prelude*, Wordsworth may have *thought* that he was carrying on from his designs back in 1799 when the prospect of researching his past seemed to bode some greater engagement with those powers of Nature that had armed him for work on *The Recluse*. Four years later, however, Wordsworth was a substantially different man and a different poet, with quite a different perspective on himself as poet, and it is consequently another purpose that is driving him on. His powers of Imagination *had* been affected by his confusion over years about his direction, and one main impulse in his undertaking of *The Prelude*, which always was and continued to be to show how Nature had gone into making him from infancy—that impulse was *now* being subordinated to the more decisive *theme* of confounded powers. Clearly even his ability to write poetry had been affected, inasmuch as he could no longer properly understand in what his poetic task should consist. His *poetic* powers had been confounded: a certain way of being himself as a poet turned out to be inseparable from his experience of a continuous visionary influence streaming into the present out of his childhood past, his poetic 'faith' being grounded in this experience out of which he wrote, and it was just this influence that was no longer working in him. It is also the case, as we shall see, that diverse powers of *perception* are involved relating to the variegated way in which this visionary influence bore fruit in him in the past. It was all supposed to have been an account of how his present powers as a poet had come into being, but it was turning into an account rather of what it remained for him to do now that his primal experience as a poet had been confounded:

I am lost . . .

. . . .

12

> . . . . *the hiding-places of my power*
> *Seem open; I approach, and then they close;*

(Bk.XI.330)[12]

Wordsworth was, by now, more profoundly aware of being Imaginatively dispossessed than he had been when he first set down his thoughts about this in the first part of *Intimations*, and paradoxically his deepening consciousness of this was to put a damper on the resentment he felt towards Coleridge from the effects of the latter's imposed task. Wordsworth knew[13] by now that it was that task that had confounded him and separated him from his Imaginative powers of old; those effects thus constituted real grounds for resentment. However, just because he could see that the situation was irreversible, he grows progressively more conscious of the depth of his partnership with Coleridge, with whom he has shared *also* an experience of tragic dispossession, so that everything becomes centred in time in the profound significance of the association they constituted. They knew, as no others could, from what shared world it was that they had fallen, which Wordsworth now especially wished to commemorate.[14]

A New Anxiety

This acknowledged new vision of confounded powers in *The Prelude*, to which Wordsworth is already giving himself by late winter 1804, underpins much of what he is presenting especially from Bk.IV onwards. It is the new subtextual sense in which we understand his need, as expressed half-way through that book, to be "solacing" (249) himself in looking back on his formative years. Often he claims to be "perplex'd" (254) in his effort to see his past life clearly, bringing us back, indirectly, to the initial "perplexity" he had wrestled with when he was struggling to break out of his confusion about his direction. There is now a strange acceptance of his bated powers, and so he can speak in this passage of the "success"(264) he has been having even though his achievement to this point has been only very partial, as he confesses.[15] Such a view combines with many feelings, some of which are more plangent if not at times downright rebellious. In Bk.IV acceptance prevails, as reflected in Wordsworth's account of the Dismissed Soldier who lives himself in "a strange half-absence" (475), "Remembering the importance of his theme/ But feeling it no longer." (477). But at other times, Wordsworth's attitude grows desperate, as when he elaborates, in Bk.V, on the Dream of the Arab about the imminence of some great apocalyptic "overthrow" (158), some great "gathering" of "the waters of the deep" (130) that threaten, of which Wordsworth feels he must take stock and about which he feels he must alert us. This episode communicates subtextually Wordsworth's deep anxiety about an emerging world that may militate against *every* survival of creative expression (it hardly needs saying, prophetic of things to come for him). This anxiety *would* inspire desperate efforts, like his own in his *Prelude*, to salvage whatever one could of the imaginative life that had been known while one could still speak of it.

By now Wordsworth was hurried along with a significantly different purpose, bearing on where he stood in relation to his old Imaginative powers, and it is quite in keeping with his new situation that, in spite of the fact that he has committed to a survey of his past, he should be strongly diverted by all that the dream of the Arab imports about the desperation of cultural enterprise. Ironically he feels he must apologize for what will strike Coleridge as a long digression from his main subject of remembering his past:

> But I was hurried forward by a stream
> And could not stop.[16]

(Bk.V.183)

Old material, also, Wordsworth now brings into his poem, appropriated to his new purposes; he is intuiting a new import to the experiences he had already described. This is the case not only with the material of the Dismissed Soldier, where a "strange half-absence" to his former life is described but also with the material of the Boy of Winander (formerly *There was a Boy*) which Wordsworth also makes room for in this stage of his production of his poem (V.389 *passim*).[17] Another, new significance attaches to the figure of the poet who at that time "stood/Mute" (421) at the boy's grave: the poet's separation from this boy by his (symbolic) death (this boy who was Wordsworth himself) has become virtually synonymous with the poet's own separation from that capacity for Imagining *with* Nature that had once possessed him.

In Bk.V Wordsworth ends strongly, in fact, with a view of literary production ("romances, legends . . . fictions") as offering primarily consolation. Such production allows us to continue to express, in displaced form, the "dumb yearnings" and "hidden appetites" that in "childhood" one dispensed at will, when one 'sat' upon these as upon a "throne" (532). Such production, in comparison, is a mere sublimation of that primal creative "power" one directly exercised over these yearnings *in* childhood, and yet, for this very reason, it is all the more valued, as indispensible emotional support. Works produced thus are "friends"(547) in the cause of all that one might have expected of one's experience on the basis of the primal power one brought with one into the world. Wordsworth's fundamental point of view as expressed in the second part of his *Intimations Ode* has begun to show itself here[18]. And yet he cannot help but return plaintively to a time in his youth when "poems" *had* once possessed him by their complete power to "entrance" as if in unison then with the forces of Nature all around; in comparison, his almost complete "distance" from this primal experience now Wordsworth feels he can only lament:

> *I am sad*
> *At thought of raptures now for ever flown,*
> *Even unto tears I sometimes could be sad*
> *To think of, to read over, many a page—*
> *Poems . . . which . . .*
> *. . . . .are now*
> *Dead in my eyes as is a theatre*
> *Fresh emptied of spectators.*

(568)

15

The decisive experience in this extraordinary about-face in Wordsworth's poetic life is the one he had when he returned to England after Germany. Within a year of that return, he had completed the *Two-Part Prelude*, and he had also written his "glad preamble", confident that still greater things were in store for him. He had put *The Prelude* behind him, had overcome, so he thought, the temptation to go his own way with this material, and was ready for something more. But for four years nothing more came. When he finally does return to *The Prelude* in 1804 it is with a vengeance, but by then it is too late; he had, in the meantime, tragically separated himself from those very powers he was hoping once again to extol. In pretending there was still hope, Wordsworth was deliberately counteracting the evidence of lost powers that he had already bewailed in his *Intimations Ode*, composed some two years earlier, in 1802, but he could see now that it was to no avail. Coleridge's admonitions had hung over him like an interdiction and had served to repress him in the direction he was naturally inclined to take.

This direction was in the contemplation of the "visionary things" of the past in which he still had some direct stake in the present, even in the period of the writing of the *Two-Part Prelude*. Rebuffed in this aim, he loses touch with the ground on which he stands; his original powers fall away from him, and when he is brought back once again to contemplating them, on returning to *The Prelude* in 1804, he finds that they have indeed left him. From the account he gives, on first returning to his poem in 1804, of extended discouragement in his poetic aims over this whole time, Wordsworth might have known better, but he was motivated by a last, a new, if futile, hope to make things happen again. There must always have been hope over this period, even when in his bafflement he turned in 1802 to writing his Sonnets, to help relieve the burden of "too much liberty" in his contemplation of greater work. This was only some few months after he had put the great question to himself:

> *Whither is fled the visionary gleam?*
> *Where is it now, the glory and the dream?*

But at that time the issue was still only in the form of a question, a question which had yet to be conclusively answered; unanswered, it left open the possibility of reversing the situation. By 1804, when he is returning to *The Prelude*, Wordsworth is also saying that he no longer has the option of lesser work to fall back on.[19]

A New Moral, and Summary

By the time he did come around to a full comprehension of his new situation through 1804 and 1805, Wordsworth knew what the principal moral of his work must be. This he finally sets down towards the end of the *1805 Prelude* after he had fully extended his work to 13 books. They are, arguably, the most crucial words in the whole of *The Prelude*:

> *and I would give,*
> *While yet we may, as far as words can give,*
> *A substance and a life to what I feel:*
> *I would enshrine the spirit of the past*
> *For future restoration.*

These words imply, in the context of the bewailing of confounded powers to which they belong—

> *I see by glimpses now; when age comes on*
> *May scarcely see at all,*

(XI.337)

—that Wordsworth is now simply doing his poetic best to recover what extraordinary experiences he has had, both in their past and present relations. This he does in order to point the lesson of what was once possible, and may yet be possible again for others, on the basis of the record he now offers to his readers, and for whatever ways it might 'restore' the spirit of his readers in the future.

Here one must grasp that Wordsworth has fundamentally passed beyond the visionary way of living into Nature that he is otherwise celebrating in this poem. He is offering, in lieu of a further direct extension of this mode of seeing in the present, fundamentally a commemorative view, living into his past again from a position of intense poetic remembering that cannot be mistaken for a direct re-invocation of the powers of vision he is calling back to mind, however intimate he appears to be at times in his description of those powers.[20] This is so even where he claims, in the last part of Bk.XI (written in late winter, 1804) still to "stand now" (255) or (some time after that) "Once more in Nature's presence"(393). Towards the end of Bk.X (written in the fall of 1804), he likewise claims that the "strength" (925) Nature has bestowed upon him over the years is one that continues to "[uphold] [him] at this day"—"in the catastrophe" (929) of politically degrading times. But by now this "strength" has turned into a more remote 'faith' built up from an experience that has passed, and if Wordsworth can be said still to stand in Nature's presence, it is in the stricter sense of his present meditation on Her insofar as he is extolling Her for what She *once* achieved in him. He is by now in a different stage of his poetic career than when he could still live back into his past experience, as he does pre-eminently in *Tintern Abbey* (in 1798), as to a certain extent he does still in the *Two-Part Prelude* (completed by 1799)—live back, and *re-create* that past experience in a form that perpetuates it as a continuous visionary experience in the present. That line of experience could once constitute a form of 'faith'—*Tintern Abbey* offers the best account of it—that was quite different from the later one Wordsworth has assumed by 1804. This earlier faith, which he is still nursing by the end of 1799, is the one that he is 'merely' commemorating, as itself a thing of the past, by the time he is extending his poem to the greater length it would assume through 1804.[21]

The process by which Wordsworth modulates from his earlier into his later experience is subtle and highly intricate, for among the different ideas that motivated him to undertake *The Prelude* from the first was the notion that he could *still* go back to especially intense moments in his past and from these re-create some informing influence of strength or "renovating virtue" (XI.259) on which he could build to define himself in the present. We may call this mental orientation and disposition Wordsworth's *Tintern*-vision, after the poem in which he outlines it in its most elaborate and successful form. Involved in this vision was the notion that, in the very act of reconstituting his past experience as a present one, he was also laying the ground for a further direct extension of that experience in the future through his work as a poet.[22] The moments in the past on which he felt he could build in this continuous way had been, for the most part, visionary moments: moments in which he had experienced an intense communion with the spirit of Nature that at the time worked directly in him. *On* such experiences Wordsworth had built his 'genial faith'[23] of the last many years, by which he had been able to thrive as a poet and to put off every power of discouragement and debasement. Even by the time he is writing the *Two-Part Prelude*, he can speak (towards the end of the Second Part) of being still in possession of this original faith in an *un*-broken line of influence stemming out of his whole past.[24]

What's more, the form this influence took involved him in the sense that he could be expanding infinitely in soul capacity, so that 'what' he was experiencing at any stage, or on what basis, had always seemed to him less significant than that the experience was *unfolding*. It was taking him to progressively more and more 'sublime' heights of "shadowy exultation" (II.362).[25] It was an experience that Wordsworth was having for its own sake; in its essential form it would come upon him "unsought"(II.5), and would take its own direction in him (he returns to this notion of "something evermore about to be" in a later section of his poem—in Bk.VI.542). Indeed, from the first period in which his attention was directly turned to Nature in his early youth, he complied in this process without "knowing why" (II.323).[26] *Allowing* the experience over the years simply to unfold, he had had no consciousness of any separation from it, and while still under its spell could, therefore, have no special need to look further into the process of it. This was Wordsworth's case, in fact, right up to late 1799, until Coleridge's demands began to prevail in him. Coleridge's incitement to present a philosophical view of his experience and to think on origins and process more systematically ran directly counter to the whole spontaneous form Wordsworth's experience had taken, and from one point of view it was an impossible contradiction of the whole way this experience had emerged. There is already, in the Second Part of the *Two-Part Prelude*, some significant revolt in him against the whole idea, where (echoing Milton's Raphael when faced with the task of conveying to earthly ears heavenly realities[27]) he questions if an analysis is even possible: "Hard task to analyse a soul, in which/ . . . / . . . each most obvious and particular thought—/ . . . / . . . Hath no beginning."(II.262) Or again: "How shall I trace the history, where seek/The origin of what I then have felt?"(II.395)[28] At the same time, Wordsworth could hardly have rejected Coleridge's demands outright, for this would have amounted to an admission very simply that he was not philosophically serious.

And yet those demands directly contradicted Wordsworth's whole direction with his experience, and the effect, in time, *was* his separation from it. We must note, especially, the deep repressive influence on him of Coleridge's incitement: Wordsworth is himself diverted from his own creative direction, and beyond this point continuity of vision is lost. His very status as a poet has changed. After 1799, Wordsworth is slowly and insidiously separated from his own most characteristic powers, though it takes time for him to consciously realize that this has happened. There is no consciousness of separation by late 1799, although there is at least an incipient awareness of conflict[29]. However, two years later he writes the first part of *Intimations*, definitely lamenting faded powers. He deludes himself into thinking he is still connected to them in January 1804 when he returns to *The Prelude* but finally comes to a formal consciousness of his situation by late winter. Conforming to his new vision in *Intimations*, he refers everything now to the childhood from which there has been a progressive and inevitable decline. As we have seen, this is precisely his argument as reflected in a section of Bk.V that was written in that very period when the second part of *Intimations* was also written.

(ii)

"The Things That I Have Seen
I Now Can See No More"

Wordsworth's Lost Experience, and Hauntings

When Wordsworth continued with *Intimations* in the late winter of 1804, he was now perfectly clear as to what it was that he had separated from. Significantly, the terms in which he develops his account take us back directly to Bk.I of *The Prelude*. There he had already taken note of those "Gleams like the flashing of a shield" (614), which he had "felt" spoke to him of "Remembrable things" and "joys that were forgotten"(635), and in *Intimations* he now links these, with great assurance, directly to a pre-birth existence. He claims a "Heaven" from which we have come in incarnating, which we bring down with us, and which we continue to have around us even into adolescence but which we lose sight of altogether by the time we reach early adulthood. It was Wordsworth's extraordinary destiny to have had this experience well into *his* adulthood, before it finally disappeared from sight for him also. This "Heaven", Wordsworth maintains, follows us down into the world as "the master light of all our seeing" and the ground of *all* visionary experience. In *Intimations* he conceives of this "Heaven", from which we originate and in which we pre-exist as souls, at once as an "imperial palace" and an "immortal sea". In Bk.I of *The Prelude*, he had, more intuitively, linked this world to the "sun" that shines down upon us in our infancy *from* that otherworld, and so the "charm" for him, he says, of "visionary things" that

> *almost make our infancy itself*
> *A visible scene on which the sun is shining*

> (662)

This power of "Heaven" is concentrated in our life on Earth especially in the young Child who, while this Heaven lives in him, is himself, however, unconscious of it. It remains rather for the poet, now

25

that he is *dis*-possessed of this power, to recognize it by reflection in the Child. Wordsworth is, however, by now confined strictly to a view of this power from the outside, however profound his adulation of the Child may be as the immediate bearer of this power, for knowledge has only come to Wordsworth after the fact:

> *Thou whose exterior semblance doth belie*
>   *Thy Soul's immensity;*
>
>   *. . . .Thou Eye among the blind,*
> *That deaf and silent, read'st the eternal deep,*
> *Haunted for ever by the eternal mind,—*

His argument from here is well-known. It is life's tragic irony that as children, just because we are unconscious of this possession, we are too ready to come *out* of our heavenly condition, in order to assume a role among adults long before we are required to do so. Then this condition is dissolved. It is the ultimate paradox that Wordsworth, now thirty-four, can nevertheless still affirm an ability to re-connect with this world with an imaginative force that, for a moment, *appears* to undo his final separation from it, claiming a fitful power to return:

> *Hence in a season of calm weather*
>   *Though inland far we be,*
> *Our Souls have sight of that immortal sea*
>   *Which brought us hither,*
>   *Can in a moment travel thither,*
> *And see the Children sport upon the shore,*
> *And hear the mighty waters rolling evermore.*

However it is only by force of the *poetic* imagination that Wordsworth can claim, oxymoronically, that he *has* succeeded in re-connecting with that otherworld. For it is, at best, as a reliquary memory, like the little life that remains in the embers of a fire that once burned fully[30], that

Wordsworth can pretend, as if for one last time, to have this powerful representation of the greater world that he has lost.

I shall have more to say about the profundity of Wordsworth's wishful effort here, when we consider more closely what counter-force he felt he was up against that had driven him to such desperate lengths. In the meantime, his association of this world of Heaven with 'sea' and 'sun' imagery, from the combined presentation of *Intimations* and Bk.I of *The Prelude*, allows us to fully measure his continued obsession with this world in his work, for indeed, one cannot overestimate the extent to which he remained haunted by this primal experience that he had lost. It is there once again in "the smiling sea" of *Elegiac Stanzas*, in the "gleam" and "light" that, he once thought, day by day continually lay over the sea in the area of Piel Castle when he visited there on holiday in his youth. Then was a "sea that could not cease to smile" from the effects of "sunbeams that did ever shine", or so Wordsworth imagines himself painting that scene at that time, when, he says, he might have thought his otherworldly experience a real one. At the time he is writing *Elegiac Stanzas*, when he was feeling embittered by loss at a number of levels, he pretends that he cannot credit such an experience as having ever been real (cf. "the light that never was"); in his youth he did not, in any case, fully comprehend the value of the experience he was having. We shall have to consider more closely at some point precisely how we are meant to take this apparent disavowal of his experience only some two years after *Intimations* was completed, but in the meantime we may note how Wordsworth's tortuous account throws an extraordinary aura over Piel Castle when it is projected in the midst of such a scene, as if here were another version of the "sunny dome" depicted in Coleridge's *Kubla Khan*:

> *Thou shouldst have seemed a treasure-house divine*
> *Of peaceful years; a chronicle of heaven;—*
> *Of all the sunbeams that did ever shine*
> *The very sweetest had to thee been given.*

That Wordsworth could once again immerse in this projected experience, to the elaborate extent he does in this poem, is already some indication that he continues to think more of it than he outwardly professes here. Experience of this otherworld is also reflected in some of the Sonnets he wrote some few months after the first part of *Intimations* was composed, when there was no question of his thinking this lost world an unreal projection. Once again there is a significant distance from and diminution of the experience, conveyed, for example, in *It is a beauteous Evening* in part through the image of a sun that is "sinking down" into the sea. But the effect still suggests strongly a reflection in the material world of the greater spiritual reality that once informed it:

> *It is a beauteous Evening, calm and free;*
>
> *. . . .the broad sun*
> *Is sinking down in its tranquility;*
> *The gentleness of heaven is on the Sea;*
> *Listen! the mighty Being is awake*
> *And doth with his eternal motion make*
> *A sound like thunder—everlastingly.*

Out of the extraordinary "calm" and "tranquility" of this moment, comparable to that which he will cite in *Intimations* as a basis for a fitful reconnection to that otherworld, the sun suddenly reflects here its heavenly form, while the sea anticipates, also by reflection, the effects of those "mighty waters" Wordsworth will seek to approach directly in the later poem. But it is all a memorial reflection only, paradoxically even somewhat disturbing, because of Wordsworth's consciousness of his distance from the otherworld, given his actual position in the world as it has become for him. Yet another aspect of the theme of *Intimations* is anticipated here, where he is ready to allow, by reflection in his uninspired daughter, that the primal reality nevertheless still *remains*, deep down, even if, like her, in a fundamental sense by now "we [all of us] know it not".

Other work by Wordsworth, both at this time and later, constitute more displaced expressions of his lost experience—among the most notable cases, his *Westminster* sonnet and *Daffodils*.[31] The profound experience that comes over him while riding out of Westminster in the early hours of the morning is conveyed in terms that likewise point to the primal experience insofar as the "sun" breaks through at this moment once again "in his first splendour", in intimate kinship with the "river" that is suddenly gliding "at his own sweet will" out of the pure depths of the primal impulse that is driving it towards the sea. All is in relation to the fact that the dwellers of this usually immensely busy City are themselves presently silenced, plunged in deep sleep, thus allowing "the mighty Being" at the heart of their existence to break through in spite of themselves.[32] We are at a somewhat greater remove from Wordsworth's primal terms in the case of *Daffodils*, although even there one feels an eruption of these terms amidst the displaced detail of "daffodils" and "sparkling waves"—in daffodils that, in "outdoing" the waves of the lake by the splendour of their "gaiety", incorporate into Wordsworth's consciousness both those "waves" *and* the sunlight the waves bear in them in their "sparkling" reflection, as an echo of the primal world that he once knew.[33]

In these poems, it may argued, Wordsworth is (in spite of himself) allowing something of his former relation to the primal scene to break through remotely, by reflection, among the details of the material circumstances into which he has been thrown out, as it were. In *Elegiac Stanzas*, as we saw, he pretends that his former absorption in the primal scene never was real, happy to think that he is now free of his illusions and that he knows himself to be in a condition that relates him to all the rest of his fellow mortals, quite properly. However, if any evidence were required to show that Wordsworth continued to pine for the world that he had lost, or that he thought this world altogether real, one would only need to cite his later *Ode Composed on an Evening of Extraordinary Splendour and Beauty*, written twelve years after *Elegiac Stanzas*. In this poem, there is once again, and for the last time it would appear, a memorial "glimpse" of the primal "gleam", which is, typically, accompanied by a "deep/And solemn harmony" that pervades the scene. It is a particularly weakened form of memory of it, conveyed by Wordsworth in advanced middle age (the quality of the poetic expression bears this out), but it

29

represents a kind of formal final acknowledgment, nevertheless, that the experience was far from ever being undesired:

> *This glimpse of glory, why renewed?*
> *Nay, rather speak with gratitude;*
> *For if a vestige of those gleams*
> *Survived, 'twas only in my dreams.*

> *Dread Power! Whom peace and calmness serve*
> *No less than Nature's threatening voice,*
> *If aught unworthy be my choice,*
> *From thee if I would swerve,*
> *O, let thy grace remind me of the light,*
> *Full early lost and fruitlessly deplored;*
> *Which at this moment on my waking sight*
> *Appears to shine, by miracle restored!*

The greater world of Heaven from which we emerge, in Wordsworth's view, at a certain point finds itself reflected, and is immediately expressed, in the material world around us. That possibility of correspondence is what offers any basis at all for Wordsworth's displaced memories of this greater world in his subsequent, alienated condition. These memories are themselves, however, merely other versions of an experience that at one time *was* the immediate thing for him, the most remarkable account of which perhaps is given in Bk.I of *The Prelude*—the "moon" standing in, in this account, where the "sun" could just as easily be.[34]:

> *The sands of Westmoreland, the creeks and bays*
> *Of Cumbria's rocky limits, they can tell*
> *How when the sea threw off his evening shade*
> *And to the shepherd's huts beneath the crags*
> *Did send sweet notice of the rising moon,*

30

How I have stood, to fancies such as these,
Engrafted in the tenderness of thought,
A stranger, linking with the spectacle
No conscious memory of a kindred sight,
And bringing with me no peculiar sense
Of quietness or peace—yet have I stood,
Even while mine eye has moved o'er three long leagues
Of shining water, gathering, as it seemed,
Through every hair-breadth of that field of light,
New pleasure, like a bee among the flowers.

(594)

Of this kind of experience Wordsworth would claim that

. . . .even then I felt
Gleams like the flashing of a shield. The earth
And common face of Nature spake to me
Rememberable things . . .

(613)

It is the kind of experience that he feels sure

must belong
To those first-born affinities that fit
Our new existence to existing things
And, in our dawn of being, constitute
The bond of union betwixt life and joy.

(581)

That account focuses *one* form in which the primal world manifested itself to Wordsworth through the material world of Nature. It was his

31

most direct form of the experience, the one in which this world presented itself as itself, as it were, a form of the experience as it arises out of the "peace and calmness" of which the later *Ode* speaks. More famously, Wordsworth's visionary experience manifested itself through "Nature's threatening voice", the later *Ode*'s other term, especially through those "severer interventions" (*The Prelude*, Bk.I,370) which Wordsworth maintains were especially instrumental in making him into the visionary poet he became. He had come to see *all* of his visionary experiences in the past in terms of an informing "light" that cast its "gleam" from within. This is the case also with those 'dark' episodes which he especially re-lives in these Books: the bird-and bird-egg-stealing episodes, and the boat-stealing episode—all those moments of "visionary dreariness" among which are also the one involving the girl walking through an intense wind with the pitcher on her head, and the simple scene involving one sheep and one tree that forever marked itself on Wordsworth's mind in the time that his father died. It is all to the point that these episodes have been described by one critic as both '*luminous* and enlarging experiences'[35]; the primal light is working directly through them also, and one feels also directly through Wordsworth's account of them—at least in the original representations of them of 1799. In *Intimations* it is especially *this* form of the experience in terms of which Wordsworth recognizes the "Dread power" at work in him in his youth. At the poem's climax, he re-invokes, by way of summarizing what he has lost, "Those shadowy recollections" of another world, "before which", he says,

> . . . .*our mortal nature*
> *Did tremble like a guilty Thing surprised.*

In each of these 'dark' episodes it is as if Wordsworth had come up against the limits of his adventurous spirit, where a seemingly unlimited freedom was suddenly bounded on the one hand by guilt and on the other by a dreary solitude and an awareness of mortality. Paradoxically, it was in these very moments that the primal Spirit revealed itself to him and informed him of its directing presence and influence, working in this case through the depths of darkness. This was clearly an educative process, designed to lead to a moral grounding in an otherworldly life streaming through *all* of Nature. Through episodes of this sort

Wordsworth was reached through a kind of "fear" or awe, that effect being rounded out from the other side by the typical episode which we have just looked at, in which his "eye" "moved" over "shining water", with an effect of "love". Effects of "love" and "fear" are how he came to represent this whole situation over time.[36] It strikes us how, in each of the dark episodes, one has to do with the Spirit present, in direct contrast with the deep "calmness" of the light episodes, in the form of a deeply troubling movement or "motion" (this word recurring in a good number of them). In some cases these episodes are explicitly associated with a strong wind or a stormy scene:

> . . . .*and when the deed was done,*
> *I heard among the solitary hills*
> *Low breathings coming after me, and sounds*
> *Of indistinguishable motion, steps*
> *Almost as silent as the turf they trod.*

> (Bk.I.328)

> ⁚ . . . .*oh, at that time*
> *While on the perilous ridge I hung alone,*
> *With what strange utterance did the loud dry wind*
> *Blow through my ears; the sky seemed not a sky*
> *Of earth, and with what motion moved the clouds!*

> (Bk.I.346)

> . . . .*the huge cliff*
> *Rose up between me and the stars, and still*
> *With measured motion, like a living thing,*
> *Strode after me.*

> (Bk.I.409)

> . . . .*I left the spot,*
> *And, reascending the bare common, saw*

A naked pool that lay beneath the hills,
The beacon on the summit, and more near,
A girl who bore a pitcher on her head
And seemed with difficult steps to force her way
Against the blowing wind . . .

       . . . .her garments vexed and tossed
By the strong wind.

(Bk.XI.301)[37]

And afterwards the wind and sleety rain
And all the business of the elements,
The single sheep, and the one blasted tree,
And the bleak music of that old stone wall,
The noise of wood and water, and the mist
Which on the line of each of those two roads
Advanced in such indisputable shapes—
All these were spectacles and sounds to which
I often would repair . . .

(Bk.XI.375)

One might well ask how any form of 'gleaming' presence can be said to appear in those episodes, but we shall find that this is the case, as soon as one brings into focus the intense application in 'seeing' and in 'hearing' that is going on in this young boy as the scenes unfold. "[T]hrough the gloom/I saw distinctly" is the basic formula of these many experiences (this phrase taken from the episode that relates a drowning in Esthwaite's Lake):

I heard among the solitary hills
Low breathings coming after me . . .

34

With what strange utterance did the loud dry wind
Blow through my ears;
> *. . . .and with what motion moved the clouds!*

the huge cliff
Rose up between me and the stars . . .

I left the spot
And, reascending the bare common, saw
A naked pool . . .

I watched,
Straining my eyes intensely as the mist
Gave intermitting prospect . . .

> (Bk.XI.360)

(this last instance from the episode associated with his father's death, marked by the one sheep and tree). Indeed, everything that the boy experienced, of both a light and a dark nature, was brought into distinct view through the complementary effort which he himself brought to bear on his experiences as these dramatically awakened the power of vision in him:

An auxiliary light
Came from my mind, which on the setting sun
Bestowed new splendour . . .
> *. . . .and the midnight storm*
Grew darker in the presence of my eye.

> (Bk.II.387)

In this last instance especially, we have the paradox of the light at work through an effect of darkness impressively accounted for. [I offer more on the great variety and complexity of Wordsworth's experiences in his youth below in Appendix I].

Wordsworth had thus had an experience of the light in and of itself and an experience of the light working through the darkness. Then he awakes one day to discover, in *Intimations*, that the "gleam" that had lived for him in all things is no longer there. Wordsworth is here speaking in a typical way:

> —*But there's a Tree, of many one,*
> *A single field which I have looked upon,*
> *Both of them speak of something that is gone:*
>   *The Pansy at my feet*
>   *Doth the same tale repeat:*
> *Whither is fled the visionary gleam?*
> *Where is it now, the glory and the dream?*

If one looks for what it is that gives the visionary experiences Wordsworth records in *The Prelude* their indisputable power and persuasiveness, we shall find it in those passages which, in his later presentations of *The Prelude*, survive intact from the original of 1799, word for word, at the climax of each account. There is a preternatural inevitability about these passages which he himself recognized, for they were always drafted virtually without alteration into the poem's later versions.[38] These passages bear witness to Wordsworth's complete identification with the process of universal influence he is tracing through them, and it is these passages that fully bear out, at the time they were written, his theories about the renovating power of those "spots of time" (Bk.XI.257), visionary experiences that continued to cast their influence into his present. At the time they were written in 1799, these passages had this power in themselves, but by 1804 things had changed; a new hand lies over his accounts, in the form of the many additional commentaries that now accompany Wordsworth's presentation of the experiences he had known. The power to absorb these experiences, so that a continuity is created, is gone. One can see that this power is gone from the way the light and the darkness are now presented; not, as in 1799, in an inevitable relationship one to the other but, in almost every case, through some form of additional reference that Wordsworth feels he must supply in order to suggest an optimistic unity which he no longer sees in his original experiences.

At the Crossroads

It is, indeed, almost as if these experiences no longer contained the moral integrity that he had otherwise assigned to them. Thus in some cases the greater emphasis put on the element of transgression in the experience, either by referring his actions to some standard of "peace" and "better reason" that has been violated by them, or a view of himself as "plunderer", where before he had been a mere "rover". [39] An intensified perception of the disturbing quality of the latter experience drives him to expand on the mystery by which discordant elements are in the end absorbed by the personality into a "calm existence"(360) in a passage in which it is far from clear that Wordsworth is fully confident about this transformation. His imagination seems to be overwhelmed in this instance rather by the burdensome thought of the extent to which he was challenged by all the "Regrets, vexations, lassitudes" to which he was *at this later time* exposed. [40] Among the more dramatic instances of Wordsworth's new distance from the early experiences he is reviewing by 1804 is the fresh take he offers on his experience of the drowned man at Esthwaite. In the original account, from the *Two-Part Prelude*, all the facts speak for themselves, and the whole description originates out of one unified experience:

> *At length, the dead man, 'mid that beauteous scene*
> *Of trees and hills and water, bolt upright*
> *Rose with his ghastly face.*

> (I.277)

In this description Wordsworth is himself identified with the universal process that at the time brought the dark facts of the drowned man's appearance into direct harmony with Nature's beautiful scene all around.[41] Already in the way the facts are presented, the darkness and the light merge into one process here. However, in re-presenting this account in 1804, it is as if Wordsworth felt he had to explain further just how, as a young boy, he could have absorbed such a gruesome sight as this of the dead man. To explain this, he resorts to the view that it was his previous reading in Romance literature that had prepared him for it:

> *And yet no vulgar fear,*
>
> *Young as I was, a child, not nine years old,*
>
> *Possessed me; for my inner eye had seen*
>
> *Such sights before among the shining streams*
>
> *Of fairyland, the forests of romance—*
>
> *Thence came a spirit hallowing what I saw*
>
> *With decoration and ideal grace,*

(Bk.V.473)

Whatever light these Romances may have cast over Wordsworth's imagination as he was reading them, it is very unlikely that it was *their* influence that prevailed in him at the sight of this dead man's body bolting upright before him in actual life. "[D]ecoration" and "ideal grace", as literary qualities intrinsically associated with those Romances, are hardly consistent with the impression of elemental facts that Wordsworth's original account conveys. In fact, Wordsworth passes here from the integral unity of the original experience, which he so faithfully records in his account of 1799, to a new theoretical view of the experience which seems quite wishful (if not merely wistful) in comparison, even if, artistically, it falls in with the presentation he is making in Bk.V, where this episode was finally placed, about the crucial value works of art do have in our lives.

More to the point still is what Wordsworth finally does with the episode involving the girl with the pitcher and the 'dreary' vision he had of her when, as a young boy, he stood stranded and lost under the

Penrith summit, in the midst of a blustery wind. To this episode he now
appends an account of a visit to this scene which he made with his sister
and with his future wife who was then but a young girl, as he declares,
"[l]ong afterwards", "in the blessed time of early love" when Wordsworth
was eighteen or so (he had had the experience at Penrith when he was
about five). In that later period, from the influence of that love, over that
scene at Penrith, "Upon the naked pool and dreary crags,/And on the
melancholy beacon", he says, now

> *fell*
> *The spirit of pleasure and youth's golden gleam—*
> *And think ye not with radiance more divine*
> *From these remembrances, and from the power*
> *They left behind? So feeling comes in aid*
> *Of feeling, and diversity of strength*
> *Attends us, if but once we have been strong.*

> (Bk.XI.321)

Recounting the import of this later experience, Wordsworth thus re-affirms
his characteristic philosophy of vision, according to which the visionary
experience of one time could be revived and built upon at another. But
significantly it is at just this point that he takes us through an extraordinary
shift in viewpoint. He launches into a characteristic paeon to the mystery of
Man's integral connection to the Universe, only to break down suddenly to
acknowledge that, in relation to the philosophy he has sought to re-live again
with this memory, he is now "lost"—capable, as he says, of comprehending
at least structurally whence the power of man's life comes, but otherwise
without the power to think himself into it any longer:

> *Oh mystery of man, from what a depth*
> *Proceed thy honours! I am lost, but see*
> *In simple childhood something of the base*
> *On which thy greatness stands . . .*
> *. . . .The days gone by*

39

Come back upon me from the dawn almost
Of life; the hiding-places of my power
Seem open; I approach, and then they close;
I see by glimpses now; when age comes on
May scarcely see at all; and I would give,
While yet we may, as far as words can give,
A substance and a life to what I feel:
I would enshrine the spirit of the past
For future restoration.

(Bk.XI.328) [42]

It is in recounting this particular memory that Wordsworth declares his new purpose in undertaking his account of his life in *The Prelude* as a whole. It is particularly fitting that he should declare his purpose here, because it is just here that he especially sensed how far he had come from his former experience of the continuity of vision. Could there be a more poignant measure of his helpless distance from that experience by 1804 than with reference to that time when he stood before the Penrith scene again with his first love? It compares with the time when he made his visit back to Tintern Abbey with his sister ten years later, except that at that time *Tintern Abbey* was produced as a complete record of that occasion whereas by 1804 Wordsworth is unable to say how the Penrith scene worked itself into the later visit associated with it, except for vague references to "remembrances" and "the power they left behind", which leave us asking what form precisely those "remembrances" took. No wonder that his real position, as one who from 1799 onwards has been severed from the continuity of visionary experience, suddenly breaks through here. At the same time, here is yet another instance in which Wordsworth felt he had to expand on the original visionary experience that is the putative focus of his account. Once again, he brings in another experience as if he felt he had to link the 'dreary' original to a more positive impression, which the "golden gleam" of the youthful happiness that later became associated with that scene provides.[43] All that was *intrinsically* positive about the original experience, a complete experience in itself, in the meantime has fallen away. It is referred, as in the other instances, to a new future-oriented purpose, both cheerful and moralizing, with which he is, strenuously, endeavoring to associate himself. Wordsworth would give himself up to this new purpose, in fact, with the same studious obsessiveness with which he had earlier committed to his visionary origins, and indeed the whole of the evolution of *The Prelude* may be said to be predicated on the way one obsession is inextricably involved in the other.[44]

Of further special interest, then, must be how Wordsworth comes to terms with the loss of his former visionary life, how he responds to his loss, for indeed much of *The Prelude* may be said to be about what he could still conceive for himself in spite of this loss.[45] But however far he extends himself with his further purpose in this poem, and however grand in the end is his projection for the future (and there seems to have been no limit to what he felt he could claim on behalf of the Poet of Nature to make up for what he had lost, as we shall see towards the end of this study), primarily his identity had been shaped by his disconnection from his past. Wordsworth's obsession with what he has lost prevails over his sense of purpose in *The Prelude* to this point: that he becomes, by 1804, *centred* in what he has lost, in relation to which his continuing account in *The Prelude* is ultimately reactive: he must try to summarize and abstract the history, and generalize the life he has lost, for future reference, before it is too late.[46] In the meantime the essential Wordsworth *remains* the Wordsworth who at a certain point turns his attention back, yearningly, to the "visionary gleam"—in *Intimations*. He thereby becomes the great poet of the 'light', in this sense of looking back, which becomes for him a way of seizing 'again' on what we bring into the world as an impulse of 'life'. His looking back to the light would remain his most cherished impulse *just because* he had had it and lost it when diverted from his own spontaneous development, as we have seen. Just when he turned his attention to the visionary life that had principally gone into making him as a poet, he found that he had been separated from it. That he had had it so close to hand, just before he could see that he had lost it, is what makes him subsequently yearn for it all the more, especially as he sees it all from the outside now, except for the occasional wishful flashbacks, and the impulse he has yet to poetically remember. What is more, a sudden new sense of death intensifies and is itself intensified by the thought of what he had, once, of the power of light and life. Wordsworth as the poet of the visionary life is lost, and it concerns him all the more now that he feels he faces death and a new darkness, "the darkness of the grave", without the light that he once knew.

(iii)

Death and "Dim Sadness" or *Tristitia*, and Resolution

Life Against Death

Here, however, we face another of our established prejudices about Wordsworth. Thus far, I have been dealing, implicitly, with one of these: our disposition to *over*-value the achievement of *The Prelude* at the expense of what Wordsworth presents about himself in *Intimations*, to which *The Prelude* is referred. Whatever else he may, in the long run, have achieved of grandeur in *The Prelude*, it may all of it be said to be, in the last analysis, derived from what he comes to lament as the final failure of the visionary experience that had made him into a poet of grandeur in the first place.[47] Another key prejudice about Wordsworth has led us to believe that his fundamental reaction to his separation from his visionary experience was that it was all for the better and that he had, in any case, been over-involved in that experience at the expense of a more proper concern with his own mortal kind. Surely he himself says as much in *Elegiac Stanzas*?

> *Farewell, farewell the heart that lives alone,*
> *Housed in a dream, at distance from the Kind!*
> *Such happiness, wherever it be known,*
> *Is to be pitied; for 'tis surely blind.*

Years later, in *Surprised by Joy*, he would take himself to task for losing sight, in a moment of renewed transport, of the grievous loss of his daughter, Catherine, who was barely three years dead:

> *Through what power,*
> *Even for the least division of an hour,*
> *Have I been so beguiled as to be blind*
> *To my most grievous loss?*

At the time of the writing of *Elegiac Stanzas* Wordsworth was but one year beyond the death of his brother, John, and there he similarly defers to this loss. But a contrary emphasis might as easily be put on the fact that in both cases he *is* diverted by a visionary "power" that *has* succeeded, if momentarily and in shadow-form, in absorbing him again by its own inherent value. The impulse to share himself in his renewed memory of this power, as in *Surprised*, has not died, any more than the memory of his daughter has died:

> *Surprised by joy—impatient as the Wind*
> *I turned to share the transport—Oh! with whom*
> *But thee, deep buried in the silent tomb,*

Likewise, in *Elegiac Stanzas*, as we have seen, the lengths to which Wordsworth does go in re-living the whole condition and bearing of the visionary world he had known, in spite of his sense of tragic loss in that moment, itself strongly testifies to the continuing worth, and reality, of that world, notwithstanding his decision to formally disavow it in this poem. There is, as we have seen, also the further evidence of the later *Ode* to cite in support of a view of his continuing obsession with this same world.[48]

On one side of the question, one surely recognizes the complete depth and sincerity of Wordsworth's grief over the loss of his brother and of his daughter, also the utter genuineness and pathos of his feeling that such realities must have a stronger claim on our sympathies as a simple emotional fact and a fact of life. In comparison with these unambiguous realities, a concern with what one knew of an extraordinary condition of being that has passed away *could* appear to be merely a poetic abstraction, especially to the more realistically- and worldly-minded souls who would see in that concern only the unreal self-absorption of which Wordsworth suspects himself. And it is easy to understand how, given these realities that pressed in on him at just this time, Wordsworth would respond by deciding that it is they that rather deserved his complete attention and devotion from the beginning. But this is to commit, or pretend to commit, to a direction in life that is no less abstract, for it amounts to believing that one is ever free to decide on any such one-dimensional course—to commit, for example, to perfection of the life at the expense of perfection of the work, or vice versa, which is hardly how it can ever turn out. On the other side of the question, one could as easily argue that Wordsworth's preoccupation with his former visionary life could only have intensified with his renewed encounter with the realities of mortality[49]—especially in the intensely private forms which he knew in this period of time. More to the point, one might say that the experience of mortality was bound to awaken in him all the more intensely the wonder of having ever had another experience that appeared to stand over and against death.[50] Indeed, given the great depth of his experience of visionary realities in his youth, which one dares to say was the equal of what he experienced in later life of grievous loss, it was inevitable that the impulse to know 'life' again, as he had known life, would have grabbed hold of him all the more hauntingly. This was especially the case as this visionary life, as we have seen, at one time reconciled *in itself* the apparent extremes of life and death, light and darkness. The incontrovertible value of that experience will explain, among other things, why Wordsworth's sense of the visionary life he had known grows only the more intense the more he appears to be on the verge of renouncing it, and why years later it is clear that his impulse to remember has never left him.

Outwardly, Wordsworth pretends to have renounced his visionary life, for the simple reason that it would have committed him to a task of further research and revelation for which he was no longer the equal—certainly not by this point when he was already defeated.[51] His attachment to this life, nevertheless, *remains* inwardly, as something he could only wish he *could* have carried over, likewise for the simple reason that it offered to preserve for him the other half of the equation of our existence, linking life to death. He had already offered his best effort of recovery in *Intimations*, where he is so bent on thinking at one point that his poetic remembering *has* taken him back:

> *Hence in a season of calm weather*
> *Though inland far we be,*
> *Our souls have sight of that immortal sea*
> *Which brought us hither*
> *Can in a moment travel thither,*

> And see the Children sport upon the shore,
>
> And hear the mighty waters rolling evermore.

However, *all* that he could manage by way of an effort has gone into his getting back here, just because he realizes that from hereon in he faces death—

> *In darkness lost, the darkness of the grave;*

without any notion that he has anything to meet it with. There is thus, as it were, a last-ditch attempt, and a very grand one, to roll back time, now that death looms before him without relief, and as unmitigated darkness—even before he will have to deal with the loss of his brother. Indeed one could say that Wordsworth's poem comes to a virtual *stop* here, in a massive caesura effect that suddenly lands him in a condition the exact polar opposite of that which he has been celebrating in the blessed Child:

> *Thou whose exterior semblance doth belie*
>
> > *Thy Soul's immensity . . .*
>
> > > *. . . .thou Eye among the blind,*
>
> *That, deaf and silent, read'st the eternal deep,*
>
> *Haunted for ever by the eternal mind,—*
>
> > *Mighty Prophet! Seer blest!*
>
> > *On whom those truths do rest,*
>
> *Which we are toiling all our lives to find,*
>
> **In darkness lost, the darkness of the grave;**
>
> *Thou, over whom thy Immortality*
>
> *Broods like the Day, A Master o'er a Slave,*
>
> *A Presence which is not to be put by;*
>
> *Thou little Child, yet glorious in the might*
>
> *Of heaven-born freedom on thy being's height,*
>
> **Why** *with such earnest pains dost thou provoke*

The years to bring the inevitable yoke
Thus blindly with thy blessedness at strife?

Wordsworth has been focusing on the primal inborn life of this Child, when suddenly the thought of death shoots in to arrest the flow of his encomiastic address, which he knows is by way of a valedictory tribute. And if, with a deliberate effort, after this disruption, he resumes this address, recovering its flow, it is only by way of leading to the all-decisive, bewildered question that marks the climax to this passage, which points the *way* to death.

It is arguably the great pivotal moment in Wordsworth's poetic career. On the one hand, all that was formerly known of the primal world and has now passed away from him for good is brought into focus in the Child, in the intensest form of knowledge he had ever expressed about that world, just as, on the other hand, death appears as its own doorway to another world before which Wordsworth stands completely bewildered because he is without any form of redress in the face of it. At this point a primal life and the reality of death appear completely polarized in his Imagination, the former falling away into its own sphere back into the past from which it emerged while the latter raises its ugly head from a future that is pure darkness, without light. The light that *would* serve to illuminate it, Wordsworth can see, we have left behind us, symbolizing it all in the Child

On whom those truths do rest,
Which we are toiling all our lives to find,
In darkness lost, the darkness of the grave;

It is, indeed, the chief tragic mystery of our existence that we leave behind us that primal visionary life that would have served to illuminate death, as it had for Wordsworth on a number of occasions.[52] Wordsworth realizes this himself more or less *fresh* from the experience of having finally left that life behind, and it is only understandable that, being the great poet that he was, *and himself at the time so close* to what he has lost, he would

49

wish so grandly to take us back, in a last-ditch effort to 'remember' those sources from which the primal life came.

It is, in a paradoxical sense, the climax to Wordsworth's long journey ever since the thought was sown in him that he should apply himself to the writing of *The Recluse*. Diverted in this way from the course of his natural development, he suddenly finds that he has separated from the primal life in which he shared, is made thereby the *more* conscious of what there had been, and *in* that intensified consciousness makes himself the more intensely and poignantly into the great poet of that life, for which we remember him. He thus lives back into the stream of that life with a more understanding consciousness, and with a more penetrating effect, than he might have if his own natural process of development had simply runs it course, to finally exhaust itself. It is how Wordsworth should principally *be* remembered, as the poet who went further than any other in re-connecting us, as far as he could, with those all-illuminating forces of life by which we are brought into the world and justified therein. *In* this context, the darkness and complete alienness of death is then, likewise, felt and understood all the more intensely, and *no bridge can be seen between these two spheres*. The darkness with which Wordsworth is suddenly confronted, which is terminally associated with "the darkness of the grave", forecasts an experience of pure material emptiness, amounting to the prospect of his own annihilation in a world become purely alien. It is without any hint whatever of the kind of spiritual influx which Wordsworth has known attached to it, and it brings to mind that whole other, *alien* world that momentarily broke in on him when he sat down to write *Resolution and Independence* two years earlier, a poem in which, it would appear, he uncannily anticipates his whole future inward condition.

The situation Wordsworth suddenly falls *out* of in *Resolution* (at this point, at least in his mind) suggests that whole form of genial, visionary life that he has known until now, from which he still does not see himself separated, as he does in *Intimations*:

> *My whole life I have lived in pleasant thought,*
> *As if life's business were a summer mood;*

> *As if all needful things would come unsought*
> *To genial faith, still rich in genial good;*

It is as if the tragic perception of himself as registered in *Intimations* had not yet fully sunk in or had not quite yet become incontrovertible. This we know to have been the case for as much as two more years, right up to late winter 1804 when the rest of *Intimations* was finally filled out. In *Resolution* Wordsworth still sees himself as possessed of that form of life which in *Intimations* he has already begun to fear is past; still he counts himself among the children who in their joy are bounding carelessly about him:

> *Even such a happy Child of earth am I;*
> *Even as these blissful creatures do I fare;*

Wordsworth's life is thus here still one uninterrupted continuity— *except for* the disturbing thoughts that suddenly take him over, which might easily be those that would naturally open out for him from the time he begins to doubt himself in *Intimations*:

> *And fears and fancies thick upon me came;*
> *Dim sadness—and blind thoughts, I knew not, nor could*
> *name.*[53]

He has been borne up by the genial powers on which he has always been able to count, but another prospect looms before him now, in the form of a world in which he sees himself potentially radically *dis*-possessed, and it is the peculiar terms of this world that should concern us, for they are altogether remote from those Wordsworth has been a part of thus far.

Poets, he declares, come into the world already well-supported because possessed of abilities that naturally incline them towards happiness and joy, but such natures are consequently all the more afflicted and weighed down when this good fortune gives way to hardship or sudden despondency, and bafflement.[54] The effect of a sudden fall into misfortune will on occasion drive the poet to madness and even—death, and one might actively bring on this condition simply from the fear that it will happen, as is Wordsworth's case in this poem. It is when he himself is immersed in such foreboding feelings that the Leech-Gatherer appears to him, as if to exhort him to a life of courage and endurance—this Leech-Gatherer who has had "many hardships to endure". Wordsworth looks to him for some comforting insight to help see himself through his newly "perplexed" condition. And from this intensely enigmatic figure Wordsworth *will* derive a powerful image of that firmness of mind he will wish to cultivate as he looks ahead to a future that must remain uncertain. By the end of the poem, in fact, he says he could "laugh himself to scorn" for the weakness he has shown in his doubts about himself and about the order of the world.

But what world exactly *has* materialized in and around this figure of the Leech-Gatherer? He himself is described as

> not *all alive nor dead,*
> *Nor all asleep—in his extreme old age:*
> *His body was bent double, feet and head*
> *Coming together in life's pilgrimage;*
> *As if some dire constraint of pain, or rage*
> *Of sickness felt by him in times long past,*
> *A more than human weight upon his frame had cast.*

It is not difficult to see that the figure who appears before Wordsworth symbolically embodies the condition of his own fear. One grasps the full force of the figure Wordsworth here imagines especially when one lays him alongside the glorious image of the Child as He is pictured in *Intimations*. The latter embodies the full radiance of those life-forces one brings with one into the world; "coming together in life's pilgrimage", at that point where life meets death, the Leech-Gatherer is, contrastingly, the image of what life, at its extremity, will have come to, once *dispossessed* of that earlier radiance and grandeur. The cycle of life will have come around to this final spectacle. All revolves around that condition of "dire constraint" which the Leech-Gatherer is said to have endured from a certain moment in his life, and which we easily associate with the fateful turning-point through which Wordsworth is living in this moment.

More significantly, this Leech-Gatherer is characterized in terms that link him directly to that world of a purely material, or biological, evolution that Darwin was to bring forward some fifty years later, the Leech-Gatherer appearing as if he might be

> *A sea-beast crawled forth, that on a shelf*
> *Of rock or sand reposeth, there to sun itself;*

Needless to say, something drastic has happened to the imagination of the "sun" that Wordsworth had so choicely and grandly linked from the beginning to that sphere of otherworldly life that he once perceived surging through Nature from beyond, from the time we come into the world, at the other extreme of the cycle. How else, however, could the world appear to him once that otherworldly life had died out and was no longer seen to operate through the world as it once did? In relation to that dire prospect, which has suddenly captured Wordsworth's imagination, the Leech-Gatherer appears as a consoling figure, as a dream-presence might whose purpose was to calm and reassure one in the face of one's worst fear, and as if there might still be some other greater cause that would appear to justify having to confront even so bleak a world as this.[55]

Consoling Imaginations

Wordsworth's tendency in this general period was to deal with the extreme dilemma into which he had been placed with *numerous* forms of consoling or reconciliatory imagination, as he desperately sought to find his own balance in the midst of his life-crisis. Over the two years after *Intimations* was completed there would be other unifying dreams in which the sphere of visionary life and the sphere of death are projected as reconciled. Some of these are poignantly tender, as in *The Solitary Reaper*, and *She Was a Phantom of Delight*. There is indeed the most intense poignancy to Wordsworth's outcry especially as regards his solitary reaper:

> *Will no one tell me what she sings?—*

This is because, in *her*, "natural sorrow, loss, or pain" and also "unhappy far-off things" are brought together into *one* form of "single"-ness, and

> *As if her song could have no ending;*

She is the *new* unitary experience after which Wordsworth now anxiously seeks, the *new* "music in his heart" which would ideally incorporate his own melancholy separation from the unitary life that he once knew, compounded as this melancholy is also by his personal angst over the enigma that now faces him of "natural sorrow, loss, and pain". On a less anguished plane, there is also the figure whom Wordsworth idealizes as a "phantom of delight" and

> *. . . lovely Apparition, sent*
> *To be a moment's ornament.*

whom some have regarded to be an idealization of his wife, Mary. This figure is herself projected as a

> *A Traveller betwixt life and death*

though this is a less challenging, and safe, figure. She could hardly fully satisfy Wordsworth's needs in the depths of his being, for in her one of the two polar elements that comprise the challenge of his existence is clearly diminished; thus she is, somewhat too nicely

> *A Creature not **too** bright or good*

> For human nature's daily food;
>
> For transient sorrows . . .

If only Wordsworth could have been reconciled to his situation by a simple, straightforward embracing of a lesser, more easily manageable complex of life.[56]

There would be no lack of ways to reconcile himself to the extremes of a polar existence. Thus in *Intimations* itself, he makes use of his 'return' to the source of life also to gather, if only to the extent that he can, a "faith" in the primal beneficence of the universe which he subsequently brings to bear on the prospect of death that now confronts him—what he famously formulates as "the faith that looks through death". Wordsworth goes so far as to deduce *from* his "recollections" of Childhood—that is, from those moments in which he had directly participated back to the otherworldly source of life, and which he strives strenuously to "remember" in this poem—"intimations" of the immortality that we must think must—therefore—await us beyond death.[57] Intricately involved in Wordsworth's projection along those lines is the associated idea that "out of human suffering" come "soothing thoughts": if that is the case, and this is often (though not always) borne out from experience, it is because the process of suffering to which we are subjected, and which leads to death, carries within itself a transformational element in which one *could* see the influence of those forces of life that seem to have fallen away. Death could in that case carry in *itself* the same transformational element, which in this ultimate sphere would translate into immortal life. This is the further basis for the case Wordsworth brings forward in this poem on behalf of a "faith that looks through death". On a more intricate, existential level also, beyond the calculations of a purely philosophical deduction (by which something "having been must ever be"), life may be thought to re-emerge from death. Finally, on the basis of this faith, strengthened from the experience over years, one could have developed the kind of "philosophic mind" that would allow one to accept the commonness of life, after life's forces have left us in their primal power. Something of that primal power must yet survive even in the "meanest flower that blows", because that power dynamically informed it when it came into life, and must therefore still lie somewhere in it while that flower has any life in it at all. Confronted subsequently with the residual spectacle of the mere commonness of life (it might, alternatively, be Wordsworth's "single field" or "tree" that at one time directly bore the influx of the primal power but does so no longer) one might weep for the loss of grandeur. However, in Wordsworth's projection one does not, because the philosophic mind 'knows' that a primal influence lies buried within, the same influence by which we could see ourselves, potentially, ultimately transformed, through our suffering over the course of our lives and by our deaths in the end.[58]

There is, however, one other line of thought which involved Wordsworth in considerations at the complete other extreme from a final acceptance of commonness. In *The Prelude*, so far from deferring to the commonness of things, he continued to seek on behalf of the visionary Mind or Imagination a form of recognition that would immerse us in the grandeur of *its* seemingly *limit*less power—and all this, in spite of the actual position he had inherited. There is the especially well-known instance of the Mount Snowdon episode, which belongs originally to Bk.V of the *Five-Book Prelude* and was later transposed to Bk.XIII in the 1805 text, virtually at the end of the work. In his strenuous climb up that mountain, Wordsworth found himself engaged by a scene of great sublimity, with the Moon shining immensely above, and a gigantic sea of mist suddenly at his feet and spreading out for miles around below him, usurping upon the *real* sea that lies in that region—the surrounding hills also gigantically breaking through the mist in that extraordinary, luminous moment:

> *I looked about, and lo,*
> *The moon stood naked in the heavens, at height*
> *Immense above my head, and on the shore*
> *I found myself of a huge sea of mist,*
> *Which meek and silent rested at my feet.*
> *A hundred hills their dusky backs upheaved*
> *All over this still ocean, and beyond,*
> *Far, far beyond, the vapours shot themselves*
> *In headlands, tongues, and promontory shapes*

Into the sea, the real sea, that seemed

To dwindle and give up its majesty,

Usurped upon as far as sight could reach.

(40)

Likewise a great "chasm" had presented itself in the midst of this sea of mist, from which innumerable water-sources had sounded out as with "one voice":

and from the shore

At distance not the third part of a mile

Was a blue chasm, a fracture in the vapour,

A deep and gloomy breathing-place, through which

Mounted the roar of waters, torrents, streams

Innumerable, roaring with one voice.

The universal spectacle throughout

Was shaped for admiration and delight,

Grand in itself alone, but in that breach

Through which the homeless voice of waters rose,

That dark deep thorough-fare had Nature lodged

The soul, the imagination of the whole.

(54)

Wordsworth's presentation here[59] does nothing less than recreate Coleridge's far-reaching presentation of the Imagination in *Kubla Khan*. There is a direct association between Wordsworth's "chasm" in his account, this "deep and gloomy breathing-place" from which rises the roar of innumerable waters, and Coleridge's own subterranean world of moving waters in his poem. Another association is between the mist that in Wordsworth's presentation extends itself over and throughout the scene, as far as the eye can see, and the course Coleridge's Alph takes through Kubla Khan's walled garden on its way back down to the "sunless sea"; likewise, Wordsworth's "mist", which arises from these waters, shoots itself "In headlands, tongues and promontory shapes / Into the sea, the real sea", of which Wordsworth says further that it

> seemed
>
> *To dwindle and give up its majesty,*
>
> *Usurped upon as far as sight could reach.*

As the years progressed Wordsworth would appear to have been especially haunted by Coleridge's sublime Imaginative landscape, and all this, it would appear, because Wordsworth was in reaction, "lost", and among other things reverting to Coleridge also for support as a former associate and "joint-labourer" (Bk.XIII.439) in the cause. In *Elegiac Stanzas*, Wordsworth supplies the last part of Coleridge's picture, where, as we have seen, he brings Piel Castle forward, in his own recollectively wishful picture, as

> a *treasure-house divine*
>
> . . . . *a chronicle of heaven;—*
>
> *Of all the sunbeams that did ever shine*
>
> *The very sweetest had to thee been given.*

thus invoking Kubla's "sunny dome".[60]

Let us step back to bring into focus this great tableau of the Mind's relationship to Nature, among the very great presentations English literature has had to offer. From the one side, from the "sun" of an *other*worldly source, come the streaming life-forces that, with our births, work their way into Nature through us. They are, as it were, 'caught' by the visionary Mind that builds its own sphere of creative culture out of them, "that sunny dome" that, among other things, casts its own shadow through and over Nature, making (to quote from Coleridge's poem) Nature's own "gardens [the more] bright" and "sunny". At some point these forces are in turn met from the other side, from that "chasm" of subterranean "waters" that derive from their own source from the deep earth itself, by the "river" of those creative forces that stream *out of* the earth that likewise resound through the Mind. *Together* these two forces make possible a form of creative civilization that would not only permeate living Nature but in time also usurp upon dead nature, that "real" or "sunless sea" of pure matter—material existence as such, which to all appearances would seem to defy any possibility of transformation by the Mind's forces.[61]

Thus did Wordsworth's deepest fear, which arose from his despair of being cut off from the visionary realities that had attended on him from birth—his fear of a material world that had become emptied of those realities and completely alien to them—find its antidote in this far-reaching Imagination shared with Coleridge. But Wordsworth would finally assume a very different position in relation to the opposed elements of that grand tableau we have been considering, and it is *Elegiac Stanzas* that best represents that position. On the one side, there had been that glorious primal life that he had known so uniquely and had so heroically re-visited after so dramatically losing his connection to it, that first world of his that Wordsworth might have been too happy, in later life, to throw over Piel Castle as its proper setting, endowing its environs with a "shining sea" that would have been the immediate earthly reflection of our heavenly origins. But on the other side, there now threatened, irreversibly it would seem, alien Nature, that "real sea" that, among other things, had claimed the life of his own sailor-brother, John. Beaumont's painting had so aptly captured this other side to Wordsworth's life-experience:

> *This sea in anger . . .*
> *The Hulk which labours in the deadly swell*
>
> *And this huge Castle, standing here sublime*

—"standing here sublime" in that it heroically braves the elements that threaten it from without:

> *I love to see the look with which it braves . . .*
> *The lightning, the fierce wind, and trembling waves.*

Such indeed had been Wordsworth's past, and such the destiny he had inherited in the present, and it had led him to renounce his former involvement in an otherworldly radiance—in which he had lived so intensely and so intently at one time—as a mere "dream", in comparison with the "reality" of our shared mortal existence with which we struggle together, while Nature is the alien force that it continues to be.

But Wordsworth's decision to go with one world at the expense of the other was, in the end, capitulation, and it could hardly have failed to rankle with him in the depths. Eschewing the deeper conflict in himself, and the deeper challenge, he had come to think that there remained but the one task of heroically enduring the inevitable prospect of human suffering. But even as he determined deliberately on this course, he knew that his had been a "dream" that could never die, and his the hope that one day the visionary Imagination might do more about the sad reality of our alien lot. Confronted as he was, at a certain point, with the prospect of death as such a dark entity, a certain stoical pessimism, combining with compassion for all humankind, was bound to take him over, and there is much evidence to suggest that he felt it morally incumbent upon him to associate himself primarily with this prospect, in sad sympathy with his mortal kind[62]. But there is much evidence, likewise, that Wordsworth throughout his life continued to confront death profoundly, at every stage fighting it off with his own characteristic powers, if only to the limited extent that remained to him. In this attitude he would not give up the earlier vision so easily, and he could only have wished he had been able to make more sense of the whole that included also that extraordinary spiritual grandeur he had once known and that had so suddenly gotten away from him. He had been so much about wanting to come through.

APPENDIX I
More On Wordsworth's Youthful Experiences

Each of Wordsworth's fundamental experiences, in connection with "fear" on the one hand and "love" on the other, has an additional dimension to it, in keeping with the profound realistic depth of his presentation. Thus the experience of "fear" involves the deeper polarity of "danger" and "desire". Relevant here are those episodes in which Wordsworth is brought face to face with the limits of his adventurous spirit by being exposed to "danger" in various forms, the effect of which is to curb impulses of "desire" which have grown too free. These latter impulses otherwise have their own proper creative function. For example, in an experience like the one he records in connexion with his ice-skating on Esthwaite's Lake, desire is given uninhibited rein. In this more innocent form it is no less creative of visionary experience than his more 'transgressive' expressions of it. Something of the extent of Wordsworth's desire in this episode is conveyed where he describes himself skating "across the image of a star" (i.e., across its reflection on the lake). Free desire leads up in this account climactically to the experience he would have when he very suddenly stopped himself from skating, and the landscape continued to "wheel" past him, "as if the earth had rolled/With visible motion her diurnal round". (Bk.I.474 *passim*) Thus Wordsworth can speak, in connection with his experiences in this *first* fundamental kind, generally of "Presences of nature" that

> Impressed upon all forms the characters
> Of danger or desire, and thus did make
> The surface of the universal earth
> With triumph and delight, and hope, and fear,
> Work like a sea . . .

> (Bk.I.497)

Likewise, in the case of the fundamental experience that Wordsworth would eventually classify under the effect of "love". Involved here are numerous moments of "pleasure, and repeated happiness" (632), among which we may count "every change /Of exercise and play to which the year/Did summon us in its delightful round." (502). Of these moments Wordsworth says that

> *the sun in heaven*
> *Beheld not vales more beautiful than ours,*
> *Nor saw a race in happiness and joy*
> *More worthy of the fields where they were sown.*
>
> (505)

Here we see how a more complex level of "desire" and "delight" could also merge with experiences of "pleasure" and "happiness". With this group of experiences we might include also the passion for

> *the rod and line . . .*
> *Which with its strong enchantment led us on*
> *By rocks and pools, shut out from every star,*
> *All the green summer, to forlorn cascades*
> *Among the windings of the mountain-brooks.*
>
> (511)

With "forlorn cascades" and what follows, we seem, in turn, to have reached the limits of the world of happiness, where a more complex delight is already turning towards darker areas, thus implying a line of continuity linking back to the other pole.

Wordsworth's presentation would appear, indeed, to be based in a clear concept of the full *round* of his experiences, highlighted at key points by a direct contact with the Spirit at work in Nature. We have seen (in the main body of my text) how this Spirit reveals itself dramatically through episodes of a dark nature involving "fear" and "danger". This is likewise the case among the many different forms of experience that identify themselves as experiences of "happiness", and among which there were very many (re: from the *Two-Part Prelude* : "All these, and more" (I.247); the Second Part of that *Prelude* itself adds many more to the compendium). However, among these experiences, of "pleasure and repeated happiness", there would emerge from time to time, as we have seen, that more definitive sort in which his "eye" "moved" over "shining water" (605), which brought Wordsworth his very deepest intimations of the otherworldly Spirit at work through his experiences, as if, in this case, he were being brought back to the source. Thus in a *second* fundamental sphere the Spirit likewise works in a two-fold way:

> *By pleasure and repeated happiness—*
> *So frequently repeated—**and** by force*
> *Of obscure feelings representative*
> *Of joys that were forgotten . . .*

(632)

Only in the sense, then, of the most comprehensive and varied experience, which Wordsworth had systematically in hand, should we understand his idea of a Spirit actively shedding Its influence in him through effects of both "fear" and "love".

"[F]ear" and "love" are how he came to represent this whole situation over time—by the spring of 1805, and in his final understanding of it (in the "Conclusion" in Bk.XIII) fear is ultimately referred to love

> *To fear and love*
> *(To love, as first and chief, for there fear ends)*

(143)

Thus is Nature's "threatening voice" ultimately subsumed in an all-resolving "calmness" (Wordsworth's terms from his later *Ode*; see above p.32). Wordsworth had come to see it in that way also as early as January of 1804 when he resumed with *The Prelude*, but the terms in which, at that time, he conveys this view bear more on his present distress, struggling as he was from his peculiar "perplexity" of this period, for one cannot imagine the youthful Wordsworth really exposed to "miseries", or suffering from "lassitudes":

> Ah me, that all
>
> The terrors, all the early miseries,
>
> Regrets, vexations, lassitudes, that all
>
> The thoughts and feelings which have been infused
>
> Into my mind, should ever have made up
>
> The calm existence that is mine when I
>
> Am worthy of myself. Praise to the end,
>
> (Bk.I.355)

A final 'calmness' served Wordsworth at this time rather as his projected or desired ideal, on the basis of what Nature seemed to accomplish:

> There is a dark
>
> Invisible workmanship that reconciles
>
> Discordant elements, and makes them move
>
> In one society.
>
> (352)

Yet what Wordsworth was *straining* after here, as a perception of how man is brought to unity in himself, Nature Herself effortlessly accomplished for him in his youth, as in this detail from the episode, as related in 1799, which recounts the drowning at Esthwaite's Lake:

> . . . .meanwhile the calm lake
>
> Grew dark with all the shadows on its breast,
>
> And now and then a leaping fish disturbed
>
> The breathless stillness.

(I.271)[63]

Here we can certainly speak of a 'reconciliation of discordant elements', but it is not so clear that one term ("dark") is subordinated to the other ("calm"), as in Wordsworth's later monism. His earlier presentation invokes rather a mutual *interpenetration* of terms, one term as it were flowing into the other. His late presentation of the matter, in the *Ode on an Extraordinary Evening*, implies dualism:

> *Dread Power! whom peace and calmness serve,*
>
> *No less than Nature's threatening voice*

Significantly, however, nowhere in Bk.I in those passages which date from the time of their original composition in 1799, shall we find any suggestion of the subordination of the dark element to the light, or of "fear" to "happiness" etc, but rather an emphasis on simultaneous, equivalent presence and influence.

APPENDIX II
Wordsworth's 'Awful Doubt': In the Simplon Pass

Also to be considered in the context of his deep anxiety about the future condition of Nature is Wordsworth's narration of his passage through the Simplon Pass in the Alps, as given in Bk.VI of *The Prelude*. *Thirteen years before*, in 1791, anticipating that he would soon be crossing into the Alps, he discovered that, without knowing it, he had already done so, and in his disappointment and frustration of the moment was suddenly displaced in time and space, transposed into another sphere in a way that was typical of his early experience. *Thirteen years later*, Wordsworth once again draws his inevitable view of that event:

> *here that power,*
> *In all the might of its endowments, came*
> *Athwart me. I was lost as in a cloud,*
> *Halted without a struggle to break through,*
>
> *And now, recovering, to my soul I say*
> *'I recognize thy glory'. In such strength*
> *Of usurpation, in such visitings*
> *Of awful promise, when the light of sense*
> *Goes out in flashes that have shewn to us*
> *The invisible world, doth greatness make abode,*
> . . . .
> *Our destiny, our nature, and our home*

Is with infinitude—and only there;

With hope it is, hope that can never die,

Effort, and expectation, and desire,

And something evermore about to be.

(527)

After this great paeon to hope, with its basis in a view of the mind's link to the inspirational influences of the visionary world, Wordsworth suddenly turns his attention to the acutely stark impression made by the Arve Ravine, a shift that is as startling as anything else in this astoundingly multi-faceted, meandering poem, but Wordsworth's imagination was at this time in a great swirl[64]:

The immeasurable height

Of woods decaying, never to be decayed,

The stationary blasts of waterfalls,

And everywhere along the hollow rent

Winds thwarting winds, bewildered and forlorn,

The torrents shooting from the clear blue sky,

The rocks that muttered close upon our ears—

Black drizzling crags that spake by the wayside

As if a voice were in them—the sick sight

And giddy prospect of the raving stream . . .

(556)

It would indeed be hard to say just how it was that Wordsworth, after his latest typical paeon to the visionary world, could turn his attention to such an alien scene (alien in terms also of his whole poetic world up to that point), but, as we saw, *unconsciously* his attention *had* shifted, to the real, physical Nature that, in its dark materiality, is the direct *antithesis* of the Imagination, as Shelley himself later saw it. In Shelley's case there is, already from early on, the presence of this oppressive antithetical concern, which *he* would bring to consummate expression in *Mont Blanc*. Shelley has himself been standing on a bridge looking over the River Arve: a deep ravine and the valley below, the mountain and glacier above:

> *awful scene*
>
> *Where Power in likeness of the Arve comes down*
>
> *From the ice gulphs that gird his secret throne,*
>
> *Bursting thro' these dark mountains like the flame*
>
> *Of lightning through the tempest*

Climaxing Shelley's presentation in his poem is a perception of alien Nature's overwhelmingly destructive power over man in time, such that Nature can only, in his own words, teach an "awful doubt"[65]:

> *The glaciers creep*
>
> *Like snakes that watch their prey, from their far fountains,*
>
> *Slow rolling on; there, many a precipice,*
>
> *Frost and the Sun in scorn of mortal power*
>
> *Have piled: dome, pyramid, and pinnacle,*
>
> *A city of death, distinct with many a tower*
>
> *And wall impregnable of beaming ice.*
>
> *Yet not a city, but a flood of ruin*
>
> *Is there, that from the boundary of the sky*
>
> *Rolls its perpetual stream; vast pines are strewing*
>
> *Its destined path, or in the mangled soil*
>
> *Branchless and shattered stand: the rocks, drawn down*
>
> *From yon remotest waste, have overthrown*
>
> *The limits of the dead and living world,*
>
> *Never to be reclaimed. The dwelling place*
>
> *Of insects, beasts and birds, becomes its spoil;*
>
> *Their food and their retreat forever gone,*
>
> *So much of life and joy is lost. The race*
>
> *Of man flies far in dread; his work and dwelling*

> *Vanish, like smoke before the tempest's stream,*
> *And their place is not known.*

In such a sublime imagination—in its own way as sublime as anything in *The Prelude*—Shelley is the great successor to the newly engaged Wordsworth who had emerged from his lost years unconsciously with the same disturbed perception about Nature, though he himself would not plumb the matter any further. In fact in his own Simplon account viewed as a whole, Wordsworth *thinks* himself still in the vein of his unitary Imagination of old. But here is suddenly *another* world quite distinct from the one he had for long been typically contemplating, a whole new world of *alien* Nature, the very world that Shelley would maintain *resists* the cheerful sense of unity which Wordsworth would insist on associating himself:

> The immeasurable height
> *Of woods decaying, never to be decayed,*
> *The stationary blasts of waterfalls,*
> *And everywhere along the hollow rent*
> *Winds thwarting winds, bewildered and forlorn,*
> *The torrents shooting from the clear blue sky,*
> *The rocks that muttered close upon our ears—*
> *Black drizzling crags that spake by the wayside*
> *As if a voice were in them—the sick sight*
> *And giddy prospect of the raving stream,*
> *The unfettered clouds, and region of the heavens,*
> *Tumult and peace, the darkness and the light*
> *Were all like workings of one mind, the features*
> *Of the same face, blossoms upon one tree,*
> *Characters of the great Apocalyps,*
> *The types and symbols of Eternity,*
> *Of first, and last, and midst, and without end.*

One will wonder at Wordsworth's effort here to suggest a greater unity when the greatest portion of his account is immersed in Nature as a scene of unrelieved darkness, except for the single references, in that final shift, to "unfettered clouds" and the "region of the heavens", which barely allow the effect he intends of bringing the whole back to unity. Even the earlier reference to "the clear blue sky" one will feel partakes of the stark coldness of the rest. But it is a measure of the conflict in himself by this point: between his old faith, which would die hard, and the hidden depths of a new anxiety much too disturbing, after the old life, to bring immediately into consciousness. But this is precisely what Shelley *would* do.[66]

The Composition of *The Prelude* in relation to *Intimations:* A Working Chronology[2]

Oct.1798-Feb.1799	The First Part, which is to become Bk.I, parts of which are transferred to Bk.XI by spring 1805
Late 1799	The Second Part, which remained substantially unchanged when it became Bk.II (**the *Two-Part Prelude* completed**)
Spring 1802	*Intimations*, Stanzas I to IV
Jan. 1804	The First Part, become Bk.I, revised and added to, Bk.III
Mar. 1804	Bk.IV, which becomes Bk.IV and Bk.V by spring 1805
	Intimations, Stanzas V to XI
	Bk.V, which becomes the last two-thirds of Bk.XI and the first half of BK.XIII by spring 1805 (**the *Five-Book Prelude* completed**)
Apr. 1804	Bk.VI

---

[2]   For full details see *The Prelude, 1799, 1805, 1850*, ed. Wordsworth, Abrams, Gill, 512 *passim*.

June 1804	Bk.IX and first half of Bk.X
Oct. 1804	Bk.VIII
Nov. 1804	Bk.VII
Dec. 1804	rest of Bk.X
May 1805	rest of Bk.XI, Bk.XII, rest of Bk.XIII, Conclusion (*1805 Prelude* **completed**)

ENDNOTES

1   During his confinement in Germany, Wordsworth may well have felt the threat of an extreme suffocation of his creative faculty suggestive of the one he had known years before when he experienced his great crisis of moral despair over the disastrous direction the French Revolution had taken. It was at that very time that Nature had 'returned' to him to save him, thanks to the intervening graces of his sister who already saw in him the poet of Nature he was destined to be, the very Nature from which Wordsworth was once again radically separated while in Germany.

2   This is to address in other words the import of the enigmatic opening of which Seamus Perry in *The New York Review of Books* (Vol. 30 Number 24) has given his own account, summarizing the mainstream view: "'This' is a disorienting sense of sudden disability, of colossal hopes unexpectedly embarrassed.' (26)

3   It is generally thought that Wordsworth had *The Recluse* in mind where he refers, in the "glad preamble" which opens *The Prelude*, to *the hope/.../ Of prowess in an honorable field* (50). The text with which, in 1804, he takes up again from his "glad preamble" also makes immediate allusion to this major preoccupation: *nor did I fail/To add meanwhile assurance of some work/Of glory, there forthwith to be begun* (85).

4   See:

> *And now it would content me to yield up*
> *Those lofty hopes awhile for present gifts*
> *Of humbler industry. But...*
> *The poet…..............*
> *Hath….his unruly times—*
> *...........................*
> *Unmanageable thoughts*

> (142)

Already at the time of the writing of the (first) Sonnets (circa 1802), Wordsworth had some clear sense of turning to these as a way of finding relief from the burden of his continued commitment to *The Recluse*, just because, four years later, he still had nothing to show for it. If only allusively, his *Prefatory Sonnet* would appear to confess as much:

> *Pleas'd if some Souls (for such there needs must be)*
> *Who have felt the weight of too much liberty,*
> *Should find brief solace there, as I have found.*

Wordsworth felt bound, in this period of time, to justify his return, with the sonnet, to a form of poem that had long been seen as *passé*.

5   Cf. *Lycidas*:

> *Alas! What boots it with uncessant care*
> *To tend the homely slighted shepherd's trade,*
> *And strictly meditate the thankless muse?*
> *Were it not better done, as others use,*
> *To sport with Amaryllis in the shade,*
> *Or with the tangles of Neaera's hair?*
> *Fame is the spur…*

6   *Was it for this…?* A tempting analogy suggests itself between Wordsworth returned, with these lines, to his enterprising self after putting his poem off for years, and Hamlet returned to *his* task with the 2nd visitation of the Ghost:

Hamlet
> *Do you not come your tardy son to chide,*
> *That, laps'd in time and passion, lets go by*
> *Th'important acting of your dread command?*

Ghost:
> *Do not forget….*

7   Here the analogy with Hamlet might be continued, as Wordsworth pursues his own way.

8   Wordsworth's main impulse on returning to his poem at this time is well summarized in a phrase from the original that he would have been coming across again (from Bk.I.586):

> *Yes, I remember…*

9   Thus Coleridge, in October 1799: 'I long to see what you have been doing. O let it be the tail-piece of "The Recluse!" for of nothing but "The Recluse"

can I hear patiently…' (See *Collected Letters of Samuel Taylor Coleridge*, ed. E.L. *Griggs*, Oxford, 1956-1971, vol. 1, 538.)

10   For a full inquiry into Wordsworth's expressions of resentment towards Coleridge in *The Prelude*, see Lucy Newlyn's chapter "A Strong Confusion': Coleridge's Presence in *The Prelude*' from her book *Coleridge, Wordsworth, and The Language of Allusion* (Oxford: Clarendon Press, 1986).

Coleridge, from his side, did express himself, in private, in a critique of Wordsworth's creative dallying during the period of the writing of his Sonnets, which Coleridge saw as 'hurtful' to him (Newlyn, 97); Coleridge otherwise refrained, in this overall period, from 'openly confronting' his 'disappointment'. (Newlyn, 98).

Ironically, Coleridge would seem to have been totally unaware of the immense repressive effect *he* had had on Wordsworth, which rather significantly complemented the devastating repressive effect Wordsworth had had on him, as narrated by Ted Hughes. See the latter's Introduction to his *Choice of Coleridge's Verse* (London: Faber, 1992)14.

11   The new material became, in the still greater re-working of his piece after Coleridge's departure in March 1804, Books IV and V and the last two thirds of Book XI of the 1805 text. The first part of Bk.XIII was also written at this time. There were, of course, changes, additions and revisions made along the way.

12   These lines had been composed by late winter 1804 and are thought to have formed part of the *Five-Book Prelude*.

13   Wordsworth 'knew': he may have continued to *think* that *The Recluse* was the right idea for him, but he knew.

14   Newlyn, with her eye on Wordsworth's resentment in *The Prelude*, sees the role into which Coleridge is consequently put, generally, as '[f]orced' (181). Contrastingly, Jonathan Wordsworth in *William Wordsworth: The Borders of Vision* (Oxford: Clarendon, 1982), makes much of Wordsworth's 'sense' in *The Prelude*, 'that he and Coleridge have in common of a falling-off from the shared idealism and shared certainties of spring 1798.' (337)

15   I treat this section of Wordsworth's poem more fully below, in n.44.

16   The irony here of course is that Wordsworth feels he must apologize to Coleridge for being diverted from his work on *The Prelude*, when it is work on *The Recluse*, and not *The Prelude*, that Coleridge expects of him.

17   Both *Soldier* and *Boy* had been composed by 1798.

18   All of the references in this paragraph are to material Wordsworth had written by the late winter of 1804 when *Intimations* was also completed. See Wordsworth, Abrams, Gill, 178n.2:"Wordsworth…has very probably just completed the *Intimations* ode…".

19   Re:

> *And now it would content me to yield up*
> *Those lofty hopes awhile for present gifts*
> *Of humbler industry. But…*
> *The poet…...............*
> *Hath….his unruly times—*
> (See n. 4.)

20   We need constantly to remind ourselves, along with Jonathan Wordsworth, that 'this is 1804 not 1798.' (317). There is also Wordsworth's general case: 'as so often when Wordsworth is writing at his best, there is a disparity between what one takes to be there, and what is actually claimed.' (318)

21   *Tintern Abbey*, written in 1798, offers the most powerful expression of the earlier faith. Thus, building on the primal experience of Nature he had had in his early youth, Wordsworth can still speak here of a direct line of visionary influence that climaxes in his present perception of a universal life that flows through all things:

> *And I have felt*
> *A presence that disturbs me with the joy*
> *Of elevated thoughts; a sense sublime*
> *Of something far more deeply interfused,*
> *Whose dwelling is the light of setting suns,*
> *And the round ocean, and the living air,*
> *And the blue sky, and in the mind of man,*
> *A motion and a spirit, that impels*
> *All thinking things, all objects of all thought,*
> *And rolls through all things.*

22   Re:

> *While here I stand, not only with the sense*
> *Of present pleasure, but with pleasing thoughts*
> *That in this moment there is life and food*
> *For future years.*

There is thus a weakly parodic relationship between the earlier faith and the later as represented in the following passage already quoted:

> *and I would give,*
> *While yet we may, as far as words can give,*
> *A substance and a life to what I feel:*
> *I would enshrine the spirit of the past*
> *For future restoration.*

(XI.337)

23   My phrase combines two terms from different sections of *Tintern Abbey*. Wordsworth himself uses this full expression in *Resolution and Independence* (see p.51).

24   Thus:

> *--if, in this time*
> *Of dereliction and dismay, I yet*
> *Despair not of our nature, but retain*
> *A more than Roman confidence, a faith*
> *That fails not, in all sorrow my support,*
> *The blessing of my life, the gift is yours,*
> *Ye mountains,—thine, O Nature. Thou hast fed*
> *My lofty speculations, and in thee*
> *For this uneasy heart of ours I find*
> *A never-failing principle of joy*
> *And purest passion.*

(486)

This text is still very close to the spirit, and the very language, of *Tintern Abbey*, in contrast with later expressions of similar sentiments when Wordsworth continued with *The Prelude* from a more self-alienated distance through 1804 (as I argue on p.18). Cf. with this passage from the Second Part—e.g., *and in thee.../...I find*—the following from *Tintern Abbey*: *and in thy voice I catch/...in thee what I once was.* But the Second Part is a strange mixture of original experience and a sudden, artificial abstraction of that experience that derives from a new, awkward self-consciousness about his past that overtakes Wordsworth at this time (as I illustrate in n.38). Already by late 1799 Wordsworth was on his way out of his primal world and fast moving into another.

25   And so:

> ...the soul—
> Remembering how she felt, but what she felt
> Remembering not—retains an obscure sense
> Of possible sublimity, to which
> With growing faculties she doth aspire
> With faculties still growing, feeling still
> That whatsoever point they gain they still
> Have something to pursue.

(II.364)

Cf., also, the following passage from Bk.VI, written in the spring of 1804:

> Our destiny, our nature, and our home
> Is with infinitude, and only there;

(538)

26 In this and in the following paragraphs, in my main text and in the notes, it seemed more appropriate to quote from the *Two-Part Prelude*.

27 See Bk.V.563 from *Paradise Lost*:

> Hard matter thou enjoin'st me, O prime of men—
> Sad task and hard; for how shall I relate
> To human sense...invisible exploits
> ....
> ....How...unfold
> The secrets of another world...

28 Cf., also, from the Second Part:

> Who knows the individual hour in which
> His habits were first sown even as a seed?
> Who that shall point as with a wand, and say
> 'This portion of the river of my mind
> Came from yon fountain'?

(245)

For a different view, cf. Newlyn, who sees Wordsworth as happily identified with this task: 'Wordsworth is only rhetorically unsure of what he is doing. "'The unity of all", he implies, will be revealed, as *The Prelude* unfolds.' (169)

29   Cf. from the Second Part:

> *...so wide appears*
> *The vacancy between me and those days,*
> *Which yet have such self-presence in my heart*
> *That sometimes when I think of them I seem*
> *Two consciousnesses—*

(26)

One might even claim the premonition of separation from his inspirational source in the Lucy poems of 1798, all of which are based in an idea of Lucy's dramatic removal to another sphere.

In both of the instances I am citing here, the consciousness of separation is double-edged: creative of the kind of temporal depth on which Wordsworth's memorial imagination thrives (his "spots of time" have their effect precisely because they have withdrawn into the past) *and*, potentially, *threatening cleavage*.

30   This is Wordsworth's own metaphor for it, from this same poem:

> *That in our embers*
> *Is something that doth live,*

31   *Westminster* was written in the same period as *It is a beauteous Evening* (some few days before only) and may even be said to be a complement to it. *Daffodils*, a school-text title for *I Wandered Lonely as a Cloud*, makes for a more convenient form of reference to that poem here.

32   The reader will not have failed to notice that in the case of three of the poems I consider in this section, the basis for visionary memory, variously experienced, is a deep 'calmness', which Wordsworth would go on, rather ambiguously, to make into a favoured form of inspiration. I discuss this issue below in Appendix I.

33   It is an extensively moving poem inasmuch as Wordsworth goes on to speak of the ongoing inspirational influence that he has often felt since he first came upon the daffodils, thus echoing pathetically also his most famous view of that kind of unbroken effect as given in *Tintern Abbey* (see above pp. 18-19):

> *I gazed and gazed—but little thought*
> *What wealth the show to me had brought:*
>
> *For oft when on my couch I lie*
> *In vacant or in pensive mood,*
> *They flash upon that inward eye*
> *Which is the bliss of solitude;*
> *And then my heart with pleasure fills,*
> *And dances with the daffodils.*

34   One would wish it *had* been the sun. The anomaly could be explained in literal terms: the lunar setting *was* the actual scene Wordsworth was remembering. At the other extreme, assuming alternatively that Wordsworth fully envisioned a symbolic difference between sun and moon, his choice of moon over sun would convey a concern less with the otherworldly source of inspirational life than with the reflective power of his own consciousness, though not in any comfortably separate, Kantian form but as the expression of the unity of consciousness and Nature and the otherworldly life that lies behind it. There is a similar (distant) interplay of inspirational, diurnal life and individual, nocturnal consciousness in *The Daffodils*, the daffodils being themselves associated with the stars.

35   See Seamus Heaney, from his Introduction to his collection of poems by Wordsworth (London: Faber, 2005) ix.

36   In the "Conclusion" to the poem—see Bk.XIII.143, written in the spring of 1805.

37   This passage and the one that follows belonging originally to the First Part of the *Two-Part Prelude*.

38   It is significant that Wordsworth had *already* accounted for all of these experiences at the time of his original writing of the First Part of the *Two-Part Prelude*, when he first threw himself into what it was that had made him into a visionary poet. He is clearly still at that time in intimate communion with the influences that streamed through him in these episodes, it would appear just because he was not yet thinking too much about them. In comparison, it is easy to feel that in the Second Part, written some months later in late 1799, he had already become (somewhat awkwardly) self-conscious about his venture into his past, in some places merely echoing his expression in the First Part or adding to it merely in a general way by enumerating almost every other form of experience he can remember having. Cf.

> 'Twere long to tell
> *What spring and autumn, what the winter snows,*
> *And what the summer shade, what day and night,*
> *The evening and the morning, what my dreams*
> *And what my waking thoughts, supplied to nurse*
> *That spirit of religious love, in which*
> *I walked with Nature.*

(II.401)

> *Thus did my days pass on, and now at length*
> *From nature and her overflowing soul*
> *I had received so much that all my thoughts*
> *Were steeped in feeling. I was only then*
> *Contented when with bliss ineffable*
> *I felt the sentiment of being spread*
> *O'er all that moves, and all that seemeth still,*
> *O'er all that, lost beyond the reach of thought*
> *And human knowledge, to the human eye*
> *Invisible, yet liveth to the heart,*
> **O'er all that leaps and runs and shouts, and sings,**
> **Or beats the gladsome air, o'er all that glides**
> **Beneath the wave, yea in the wave itself...**

(II.445)

In the last several lines there is a crude echo of the climactic account in *Tintern Abbey.* Cf:

> *A motion and a spirit that impels*
> *All thinking things, all objects of all thought*
> *And rolls through all things.*

In the Second Part of the *Two-Part Prelude* Wordsworth is, at the same time, also separating out from his experiences of Nature that "superadded soul", or "plastic power", that "auxiliary light" (377, 411, 417) which he will later recognize as the matrix of all his visionary experience, though he does so here only very abstractly, already diverted, it would seem, by the injunction to analyze. Appropriately (and ironically), he calls upon Coleridge at the end of this Part in support, as if to vindicate his efforts to understand himself in the more studied form of this Part. Only a few passages in the Second Part in fact show the *un*-self-conscious form of the First Part: e.g., the infant-Babe passage, and the passage commemorating Wordsworth's boating-expeditions on Lake Windermere. In the meantime he had amply demonstrated his unfitness for abstraction at least at this time, being as

83

we have seen primarily made for spontaneous development. And it was already by then too late; he had already separated from himself.

[39] See from Bk.I:

> *Moon and stars*
> *Were shining o'er my head; I was alone,*
> *And seemed to be a trouble to the peace*
> *That was among them. Sometimes it befel*
> *In these night-wanderings, that a strong desire*
> *O'erpowered my better reason, and the bird*
> *Which was the captive of another's toils*
> *Became my prey;*
>
> (321)

In comparison with which the original (from the *Two-Part Prelude*) is more neutral and indulgent and even creates a positive impression of vitality:

> *Gentle powers,*
> *Who give us happiness and call it peace,*
> ....
> *...how my bosom beat*
> *With expectation! Sometimes strong desire*
> *Resistless overpowered me, and the bird*
> *Which was the captive of another's toils*
> *Became my prey;*
>
> (I.35)

Consider also, from the 1805 text:

> *Nor less in spring-time...*
> ....
>   *...when the vales*
> *And woods were warm, was I a plunderer then*
> *In the high places...*
> ....
>   *...Though mean*
> *My object and inglorious, yet the end*
> *Was not ignoble.*
>
> (333)

and *its* original:

> *Nor less in spring-time...*
> ....

> *...when the vales*
> *And woods were warm, was I a rover then*
> *In the high places...*
>
> *...Though mean*
> *And though inglorious were my views, the end*
> *Was not ignoble.*

(I.50)

40   Consider from Bk.I:

> *Ah me, that all*
> *The terrors, all the early miseries,*
> *Regrets, vexations, lassitudes, that all*
> *The thoughts and feelings which have been infused*
> *Into my mind, should ever have made up*
> *The calm existence that is mine when I*
> *Am worthy of myself.*

(355)

There is little evidence in Wordsworth's early experiences, as originally recounted, of any such weakened forms of negative import as his characterizations here suggest: *early miseries/Regrets, vexations, lassitudes*. On the contrary all of those early experiences have something portentously harmonious about them, as I argue in the body of my text: all negatives are immediately absorbed into an effect that is overwhelmingly positive, an effect supplied from within the experiences themselves. Wordsworth's characterizations at this point reflect rather on his experience in the present, which he has anachronistically (if poignantly) interpolated into his text. What, for example, do his earlier experiences have to do with "lassitude"? though the term is altogether fitting of Wordsworth's present case as he accounts for this in some of the first material he wrote when he comes back to the poem in 1804 (this I have covered above). In fact it is Wordsworth's *original* experiences which are positive, his *later* experience which has resolved into something negative, while ironically Wordsworth sees the past as harboring a negativity that he feels he must correct and would cheerfully supply the missing positive. It is only a perversely modernist view that will insist on reading back into the original account the negative suggestions Wordsworth introduces here. This Seamus Perry allows himself to do in the article quoted above, which takes its title from Wordsworth's phrasing: "Regrets, Vexations, Lassitudes"(see n.2). Thus Perry perversely polarizes the terms of Wordsworth's original account, which harmonize inherently, reducing them to stereotypes: 'the boy

85

Wordsworth is not wandering seraphically in the company of God, but is a solitary figure, bewildered, frightened, guilty, forsaken.'(27) For more on this passage, see my Appendix I.

Yet another example of Wordsworth's abstractive manipulations of his material at this later stage is where the original testifies (famously) to how in his early youth:

> *...huge and mighty forms that do not live*
> *Like living men moved slowly through* [his] *mind*
> *By day, and were the trouble of* [his] *dreams.*

(Bk.I.424)

Wordsworth's interpolation after this passage suddenly yanks us into a vastly different dimension of writing where the concrete vibrancy of the original dissolves into something more safely (and vaguely) metaphysical:

> *Wisdom and spirit of the universe,*
> *Thou soul that art the eternity of thought,*
> *That giv'st to forms and images a breath*
> *And everlasting motion—*

It is as if Wordsworth were here vaguely referring himself back to Coleridge but without the latter's more distinct perception of what these terms signified as pantheism. See, for example, from *The Eolian Harp*:

> *And what if all of animated nature*
> *Be but organic Harps diversely fram'd*
> *That tremble into thought, as o'er them sweeps*
> *Plastic and vast, one intellectual breeze,*
> *At once the Soul of each, and God of all?*

[41] At one point Wordsworth's account enters deeply into this utter harmony of setting and event:

> *meanwhile the calm lake*
> *Grew dark with all the shadows on its breast,*
> *And now and then a leaping fish disturbed*
> *The breathless stillness.*

(I.271)

[42] The Penrith episode was transposed to Bk.XI in the *1805* text from its original place in the First Part of the *Two-Part Prelude*, but along with the commentary Wordsworth added to it in the spring of 1804, just after he

had completed *Intimations* (from "I am lost" to "and they close"), it already formed part of the *Five-Book Prelude* of 1804, closing out (the then) Bk.V. See above p.13 and note 12.

43 That the original has by 1804 become remote and belongs to a secondary order in Wordsworth's immediate consciousness is even more clearly manifested in his account of the same occasion in Bk.VI. Here the original experience is expressly subordinated to his youthful love at a later time:

> *And o'er the Border Beacon, and the waste*
> *Of naked pools and common crags that lay*
> *Exposed on the bare fell, was scattered love—*
> *A spirit of pleasure, and youth's golden gleam.*

(242)

It is likewise the overlaid "golden gleam" that is uppermost in Wordsworth's consciousness in the account from Bk.XI that we have been looking at, even if this is less straightforwardly the case. (There is, incidentally, a strangely insouciant doubling of the same phrasing across the two accounts.)

44 At some point, the crossing over of these two diametrically opposed directions makes for a truly bewildering situation, as, for example, in the following, well-known material which appears half-way through Bk.IV. In this passage, Wordsworth focuses his attention directly on the whole process of his autobiographical research in writing his poem. He compares the material of his past, and most especially his youthful past, to the many items one might find at the bottom of a lake which one was in the process of searching out from a boat on the surface of the water. From time to time one can make out the objects one is attending to, but, for the most part, one is in a constant struggle to make things out because of the many different reflections that appear on the water from one's immediate surroundings:

> *As one who hangs down-bending from the side*
> *Of a slow-moving boat, upon the breast*
> *Of a still water, solacing himself*
> *With such discoveries as his eye can make*
> *Beneath him in the bottom of the deeps,*
> *Sees many beauteous sights—weeds, fishes, flowers,*
> *Grots, pebbles, roots of trees—and fancies more,*
> *Yet often is perplexed, and cannot part*
> *The shadow from the substance, rocks and sky,*
> *Mountains and clouds, from that which is indeed*
> *The region, and the things which there abide*
> *In their true dwelling; now is crossed by gleam*

> *Of his own image, by a sunbeam now,*
> *And motions that are sent he knows not whence,*
> *Impediments that make his task more sweet;*
> *Such pleasant office have we long pursued*
> *Incumbent o'er the surface of past time—*
> *With like success.*
>
> (247)

Apart from the problem that is created by a merely intellectual perception of his past (represented in Wordsworth's analogy by the reflection of his immediate surroundings in the water which interfere with a direct vision of the depths), there is the additional impediment created by his self-consciousness in his venture, the "gleam" of his own "image", which also impedes vision. He is held back as well by the influence of the outer world and its own inherent appeal, its own "sunbeam", including influences from the outside world of other untraceable kinds, "motions that are sent he knows not whence". Most significantly, image, sun-beam, and motions constitute together a parodic version of that deepest primal experience to which Wordsworth had at one time been able to reach out and wished to reach out again. Implicated in this irony, he thus insinuates the extent to which he feels caught up in the frustration of his own efforts, and yet can speak, nevertheless, of a pleasant success in his venture. As the critic, Jonathan Wordsworth, has put it:

> *A passage that appears to state the difficulties of getting at objective memory suggests on closer reading that there could be no point in trying. The growth of a poet's mind concerns not just the details of the period that is nominally his subject, but all those elements and experiences of the present and more recent past that confuse or refract them (for the I in altering, alters all). (335)*

And thus does the writer of epic vision cheerfully absorb and come to terms progressively with his estrangement from his visionary powers and his defeat as a visionary poet. A whole new range of sometimes bewildering feelings is being expressed about this defeated situation that is paradoxically the wonder of *The Prelude* as Wordsworth's evolving epic poem (cf. "And I would give.../A substance and a life to what I *feel*"). Freshly evolving feelings come to revolve, despite essential failure, around a new stubborn purpose of optimistic hopefulness.

45 Indispensable to Wordsworth's further purposes in *The Prelude*, of course, is the powerful new voice he brings to bear on the old material when he first re-engages with his poem in the early winter of 1804. It is all in reaction

to the creative impasse into which he had fallen over this time, which was very much connected with his dissociation from his visionary powers after 1799. Clearly, in the period between 1799 and 1804, when Wordsworth seemed not to be making any progress with his creative direction, something very grand had been gestating in him, a deeper resolve to come to terms, both with his present position and his life as a whole, that would bring forth the massively capable voice that begins to sound to us, from the first verses of his new venture in 1804, and that would continue to sound throughout the rest of his production of this poem. In this new capable epic voice we may discern an idiom that would allow Wordsworth to take on almost any range of multifarious episodes in his life, a new power to bring into a unified order whatever material might come his way, however bewilderingly fragmentary this material might appear to him to be, also at the time he first re-engaged with it. His editorial powers at this time are themselves monumental, especially in the case of his approach to Bk.I. To have brought himself back into a relationship with such fragmentary and enigmatic material as he started from—in the case of what he had written in 1799, and to be able to re-mould that material in order to bring it into line with the very different presentation of himself he had to make by 1804, after years of deep frustration: all this is nothing less than a master effort of poetic self-re-creation, and a model of poetic survival for any poet in any age. The depth of Wordsworth's determination to come through, no matter what the odds, speaks for itself. Equally grand is the way he came to contend at a later point with the knowledge of his final, decisive separation from the visionary influences that drew him back to his past in the first place. Taking on this whole new distressing situation in turn, he once again powerfully comes through, in his own way. The visionary poet had passed away; the epic poet had come through—at least, for the time being. He was nothing, however, if *not* the visionary poet.

46   A thought that Duncan Wu attributes to Wordsworth as early as January 1804. See Wu's "Introduction" to *The Five-Book Prelude*, 12, where he speaks of 'the implicit understanding [already at that stage] that [Wordsworth] has only a limited time left in which to write the great verse for which his early life has prepared him'.

47   This is hardly to discount *The Prelude* as a monumental accomplishment in its own right, whose subject in time expands to include every aspect of a life grounded in Nature, the latter seen as standing *as a whole* in a complex, dialectical relationship to Society and its corruptions. No little satisfaction must have come to Wordsworth from his having been able, in spite of his separation from his visionary experience, to recover with *The Prelude*, and with so much epic power, the whole course and tenor of his life right up to the time he completed that poem in 1805. What he had

been able to accomplish in this respect had given him fresh hope that *The Recluse* might at last be written (see XIII.370). But this was only one—the derivative Wordsworth, who narrates Nature from an alienated *distance*, *after* his separation from its primary influence. There was also *the other*, more deeply challenged Wordsworth who laments this separation, whose baffled fortunes we have been tracing, and who would soon have the better of the first, as Wordsworth's general poetic *dis*possession after 1807 bears witness. He was no longer the poet Nature Herself once fashioned him into, and *The Recluse* would never be written.

48   John Beer's view of Wordsworth's situation, which enthusiastically endorses the latter's own formal assessment of it, strikes one as reducing the extraordinary tensions in Wordsworth's experience with an extreme abandon:

> *For Wordsworth, the transience of the imagination meant automatically that it could have no place in his permanent philosophy. If he did not renounce it, he bade it farewell, content to accept the remaining glimmerings as welcome visitations, but careful to regard them merely as windfalls, not to be budgeted for in the life of common day.* (from *Coleridge the Visionary* (London: Chatto and Windus, 1959) 285.

'Automatically'; 'content to accept'; 'careful to regard them merely as windfalls, not to be budgeted' etc? Beer's black-and-white reductionism seems spectacularly inappropriate:

> *The continuance of such a consciousness as he had in childhood might have rendered him totally self-sufficient and isolate—and so, ultimately, monstrous. It is necessary that the former total possession should accede to a gentler working of that primary force.* (from *Wordsworth and the Human Heart* (New York: Columbia University Press, 1979) 107-108.

Are we really to suppose that what Wordsworth's Child inspires in him could ever have rendered him 'monstrous'? or so hopelessly oblivious to our mortal lot? the tragedy of which lot was bound to reach the hypersensitive Wordsworth as a matter of course, as indeed it already had. In fact, Wordsworth's actual, as opposed to his formal, view is that 'the continuance of such a consciousness as he had in childhood' would, on the contrary, have brought certain redemption in relation to that lot, as I argue in the body of my text, which is why the loss of such consciousness had to be felt as an absolute loss.

49   A 'renewed' encounter with mortality, inasmuch as he was already quite familiar with it, especially during his years as a spectator of the French Revolution. Coming away from the Revolution, he had been through his great moral crisis over the tragic fate of humanity. In *Tintern Abbey*, six years after his time in France and almost a decade before the time we are considering, he speaks of having *learned to look on nature... / hearing oftentimes / The still sad music of humanity*. Elsewhere in *Tintern* he enumerates the negatives of solitude, fear, pain, and grief as a possible fate for his sister in the future. Wordsworth had also lost both parents in early youth. However, in contrast with his later bereavement, at the loss of his brother and then his daughter and his son, he seems to have managed absorbing mortal realities more harmoniously in the first portions of his life. It is on considering anew where he stood with our general mortality, when brought face to face with *the darkness of the grave* in *Intimations*, that he speaks of himself as one *that hath* [already] *kept watch* [and would continue to keep watch] *o'er man's mortality*.

50   It is all to the point that Wordsworth's visionary experiences should have left him in his youth with the sense that he could not die: "Nothing was more difficult for me in my childhood than to admit the notion of death as a state applicable to my own being." (Letter from 1843 addressed to Isabella Fenwick, usefully reprinted as part of the Introduction to the *Intimations Ode* in the Wolfson/Manning Longman edition of *The Romantics and their Contemporaries*.) *The Prelude* reflects this point of view in a number of places: see, e.g., Bk.IV.154, where Wordsworth speaks of having had, in his youth, *glimmering views* of

> *How life pervades the undecaying mind,*
> *How the immortal soul with godlike power*
> *Informs, creates, and thaws the deepest sleep*
> *That time can lay upon her...*

Referring us back once again to the experience of his youth, he speaks, in Bk.V.14, of *the speaking face of earth and heaven* and of

> *...the Sovereign Intellect*
> *Who through that bodily image hath diffused*
> *A soul divine which we participate,*
> *A deathless spirit.*

51   One could also imagine him poetically exhausted at this point, or, at least, he had spent the greater part of himself.

52   It had already done so, e.g., in the case of the drowning at Esthwaithe, and at the death of his father. However, the same all-illuminating power makes itself known when he was himself perilously close to death when hanging from a cliff, or when faced with a pure primal terror, as on Ullswater (in the boat-stealing epsiode) or under the Penrith summit.

53   It has been claimed (by Lionel Trilling in *The Liberal Imagination*, New York: Doubleday, 1950, 135 *passim*) that *Resolution* **is** the "timely utterance" by which in *Intimations* Wordsworth finds "relief" from that "thought of grief" that suddenly alienates him from the blissful society in which he finds himself that morning. If so, then *Resolution* would have to have been written in the short interval of time in which he steps away from the scene in *Intimations* and then returns to it in the course, it would appear, of a single morning. This seems most unlikely. But it is perhaps enough that *Resolution* was written over the same period as the first part of *Intimations* was, and from a close structural comparison between the two poems, it reads rather more like the poem Wordsworth had come to the point of writing when he *left off* with *Intimations* rather than the poem he went off to write in the middle of it. (We are speaking here of the first part of *Intimations*.) The scene of joy with which *Resolution* **begins** has strong affinities rather with what Wordsworth makes of the scene in *Intimations* **after** his mysterious dealing with the "thought of grief". In *Resolution* he writes:

> *I **saw** the hare that traced about with joy;*
> *I **heard** the woods and distant waters roar;*
> *Or heard them not, as happy as a boy;*

Here Wordsworth returns to what he has already described in the first part of the poem, and with these lines we may compare, from *Intimations*:

> *I hear the Echoes through the mountains throng*

> *Shout round me, let me hear thy shouts, thou happy Shepherd-boy!*

which likewise shows Wordsworth returning to what there is to hear and see in the situation of that poem. What's more, *Resolution*'s **main** meditation, stemming from the point of "sadness", begins with the same form of radical qualification with which the first part of *Intimations* suddenly breaks off, while Wordsworth is in the very midst of what is a scene of joy for others:

> *But there's a Tree, of many, one,*
> *A single Field which I have looked upon,*

> *Both of them speak of something that is gone:*

with which we may compare, from *Resolution*:

> *But there may come another day to me—*
> *Solitude, pain of heart, distress, and poverty.*

One poem (*Intimations*) would (in time) look back wistfully to the past, while the other anxiously anticipates the future.

All this would leave in mystery what Wordsworth went away to do to find "relief" from the "thought of grief" that takes him over at an early point in *Intimations*.

54 It is well-known that Wordsworth's poem, in one respect, forms part of an ongoing dialogue with Coleridge that continues from the latter's *Dejection* (itself a reply to the first part of *Intimations*). The same sentiments Wordsworth gives voice to in *Resolution* Coleridge formally expresses in *his* poem. (I deliberately echo Coleridge's key term—"affliction"—in my description of this process in my text.)

55 At some point Wordsworth's Leech-Gatherer does turn into *one whom I had met with in a dream*;

> *But now his voice to me was like a stream*
> *Scarce heard; nor word from word could I divide;*
> *And the whole body of the Man did seem*
> *Like one whom I had met with in a dream.*

56 There is a remarkable emphasis, in Wordsworth's *œuvre*, on 'gaiety' as yet another, highly subtle and complex way of coping. In *Intimations* 'gaiety' is a deliberate moral choice pursued in spite of the threat of *tristitia* or grief to which Wordsworth has already succumbed. In this grief Wordsworth would not impose himself on others. He goes away to deal with it, and returns given up again to the gaiety in all around him:

> *I hear the Echoes through the mountains throng*
> *...*
> *And all the earth is gay.*

That gaiety has everything to do with Nature continuing to adorn itself, to the extent that it does, even if it now lacks any visionary depth for Wordsworth or has lost its visionary "gleam":

No more shall grief of mine the season wrong.

Oh evil day! If I were sullen
While earth herself is adorning,
    This sweet May-morning,
And the Children are culling
    On every side,
In a thousand valleys far and wide,
Fresh flowers

Wordsworth is returned to 'gaiety' in his poem on the daffodils where, as we have seen (see p.29), something of the visionary world he has left behind is actually reflected:

A Poet could not but be gay
In such a laughing company

Indeed the pursuit of 'gaiety' turns paradoxically into another (distant) way of living back into that world. This is the case also in his two poems on the butterfly. In one of these, he addresses the butterfly as *Historian of my Infancy*:

Dead times revive in thee
.................gay Creature

Oh! Pleasant, pleasant were the days,

Sweet childish days...

Set up by then at Dove Cottage, Wordsworth had created a world in which the butterfly could visit to assume this memorial function in the depths of his imagination:

This plot of Orchard-ground is ours;
My trees they are, my Sister's flowers;
Stop here whenever you are weary,
And rest as in a sanctuary!
Come often to us, fear no wrong;
Sit near us on the bough!
We'll talk of sunshine and of song;
And summer days when we were young,
Sweet childish days...

Wordsworth's deliberate pursuit of a culture of gaiety may also explain why in writing *Daffodils* he *re*-fashioned the scene as he actually experienced it with his sister. The day they came across the daffodils, the lake, according to Dorothy's Notebooks, was 'rough', the wind 'furious', the weather generally 'stormy...and in the middle of the water like the Sea—Rain came on'. Of course, other reasons could as easily be supplied for the alteration, as that Wordsworth was not up to facing the sombre reality that already threatened him, or that he wished to insist on cheerfulness, was adamant about reflecting on the past etc. It is worth noting that he had, a few years earlier, similarly altered the actual circumstances that lie behind the writing of *It is a beauteous Evening*. Dorothy describes the sea at the time as 'gloomy for there was a blackness over all the sky except when it was overspread with lightning'. In the poem we read: *the broad sun/Is sinking down in its tranquility/The gentleness of heaven is on the Sea*.

57   This deduction is along the lines of the argument Plato allows Socrates to present in the *Phaedo*: that an otherworldly life 'having been', it 'must' therefore 'ever be'. See the *Phaedo* (New York: Dover, 2007) 58 *passim*.

There may indeed be thoughts of a life that continues beyond death in the last part of Wordsworth's poem, but one needs to note at the same time that that is not how death presents itself climactically

> *In darkness lost, the darkness of the grave;*

Here death has the force rather of an impenetrable enigma. In this context, it is only too easy to feel, along with Socrates's auditor, Simmias (who insists on his dismay despite Socrates's own confidence in his position):

> *how very hard or almost impossible is the attainment of any certainty about questions such as these in the present life.*

Philosophers have come to see that Plato's point of view in his dialogues is generally more relativistic than we had supposed, and that he is far from simply endorsing the positions that Socrates takes in them. Likewise with the formal position Wordsworth finally takes in his poem. Thus one may admit of his demonstration, as Socrates's auditors do of his:

> *the existence of the soul before entering the bodily form has been very ingeniously, and as I may be allowed to say, quite sufficiently proven;*

One reserves, however, some doubtfulness about the rest of the common presentation (common to Wordsworth and Socrates alike):

95

But that after death the soul will continue to exist is not yet proven

So that at least one aspect of the presentation would appear to remain beyond demonstration:

> *That the soul will exist after death as well as before birth is the other half of which the proof is still wanting. (Socrates himself will go on to argue more, but with that enters into the much larger question of the nature of generation and corruption, which Wordsworth never approaches.)*

In comments on the poem dictated by Wordsworth to Isabella Fenwick many years after *Intimations* was completed, the notion of "a prior state of existence" itself comes in for some significant qualification. It is now treated by him merely as "a shadowy notion". These comments, combining with Coleridge's statement in his *Biographia Literaria* that Wordsworth did not believe in pre-existence, have been the source of a spate of remarks by critics as to whether Wordsworth ever took pre-existence seriously. There is no doubt in my mind—and the whole of the present book speaks on behalf of this view—that at the time of the writing of *Intimations* and *The Prelude* in 1804-1805, Wordsworth was immersed in this notion because it had been his *experience*, in some profoundly literal sense. This remains true whatever he may have said about it later when referring himself to his by then orthodox religious faith. (For an exhaustive treatment of the facts, concluding on the side of Wordsworth's identification with an otherworldly experience, see Robert Zimmer, *Clairvoyant Wordsworth* (Lincoln, NE: IUniverse, 1997)). On the other hand, Wordsworth's attempts to argue in his poem that a notion of our pre-existence can serve as a basis for a belief that we also live on after death may, as I think, be radically questioned, because of the way death is presented in his poem. Wordsworth would later reduce his notion of pre-existence to no more than "an *element* in our instincts of immortality" [italics mine]. With this formulation he was finally referring the matter to the greater certainty of the dogmatic truths assumed by the Christian faith he had by then adopted.

58 Emphasis in the poem is on the commonness of the flower, not on any thought of its mortality (or suffering), as Trilling (somewhat ludicrously) proposed: 'the meanest flower is significant now...because...it speaks of age, suffering, and death'(147). Nor is it the case that Wordsworth's emphasis falls on the flower's brevity, as Beer assumes: 'soon...it will have faded' (*The Human Heart*, 110). In Wordsworth's "meanest flower" we are not being directed forward to the problem of death but directed back to the problem of commonness which we are left dealing with while still alive. If that flower "blows" in the wind, it is in all its commonness in spite of

the suggestion of the potential for greater life all around it as suggested in that wind, a potential which actually lies beyond it (rather, as a full inspiration from Nature lies beyond Wordsworth's daughter, and himself by that point, in *It is a beauteous Evening*).

59 Given to us, somewhat abstractly, years later, for, as Jonathan Wordsworth slyly points out, years before, when the episode Wordsworth recounts took place, 'in the summer of 1791...whatever else he was thinking about, it is not likely to have been the creative imagination.' (310)

60 *Kubla Khan* was not made public until 1817, while the passage we are considering from *The Prelude* was composed in 1804. But *Kubla* was written in 1797, and it is impossible to think that this poem was not shared with Wordsworth over this time. Also for my view of how 'sun' and 'moon' interassociate in Wordsworth's poetic symbolism, see n.34.

61 As for the second source of Imaginative visionary power, stemming from the other extreme of the 'deep earth', we seem to have to do with a future accomplishment to which perhaps only Coleridge has yet to make any significant approach. In his Introduction to A *Choice of Coleridge's Verse* Ted Hughes conducts some extraordinary research into the prospect of that power as Coleridge's poems and notes outline this. The idea that the Imagination reserves the power in time to transform even dead nature is conveyed in *Kubla Khan* through the image of the displaced "rocks" that are suddenly made to "dance", as the Alph, a symbol of the visionary power of the Mind, breaks through to the surface from its subterranean sphere. The combined presentation of otherworldly sun, dome and subterranean world, as given by Coleridge and Wordsworth, is anticipated in that remarkable, enigmatic painting from the 17th century, by Rembrandt—*The Polish Rider*.

62 He sought to fight this prospect off also with his religion, as prognosticated already in the following, written on the eve of James Fox's death in 1806. These lines, in spite of their concentration on the fate of Fox, clearly bring into focus the whole question of the general fear of death that became Wordsworth's fundamental preoccupation from *Intimations* onwards:

> *Sad was I, even to pain deprest,*
> *Importunate and heavy load!*

> *The Comforter hath found me here,*
> *Upon this lonely road;*

> *And many thousands now are sad—*

> *Wait the fulfilment of their fear...*

63 Altered in the *1805* text (somewhat unhappily) to:

> *...meanwhile the calm lake*
> *Grew dark, with all the shadows on its breast,*
> **And now and then a fish up-leaping snapped**
> *The breathless stillness.*

(Bk.V.463)

64 Wordsworth's paeon to hope and his elaborate impression of the Arve are two *separate* passages that describe two distinct experiences. They are not, as Jonathan Bate once suggested (in an interview for a short documentary on *Wordsworth's Spots of Time* for Lancaster University Television, put out in 2002), inter-associated, the latter seen as an elaboration on the former. The former is, rather, its own account: another typical, extraordinary generalization *about* the old visionary experience, of which there are many scattered throughout *The Prelude* as part of Wordsworth's programme for instituting a possible "future restoration" of such an experience. The latter is Wordsworth's fresh imaginative engagement with the old scene, undertaken in terms of his new poetic situation in which a competing anxiety about Nature's emptiness breaks through in spite of his attempt to think himself back into his unitary experience, or so I argue in the rest of this Appendix.

65 As formulated in *Mt. Blanc*:

> *The wilderness has a mysterious tongue*
> *Which teaches awful doubt, or faith so mild,*
> *So solemn and serene, that man may be*
> *But for such faith with nature reconciled;*

In the case of "faith...so solemn and serene", Shelley was directly addressing Wordsworth's own settled position. Shelley could not have known of Wordsworth's Simplon passage, since *The Prelude* was kept private until 1850 (except for the occasional readings over the years to Coleridge principally). The Simplon passage was published for the first time in Wordsworth's *1845 Poems*, over twenty years after Shelley died. If Shelley *had* known of this passage, he would no doubt have cited it as proof that Wordsworth could only share in his own dark, sceptical philosophy of Nature.

It seems all to the point that Wordsworth, some two years beyond completing the 1805 *Prelude*, inserted other lines into his passage on the Simplon Pass—lines that bring out even more clearly the impact of the spirit of destruction that overwhelmingly attaches to this scene, and that by their inclusion would have pre-empted any such unitary effect as Wordsworth intended with this passage. These inserted lines almost directly evoke Shelley's own description; Wordsworth subsequently cut the lines when revising for the 1850 text over twenty five years later. (See Wordsworth, Abrams, Gill, 218 n.5):

> The immeasurable height
> Of woods decaying, never to be decayed,
> The stationary blasts of waterfalls,
> And everywhere along the hollow rent
> Winds thwarting winds, bewildered and forlorn,
> The torrents shooting from the clear blue sky,
> The rocks that muttered close upon our ears—
> Black drizzling crags that spake by the wayside
> As if a voice were in them—the sick sight
> And giddy prospect of the raving stream,
>
> **And ever as we halted, or crept on,**
> **Huge fragments of primaeval mountain spread**
> **In powerless ruin, blocks as huge aloft**
> **Impending, nor permitted yet to fall,**
> **The sacred death-cross, monument forlorn**
> **Though frequent of the perished traveller**
>
> The unfettered clouds, and region of the heavens,
> Tumult and peace, the darkness and the light
> Were all like workings of one mind, the features
> Of the same face, blossoms upon one tree,
> Characters of the great Apocalyps,
> The types and symbols of Eternity,
> Of first, and last, and midst, and without end.

One imagines Wordsworth returning to the scene he had described and remembering *how it really was*, drawn back in spite of himself into his anxious perception of Nature's alien reality, only to retire again into his unitary view of old. As a poet, and as a reader of his poetry, he knew that the inserted lines could not be allowed to stand without disturbing the rhetorical effect he intended, and he was not committed to his deeper perception about Nature's alienness, was not set up, *or* constituted, to pursue it. However, Wordsworth did leave *traces* of his deeper experience

99

in the poem as he left it. This includes the lines in which he speaks of his place of residence at the time of his visit to the Pass:

> A dreary mansion, large beyond all need,
> With high and spacious rooms, deafened and stunned
> By noise of waters, **making innocent sleep**
> **Lie melancholy among weary bones.**
>
> (577)

When Wordsworth re-visited this area with Dorothy in 1820, over 15 years after he wrote these lines, she could not persuade him to enter this "mansion" again.

62191462R00205

Made in the USA
Lexington, KY
02 April 2017